SUPPLEMENT JOURNALISM IN INDIA

SUPPLEMENT JOURNALISM IN INDIA

Pooja Rana

Foreword by

Dr Daya Thussu
Professor of International Communication &
Co-Director, India Media Centre
University of Westminster, London

PENTAGON PRESS

Supplement Journalism in India / Pooja Rana

ISBN 978-81-8274-454-7

First Published: 2010

Published by

PENTAGON PRESS
206, Peacock Lane, Shahpur Jat,
New Delhi-110049
Phones: 011-64706243, 26491568
Telefax: 011-26490600
email: rajan@pentagonpress.in
website: www.pentagon-press.in

Printed at
New Elegant Printers, New Delhi-110064.

FOREWORD

The liberalization of the Indian media industries has revolutionized journalism in the world's largest and most vibrant democracy. With liberalization have come increased competition and excessive commercialization of news and information in what is the world's most diverse and multilingual media landscape. One indication of this change is the advent of supplement journalism, a phenomenon which since its emergence in the 1990s has transformed the rather sedate and sober look of Indian newspapers.

It was that old lady of Indian journalism, *The Times of India,* which heralded the change with the launch of its 'Delhi Times,' closely followed by its arch-rival in the national capital, the *Hindustan Times,* with its own supplement 'The Delhi City.'

Both were extremely successful as they contributed to enhanced circulation of these two agenda-setting newspapers, prompting other newspapers across the country to follow suit. Consequently, newspapers throughout the land regularly and routinely carry pullouts or supplements on subjects as diverse as the arts, culture, education, agriculture, health, beauty and lifestyle.

Moreover, as the localization of content has become fashionable, more and more newspapers frequently publish city and even town-specific supplements or pull-outs, a trend particularly visible in the Hindi heartland, where newspapers have focused increasingly at a localized audience and advertising – an interesting paradox at a time when corporate India is gradually integrating with a globalized economy.

This micro localization has thrived as the 'newspaper pluses' have become money-spinners for news organizations – in some instances the advertisement rates for the supplements are higher than the main newspaper. In addition, the supplements are relatively cheap to produce and their cheerful and glossy look translates into good advertising revenue and a youthful readership, more susceptible to what I have elsewhere described as global infotainment.

Against this background, this pioneering study by Dr Pooja Rana is a very welcome addition to the literature on contemporary journalism in India. The book draws an interesting comparison between the supplements of *The Times of India,* in the globalized and networked Gurgaon, and of the *Dainik Bhaskar,* in Hisar, a town situated in the hinterland of Haryana. The book argues that supplement journalism caters to three key players - the advertisers, the media houses and the readers - through segmentation of information and a consequent fragmentation of mass audience into identifiable homogeneous sub groups.

Given its topicality and relevance, this study should prove useful for students of journalism as well as for the wider community of media scholars and social science researchers.

Dr Daya Thussu
Professor of International Communication &
Co-Director, India Media Centre
University of Westminster, London

CONTENTS

CHAPTER I

INTRODUCTION

The year 1991 is a watershed in the history of humankind. It was around this time that the world was hit by major cataclysmic events that changed the way men and women looked upon life. It was the year when the Internet burst upon the global scenario as the scarlet sun of New Information and Communication Technologies (NICTs) that gave sustenance to new initiatives and endeavours in social, political, economic and cultural life. As Stanley J. Baran and Dennis K. Davis put it, "They (new media proponents) argue that new technology can expand each person's cultural and experiential horizons. They envision newly energized, active audiences in which people find ways of making media serve them so that their lives are more interesting and purposeful."[1] It was also the time when the old world rivalries between the Cold War veterans, the then USSR and the USA, began to thaw and the USSR disintegrated. It was also the year when globalization made yet another thrust and roped in economies as large as that of India into the Free Market mould.

In other words, it was the dawn of a new era that would come to fruition in the 21st century and stood knocking at the threshold. The whole of the scenario of Indian media changed when the new media entered the scene.[2] It was in this first flush of the new found youth of growth that Indian media, part of the largely neglected culture Industry, as much as Indian business and industry, started stretching its wings for the proverbial flight. With a spurt in the activities of the Indian business and industry, the Indian media too got a boost. Spurred by greater advertising revenues, the Indian media gave up its conservative hesitation to go avant-garde. While television had already broken free from the bonds of state control, newspapers too started experimenting to retain control over their market share of the audiences. As Denis McQuail puts it, "It was almost two hundred years after the invention of printing before what we now recognize as a prototypical newspaper could be distinguished from the handbills, pamphlets and newsletters of the late 16th and early 17th centuries....The early newspaper was marked by its regular appearance, commercial basis (openly for sale), public character and its multiple purpose. Thus, it was used for information, record, advertising, diversion and gossip."[3] While earlier newspapers had a very staid and formal look, post-1991 they became flamboyantly colourful to attract attention. Some of the dailies even gave up their allegiance to the broadsheet and embraced the sleeker tabloid size. As Navneet Anand remarks, "The efforts of the newspapers to get slimmer and package stories with large display of pictures and at times story-telling through pictures are some (other) manifestations of Indian newspapers' drive towards churning out global standard products."[4] Also, where earlier there would be one weekly supplement at the most, post-liberalization newspapers launched a number of supplements and offered them in a package deal to their customers.[5] These supplements attempted to reach out to different segments of the audience and to different informational needs of the reading public. As the economy surged ahead, the newspaper industry too blossomed with a volley of new supplements.

In the light of these developments, this study attempts to analyze the phenomenon of supplement journalism by focusing attention on the newspaper supplements of two leading Indian dailies, one in English and the other in Hindi.

As Denis McQuail remarks, "The (later) history of newspaper can be told either as a series of struggles, advances and reverses in the cause of liberty or as a more continuous history of economic and technological progress."[6] Similarly, the phenomenon of supplement journalism can be understood in two contexts: one, the cultural and the other, the conceptual. Culturally, the evolution of supplement journalism in India needs to be understood against the backdrop of the economic and social changes that rocked the country in two phases of its national development: one, the post-colonial phase and the second post-liberalisation phase. Conceptually, the evolution of supplement journalism in India needs to be viewed against the backdrop of the semantic swings that the process of communication has undergone in not just India but the world as a whole. To plot the graph of this movement, one first needs to interrogate the term communication itself. This is important because the developments in communication technology resulting in the birth of the mass media have been so powerful that they have fore-grounded a conceptual terrain that has often overshadowed the original semantic landscape.[7] Before we may discuss the conceptual changes that underpinned the emergence of supplement journalism in India, it would be very much in order to analyze the cultural changes that necessitated the emergence of supplement journalism in India.

I.1. The Cultural Backdrop

Newspaper journalism in India struck roots in its nascent stage due to the need for uncensored information by a subject race reeling under the tyranny of its colonial masters. As such, the newspapers covered hard news affecting the lives of the masses. This was the time when most people in India struggled to eke out their daily livelihood. Illiteracy was rampant. So, newspapers catered to the needs of the educated middle class which was caught between their allegiance to the nation and their desire to earn a comfortable lifestyle. The middle class was a miniscule minority struggling to resolve the pulls and pushes of these two conflicting desires. Newspapers kept this miniscule minority in touch with what was happening around them in the society. Unable to resolve this conflict, they drew solace from the news of the freedom struggle reported in the press. In the era of freedom struggle, Indian press served as a vehicle for propagating nationalist ideologies. Eminent leaders like Mahatama Gandhi and Bal Gangadhar Tilak were also bringing out newspapers.[8] The symbiotic interaction between the missionary zeal of the journalists and the hunger for nationalistic news among the middle class decided the kind of newspaper produced in pre-independent India.

The social and economic landscape of India did not change overnight after independence. Saddled with a huge population living in penury and illiteracy and a huge landmass bereft of a scientific and industrial foundation, the country had to fight a number of economic and social disabilities before it could offer its citizens a comfortable and secure livelihood. The emphasis on agricultural development in the first three Five Year Plans helped to alleviate rural poverty, stimulate agricultural production and to lay down a basic rural infrastructure, helping thereby to ensure to a great extent moderate rural development. With literacy rising in the villages and a moderate prosperity blessing rural households, the reach of the print media widened to include readers in rural India. Simultaneously, the development of urban areas as a consequence of various infrastructural projects launched in the first three Five Year Plans helped to give a sense of economic security to the upwardly mobile middle class. By the 1970s, when Mrs Gandhi's control over the Congress tightened post-Nijlingappa Plan and the decisive Bangladesh victory, the Indian middle class had swollen its ranks to include the bureaucracy, the service class and the noveau-riche merchant class; all of them hungering for a share in the new found prosperity.

As political machinations ruled the roost, corruption crept into the body politic at all levels and in all shapes. This got reflected in newspapers turning professional from their erstwhile missionary zeal. Indian press became more and more commercial and competitive in approach, sharply deviating from its idealistic approach of the pre-independence era.[9] Newspapers took on positions that were either pro-establishment or anti-establishment. From being wedded to the cause of providing unvarnished and truthful news to the masses, newspapers now exercised their gatekeeping function to provide information that suited their editorial policy and business interests. The corruption that afflicted the body politic had at last claimed the Fourth Estate as well in so far as it had whittled down its commitment to objective truth on partisan grounds.

Liberalization came as a whiff of fresh air to both the media houses as well as the readers. With the private sector contributing in a major way to the growth and development of the national economy and pushing up the income levels of citizens by providing them fully productive employment, the standard of living of the people, in particular the middle class, registered a phenomenal jump. The surplus income with the service class became the target of the marketers who wished to reach out information about their products and services to every prospect. This necessitated greater advertising space which the newspapers readily provided by going in for niche supplements. The liberalization of business and industry also paved the ground for the entry of new players in the media market.[10] The mushroom growth of satellite channels on the crest of the advertising boom threatened to erode the circulation base of newspapers. This challenge was met by the newspapers by going in for flamboyant supplements that had a greater shelf life than the electronic media products did. As Om Gupta puts it, "...when the satellite and cable television hit the Indian middle class in their drawing and bedrooms suddenly the newspapers realized that their traditional role was fast losing ground to the more colourful and immediate medium. TV provided authentic information, albeit in a capsule form directly quoting the players of the event. It reduced the morning newspapers to being stale and repetitive. Hence, they started looking around for an additional function and thus came the daily supplements with a heavy dose of entertainment, glamour and useful information laced with colour and vanity."[11] The injection of advertising money into print media further altered the nature of newspapers. From the original missionary approach to the professionally correct approach and finally the economically appropriate approach, newspapers have travelled a long distance. In their new found avatar, newspapers have become an advertising medium that shores up the advertising revenues and churns out popular stuff that titillates and fascinates without attempting to tax the readers' attention with the so-called 'heavy stuff'.

The spurt in the number of newspaper supplements meant greater liberty and control passing into the hands of the readers as compared to the earlier times. As each supplement focused on a different interest/pastime of the readers, supplements started reversing the trend of massification of media messages and encouraging niche journalism. Readers could now access newspapers for the kind of information they wanted to read or see. The diversity of content helped to empower the readers by making access to different kinds of information convenient and delightful.

Having seen how the turn of events in the economic and cultural life of the nation facilitated the growth of supplement journalism, we may now proceed to unravel the conceptual implications underpinning this new phenomenon.

I.2. Conceptual Background: Interrogating Communication

Upon tracing the root of the word, communication, we find that it comes from the Latin word, *communis,* which means 'to make common' or 'of which all have an equal degree of use or advantage.'[12] Derived from it is the Latin verb, *communicare,* which means 'to impart a piece of information, an idea or a concept with a view to discovering/developing a commonality of thought and/or feeling' or 'to make something entirely common with another'.[13] Communication may, therefore, be defined as the process of interaction that helps in evolving a common ground of understanding between the communicators. Interaction as defined by Oxford Advanced Learners' Dictionary means 'reciprocal action or influence'. In other words, the relationship between the two communicators is not fixed but dynamic.

Viewed thus, communication becomes a process wherein there are no fixed producers or consumers of messages. The roles are dynamic and interchangeable. So, contrary to popular perception that communication implies speaking or writing or even showing signs to express oneself, communication involves listening as much as speaking, reading as much as writing and seeing as much as showing. As communication is interactive, it empowers both the communicators equally; giving birth to a power equality between the communicators. It follows, therefore, that communication is dialogic. In other words, the communication message is not necessarily a pre-existing entity. It could emerge from the dynamic exchange of verbal and non-verbal signals/symbols between the communicators.

And, what's more, the process of interaction could produce as many messages as are the number of communicators, depending on the idiosyncratic and cultural inputs each brings to bear on the process of interaction, leading to what has often been called the polysemy and polyphony of communication. However, as communication strives to create a common ground of understanding among the communicators, ideally it should produce one common message between the communicators. Furthermore, as communication involves the interaction of each communicator with the other, it is personalized and individualistic in nature.

I.2.1. *Osgood and Schramm*

Communication experts down the ages have testified to this nature of communication in the various models of communication that they have presented. Osgood and Schramm, who gave the earliest model of this kind, observe, "In fact, it is misleading to think of the communication process as starting somewhere and ending somewhere. It is really endless. We are little switchboard centers handling and rerouting the great endless current of information...." As illustrated, both the participants keep on interchanging their roles as encoders and decoders.

Here, none is privileged at the expense of the other. Interestingly enough, Schramm came round to this perception of the process of communication after having given an entirely different model of communication earlier, which however he discarded later. The diagram given below presents the earlier model.

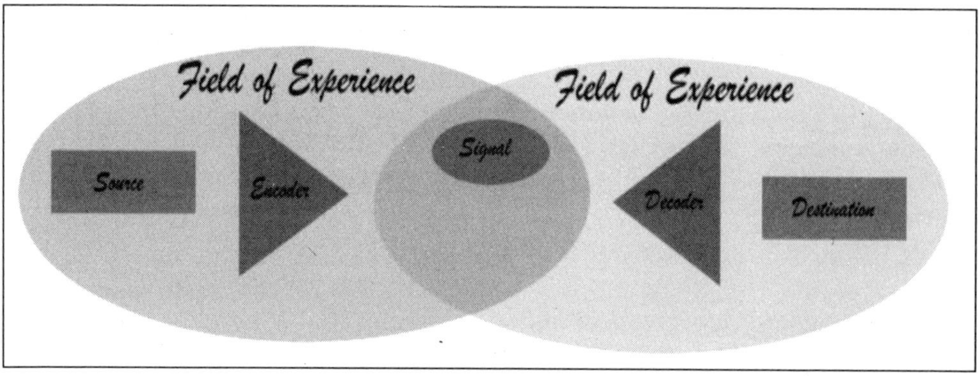

Figure I.1: Wilbur Schramm's model

Schramm revised his opinion in the light of Charles E. Osgood's work to incorporate the element of interaction in the communication process. The modified model of communication is given below:

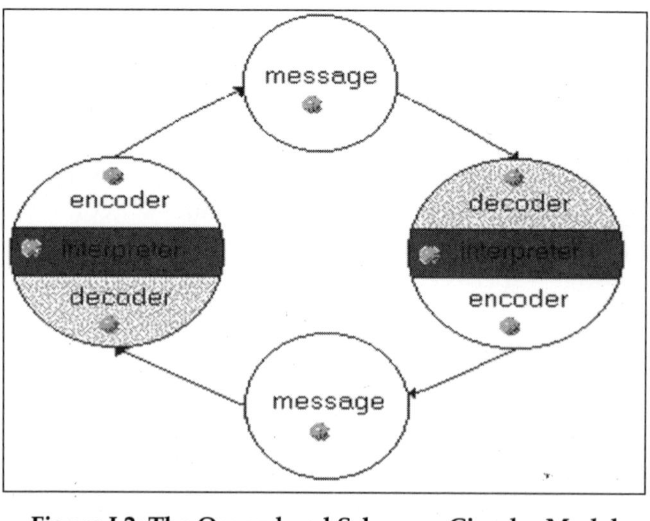

Figure I.2: The Osgood and Schramm Circular Model

I.2.2. *Convergence Model*

As the name suggests, the convergence model avers that communication leads to commonality of thought, feeling or interest between the communicators. It represents communication as a process of horizontal sharing between two or more participants within social networks.[14] The first noticeable feature of the model is that information is shared or exchanged between two or more individuals rather than transmitted from one to the other. All participants act on the same information; none are passive receivers of information. The information can be created by the action of any participant, or it may originate from a third source such as a television or a radio, or a person or an institution not directly participating such as a church, a school, a non-governmental agency and so forth.

The second feature of the model is that it lays emphasis on the important role of the perception and interpretation of participants, and thus draws upon the principles of semiotics and the hermeneutics, which treat understanding in terms of a dialogue or ongoing cultural conversation. The third feature of the model is that it represents a horizontal, symmetrical relationship among two or more participants that is created by sharing information. The outcomes of information processing by the participants are *social* – mutual understanding, agreement and collective action (see the central column of the model), as well as individual – perceiving, interpreting, understanding and believing.

And finally, the model implies a continuous, cyclical process as participants take turns creating information to share with one another and then interpreting and reinterpreting its meaning until a sufficient degree of mutual understanding and agreement has been reached for collective action to take place. 'Information' is preferred over the term 'message' to allow for both verbal and nonverbal information, unintended as well as intended information. For example, if women suddenly show up at a community meeting for the first time, this *action by itself* conveys information that can be stronger than all of the verbal comments made about "allowing women to participate." The inherent properties of this process suggest that over time most groups will converge towards a state of greater internal uniformity, also referred to as "local culture".

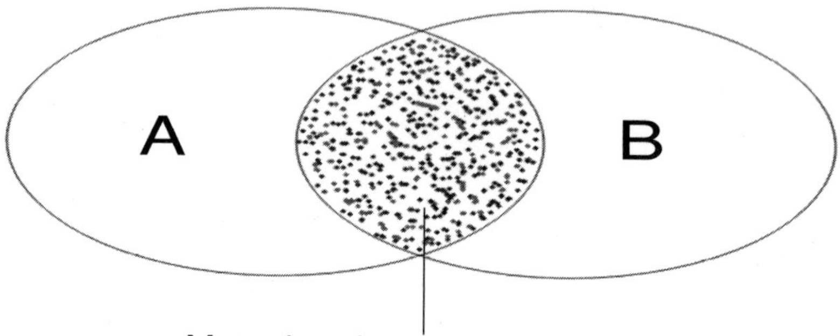

Figure I.3: Convergence Model

I.2.3. ***Participatory School of Communication***

In recent times, the Participatory School of Communication has echoed this very meaning of communication when it has emphasized the need for participation of the two communicators to arrive at a message through interaction. It has, however, gone one step further. Rooted in semiotics and the seminal ideas of Levi Strauss, participatory communication emphasizes the generation of meaning or the text as a joint exercise of the two communicators. The Participatory School of Communication sees communication as "the production and exchange of meanings". It is concerned with how messages or texts interact with people in order to produce meanings; that is, it is concerned with the role of texts in our culture. It uses terms like signification and doesn't consider misunderstandings to be necessarily evidence of communication failure—they may result from cultural differences between sender and receiver. For this school, study of communication is the study of text and culture. The Participatory School tends to draw upon linguistics and arts subjects and tends to address itself to works of communication.[15]

In the light of the preceding discussion of the meaning of communication and its explication with the help of various models that support it, we may safely observe that communication is personalized/individualistic dialogue between the communicators involving exchange of information that could be objective or/and subjective. Going a step further, the content of interaction could be verbal or non-verbal or a mix of both. And as there are no fixed producers or consumers of the verbal/non-verbal messages, the content of any single instance of communication is a product of the joint exercise of the two communicators. This makes communication a mathematical equality of power relations. None is advantaged at the expense of the other. This makes communication at once a powerful tool of 'communal' participation of the citizen, essential for the success of a democracy. Besides, as there are no fixed producers of information, their unrestrained interaction has the potential of producing content on unlimited subjects, making public discourse polyphonic.

I.3. Communication and Society

Communication in this form worked successfully as long as people lived in village/town communities which were amenable to interpersonal communication. The city states of Greece and the 'ganas' of India were testimony to this power of communication. This worked very well even in the tribal societies, where much against popular misconception, the tribes evolved a code of conduct that kept them together in a peaceful manner and ensured the sway of certain basic value systems. For, to begin with when man first learnt to verbalize his communication with his fellow beings, he communicated for the most part at the interpersonal level as the tribe or community of which he formed a part was a socially cohesive and self contained unit that staved off any foreign admixture. Even when the nomadic tribal community settled down to an agricultural mode of life in village settlements, his communication needs remained restricted to the interpersonal and small group level.

Such communication situations are a remote throwback on the modern nation-states where the sheer size of the population and the length and breadth of the geographical space localizing the nation mitigate against the successful use of interpersonal and small group communication for public participation 'in the life of the nation-community.' Self-contained, though they were, the village communities had a world-view which was not restricted to the village in which they lived. The rambling gypsies continued to widen the *weltanschauung* of the village community with the tales and fables of the world they rambled through.[16] All the same, the functional needs of the village and its inhabitants made no demands on their communicating with the world outside on a regular basis except for feeding on the romanticized tales for their entertainment.

With the expansion of the communities beyond the boundaries of the village/town, not only did the worldview undergo a change but at the same time, a hiatus also occurred in the process of communication. As the village communities gave way to the industrialized cities of the 18th century and the consequent large scale mobilization of labour force across villages and town boundaries scattered people, interpersonal and small group communication reached its bursting point. Alongside, political developments that knit the loosely agglomerated towns and villages into well-knit and cohesive nation-states of modern times called for new ways of communicating across the heterogeneous mass of people forming the nation. Developments in communication technology kept pace with these changes and as every solution looks for a problem, the solution of mass media came knocking for being used to fulfill the need.

Mass media supplanted the town hall/village green as the forum for public debate, discussion and information. Mass media sought to inform, educate and entertain its audiences. With its wide-sweeping reach, it could overcome the barriers of distance to connect the members of the community scattered over the length and breadth of a nation-state and create, thereby, the semblance of cultural cohesion. Along with the developed means of transportation, it became the instrument of building huge nation-states and of sustaining them administratively. Soon, communication that embraced interpersonal and group interaction got back-grounded from the public domain and the mass communication of messages by the mass media got foregrounded.

I.4. From Communication to Mass Communication

The advent of mass media and its attendant phenomenon of mass communication turned communication upside down. It usurped the right of the citizen to communicate in the public domain and handed over the right, read power, to communicate to either the government or corporate houses that got to control the mass media. The power equality that characterized communication turned into a power inequality in which the mass media owner monopolized the right to communicate as the 'sender' of mass media messages and the citizen was passivised as a mere recipient of those messages; the maximum extent to which (s)he could make his/her presence felt in the process of communication was to give a feedback. The content of public discourse got restricted to the agenda that the mass media organization decided, keeping in mind its editorial and business policy. The power inequality, therefore, created the communication inequality. It is this inequality that characterizes mass communication.

Besides, as the mass media messages had to reach out to a large audience, there could be no personalized communication. Mass audiences, which were heterogeneous and anonymous, called for mass messages that could appeal to the largest common denominator of such an audience. Obviously, like the factories which churned out 'standardised' products for mass consumption, the mass media came out with 'standardized' messages containing news pertaining to business ventures to begin with and political and social change in later times. Both reached out to heterogeneous mass of users submerging the small group proclivities and individual idiosyncrasies. Standardization was, therefore, a clever capitalistic euphemism for such a deterioration of quality.

The phenomena, which began with the print media, continued with the electronic media, especially television, with the exception of the radio. With a view to enhancing its TRPs, the TV channels sought to produce programmes that caught the attention of the greatest number of eyeballs. With the booming of business opportunities, and a fillip in advertising, the fight for viewers' attention became greater. In the attention economy of the twentieth century, television sold the attention of its audiences to the advertisers. Radio, though an exception to this trend, could do nothing to obviate it as it came under the guillotine of governments fearful of its power over the masses and corporate houses suspicious of its power to circumvent copyright provisions that ensure the trickling in of their revenue perennially.

Controlled by the governments, the radio too produced messages that empowered the government at the expense of the masses. In effect, mass media effectuated a breakdown in the continuity of the quintessential meaning of communication. It gave birth to models of communication that fixed the roles of the two communicators as sender and receiver and made the process largely unidirectional. The producer of mass messages was empowered at the expense of the consumer of those mass messages and the communication inequality was stabilized in the mass media for a long time to come.

I.4.1. *The Transmission School of Communication*

The Transmission School of Communication popularized this communication heresy in the various models that its proponents enunciated. The School went as far back in time as that of Aristotle to vindicate their version of the concept of communication. Aristotle had spoken about the art of rhetoric as the successful identification of the needs of the audience and the successful transmutation of ideas into linguistically palatable messages that could influence the behaviour of audiences. The proponents of the Transmission School equated rhetoric with communication to press their point ignoring the fact that rhetoric is only one form of communication in which the speaker is at a vantage point compared to the audience. In modern parlance, rhetoric would be identified as large group communication. Such a communication situation distorts the equality between the communicators as it empowers one participant vis-à-vis the other.

I.4.1.a. *Lasswell*

Nearer in time, Lasswell (1948) was the first to speak of the linearity of communication that empowers one of the communicators at the expense of the other by investing the former with the power to produce and disseminate messages. Lasswell was primarily concerned with mass communication and propaganda. So, his model traces the graph of communication as a linear route involving someone speaking in a certain channel to someone with a certain effect on the person(s) spoken to. As John Fiske observes, "This is a verbal version of Shannon and Weaver's original model. It is still linear: it sees communication as the transmission of messages: it raises the issue of 'effect' rather than meaning."[17]

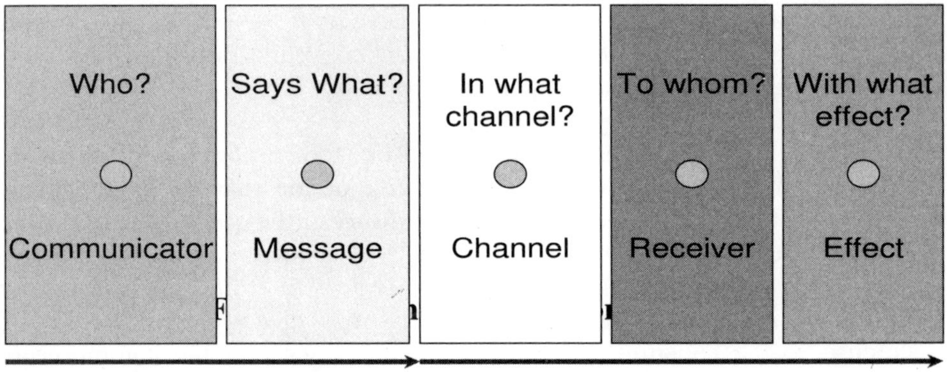

Figure I.4: Lasswell's Model

I.4.1.b. *Shannon and Weaver*

Shannon and Weaver, two engineers concerned with the fidelity of the sound transmitted across telephone lines, gave a similar account of communication to explain the efficiency of the mechanical process that they had been working on. Their model consisted of five elements: an information source, producing the message; a transmitter, encoding the message; a channel through which the encoded message is sent as signals; a receiver, decoding/reconstructing the message from the signals; and a destination/recipient receiving the message. All these elements were not unlike those spelt out by Lasswell. They, however, added a sixth element too in the form of the noise that subverts the message. Claude Shannon and Warren Weaver were not social scientists but engineers working for Bell Telephone Labs in the United States. Their goal was to ensure the maximum efficiency of telephone cables and radio waves. They developed a model of communication which was intended to assist in developing a mathematical theory of communication.

Shannon and Weaver's work was no doubt seminal. But it was more useful for the technical side of communication than for its applied part. It focussed on the capacity of communication channels to carry voice data undistorted from the sender of the messages to the recipients. It also contributed to laying the foundation of new technologies such as the new information and communication technologies (NICTs), disciplines such as the mathematical study of information as well as concepts such as redundancy of language. However, the extension of their ideas to human communication resulted in distorting its integral character. According to Erik Meeuwissen (email 26/2/98), Shannon himself was well aware of the fact that his theory did not address meaning. He offers these supportive quotations from Shannon and Weaver:

> The fundamental problem of communication is that of reproducing at one point either exactly or approximately a message selected at another point. Frequently the messages have meaning; that is they refer to or are correlated according to some system with certain physical or conceptual entities.

The word 'information', in this theory, is used in a special sense that must not be confused with its ordinary usage. As Fiske puts it, "(the) term information is used in a specialist, technical sense, and to understand it we must erase from our minds its usual everyday meaning."[18] In particular, information must not be confused with meaning. In fact, two messages, one of which is heavily loaded with meaning and the other of which is pure nonsense, can be exactly equivalent, from this viewpoint, as regards information.

Lasswell and Shannon and Weaver together spawned a host of communication theories and models that spoke of the communicator as source or transmitter or *sender* of the message and the other communicator as the recipient. John Fiske observes Shannon and Weaver's model is "widely accepted as one of the main seeds out of which Communication Studies has grown."[19]

The Shannon and Weaver and Lasswell models are typical of so-called Transmission Models of Communication. These two models also typically underlie many others in the American tradition of research, showing Source-Message/Channel-Receiver as the basic process of communication. In such models, communication is reduced to a question of transmitting information. The Transmission Model fixes and separates the roles of 'sender' and 'receiver'. But communication between two people involves simultaneous sending and receiving (not only talking, but also body language and so on). In Shannon and Weaver's model, the source is seen as the active decision-maker who determines the meaning of the message; the destination is the passive target.

It is a linear, one-way model, ascribing a secondary role to the receiver, who is seen as absorbing information. However, communication is not a one-way street. Even when we are simply listening to the radio, reading a book or watching TV, we are far more interpretively active than we normally realize. There was no provision in the original model for feedback (reaction from the receiver). Feedback enables speakers to adjust their performance to the needs and responses of their audience. A feedback loop was added by later theorists, but the model remains linear.

In short, the transmission model distorts the very truth of communication and is in fact a representation of the process of mass communication, which thwarts the inter-changeability of the roles of the sender and the recipient, by concentrating the power of producing and sending messages in the hands of the mass media owners. So, this model is of little value for understanding the dynamics of communication in the unmediated public and private spheres. This model has restrictive applicability to situations in which the mass media operates. Its reductive influence has implications not only for the commonsensical understanding of communication in general, but also for the specific forms of communication such as speaking and listening, writing and reading, watching television and so on. In education, it represents a similar transmissive model of teaching and learning. And in perception in general, it reflects the naive 'realist' notion that meanings exist in the world awaiting only to be decoded by the passive spectator. In all these contexts, such a model underestimates the creativity of the act of interpretation.

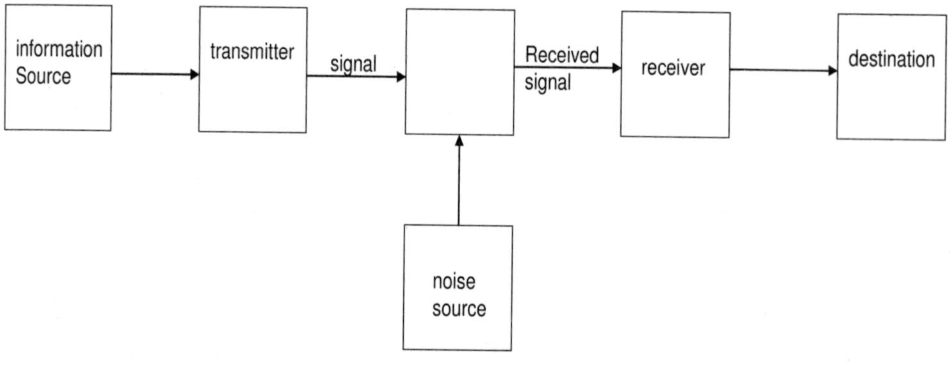

Figure I.5: Shannon and Weaver's Model of Communication

I.4.1.c. *Gerbner's Model of Communication*

Gerbner's model of communication is a variation on Shannon and Weaver's model of communication. This model, as is clear from the diagram, added the perceptual dimension to the process of communication as envisioned by the Transmission School. John Fiske remarks, "(I)t relates the message to the 'reality' that it is 'about' and thus enables us to approach questions of perception and meaning, and it sees the communication process as consisting of two alternating dimensions- the perceptual or receptive, and the communicating or means and control dimension."[20]

The event (E) is perceived by M (a man or a machine). The process of perception is not simply a matter of 'taking a picture' of event E. It is a process of active interpretation. M, the perceiver of the event E (or receiver of the message) selects from the event, paying more attention to this aspect and less to that.

This process of selecting, filtering is commonly known as gatekeeping, particularly in discussion of the media's selection and discarding of events or aspects of them. The selection is also determined by the context and the availability of such events. Based on the interpretation of the perceiver, event E 1 is formed in the mind of the perceiver. The degree of correspondence between M's perception of event E (E1) will be a function of M's assumptions, point of view, experiences, social factors etc.

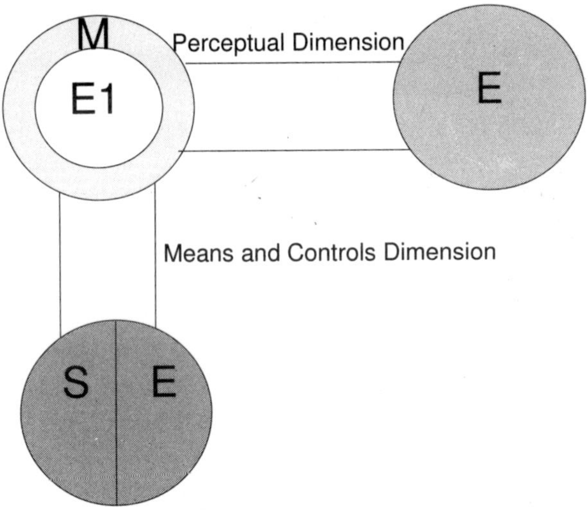

Figure I.6: Gerbner's General Model

In the next stage of the model, M becomes the Source of a message about E to someone else. M produces a statement about the event (SE). To send that message, M has to use channels (or media) over which he has a greater or lesser degree of control. The question of control relates to M's degree of skill in using communication channels. SE (statement about event) is what we would more normally call the message. S stands for Signal in fact, so in principle an S can be present without an E, but in that case it would be noise only. The process can be extended ad infinitum by adding on other receivers (M2, M3 etc.) who have further perceptions (SE1, SE2 etc.) of the statements about perceived events.

The generality of the model makes it useful for the analysis of both interpersonal and mass communication. Where the mass media are concerned, E could be potential news, M the mass media, SE media content and M2 the media audience.

I.4.1.d. *David Berlo's SMCR Model* (1960)

This model is as linear as the other transmission school models are. Berlo, however, adds one more element to this model which makes it dyadic instead of being monadic. Berlo stresses the role of relationship between the source and the receiver as an important variable for ensuring the success of communication.

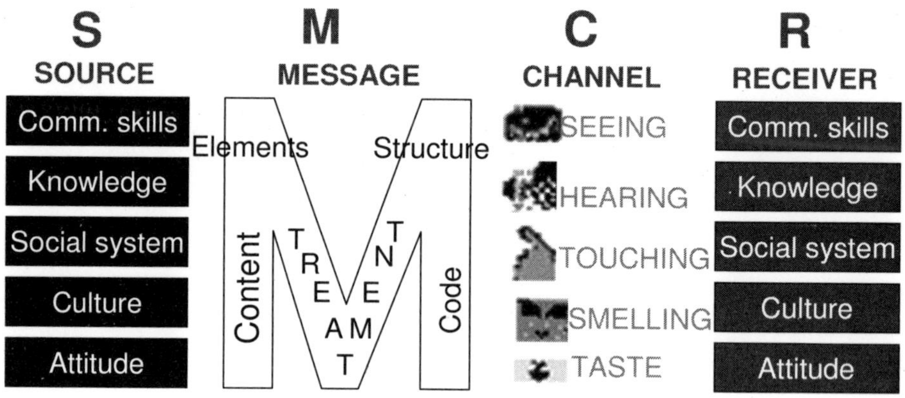

Figure I.7: Berlo's SMCR Model

Apart from this, he enumerates the factors to be taken into account at each 'end' of the communication for predicting the success of communication. These are the relative competence of the sender and the receiver in regard to communication skills, their relative levels of knowledge, the convergence/divergence of the social systems they belong to, their cultural affinities and their relative attitudes. It's not easy to make a clear distinction between the influence of culture and of the social system, so the two are often referred to as the socio-cultural system.

I.4.1.e. *Halliday* (1978)

Like others in the Transmission School, Halliday too subscribes to the linear model. However, his emphasis falls on the impact of the socio-cultural moorings of the communicators. According to him, no source communicates as a free agent without being influenced by his/her position in a socio-cultural system. People in differing social classes communicate differently. Social and cultural systems partly determine

- the word choices which people make
- the purposes they have for communicating
- the meanings they attach to certain words
- their choice of receivers
- channels they use for this or that kind of message etc.

I.4.1.f. *Maletzke's Model of Mass Media* (1963)
Just as the rest of the transmission models, the Maletzke's model of mass media has linearity built into it. The model emphasizes the commonly found elements in a transmission model, namely: Communicator (C), Message (M), Medium and Receiver (R).

It is interesting to note that Maletzke's model comprises four major elements, whereas Lasswell's model, which underlies many communication models, comprises five. Maletzke argues that the 'with what effect?' component of Lasswell's model properly belongs to sociological and psychological study of the receiver and should therefore not be introduced as a fifth component. He mentions in passing that other commentators have introduced a variety of different elements, for example Braddock has seven: 'Who says what to whom under what circumstances through what medium and with what effect? (Braddock, through further segmentation, eventually arrives at 84). McLuhan has seven: source of information, the sensing process, sending, the flight of information or transportation of information, receiving, decision-making, the action.

I.5. The U-turn: Mass Communication to Communication

During the 1970s, criticism of one-way, top-down, persuasive models of communication was well articulated by Latin American scholars such as Beltrán, (1974, 1976, 1980) and Díaz Bordenave (1976). As a consequence of this growing dissatisfaction, emphasis began to shift from audience members as individual objects to audiences as social groups, and from the action of sources on receivers to the *relationships* among participants (Schramm, 1973), to *mutual understanding* (Kincaid, 1979, 1988), and to *convergence* within communication networks (Rogers and Kincaid, 1981; Kincaid 1993; Rogers, 1995).

The Transmission School of Communication and the process of mass communication perpetuated a communication inequality wherein the sender of the messages got empowered at the expense of the recipient. The 'massification' of media messages was a pivotal element in the widespread prevalence of this model in theory and praxis. So, any attempt at restoring the balance in the communication inequality had to target this massification of messages. This got catalyzed through two important developments in mass media. One was the emergence of the new media consequent upon the advent of the new information and communication technologies and the other was the reinvention of the old media in response to the threat from the new media and the prospect of new business opportunities opened up by globalization post-WTO.[21]

I.5.1. *Emergence of New Media and the Resurrection of Communication*

The New Media was at once a democratic media that pulled the rug from under the seat of power of the 'producer' of messages and rehabilitated the user as an equal participant in communication. Tim Berger Lee's Mosaic browser was designed to enable the Web surfers to communicate among themselves irrespective of who had hosted the site. For the first time, the difference between the producer and the consumer of messages had been made to evaporate and the quintessential spirit of communication as it obtained at the interpersonal and the small group level resurrected. Obviously, it resulted in the individuation/personalization of messages, which the old mass media could never achieve. For the first time, the lumpen mass of mass communication had acquired a face, a personal and individual character.

The old mass media reacted to this development through a number of measures. One was the co-opting of the new media and its incorporation within the matrix of the old media. Newspapers and TV channels increasingly resorted to the use of mobile messages for opinion polls and for narrowcasting. Some of them went online by hosting the print editions on the web as their news sites. But, though they went on the Web they little understood the character of the new media. As a result, they ended up hosting shovel ware on their sites. As understanding of the new media dawned, the interactive options available on the news sites increased, enabling the participation of the audience in the process of mass communication. The development of blogs was another step in the direction of the empowerment of the audience as an equal participant in the process of communication. Each of these developments had the fallout of greater acknowledgement of the personal/individual element in mass communication. As individual readers accessed the various interactive options available on the news sites or communicated their views through mobile phones to the media house, the personal element in communication got strengthened.

I.5.2. *Evolution of Supplement Journalism*

There was yet another development in mass media, in particular the newspapers, which sought to redeem the individuals in the mass audience from the stigma of the 'mass'. This was the launching of supplements by various newspapers. This development was engineered by a number of factors. For one, the television had made strong inroads into the audience share of the newspapers. Secondly, with the growth of business opportunities in a post-globalised world, newspapers saw the potential of tapping the huge advertising revenues by launching supplements that targeted niche 'audiences'. The developments in new information and communication technologies greatly facilitated this move by helping in efficient content management.

This change was all the more felt in India, where for long journalism, in particular print journalism, as it had a long and hoary tradition almost in tandem with that in the West, was more a mission than a profession. The Indian print media had played a significant role in the freedom struggle of the country and it carried on this tradition of service to the society till the body politic, and the society in general, had not got infected with the virus of self-aggrandizement at the cost of nation building.

In India, newspapers saw the light of the day on January 29, 1780, when James Augustus Hickey, a disgruntled ex-employee of the East India Co. launched Bengal Gazette to expose the malpractices of the company. Although in nascent stage, newspapers soon started playing a strong political and social role, motivating people to join the freedom struggle thus broadening the base of the movement for independence. Nation building phase followed the pre-independence or the militant phase. Newspapers engaged themselves in disseminating information regarding national policies and helping the young nation take up various challenges at social, national and economic levels. It was Indira Gandhi's tenure that marked an imposing shift in journalism. In the changing milieu journalism started being recognized as a profession.

With liberalization started the wave of market-driven journalism. Today's new generation editors are the employees, following certain unwritten rules and conventions governing the running of the newspaper industry set by the people who own the controlling shares of the publication. Today, the prime consideration of many successful newspapers seems to be increasing circulation for increasing their ad tariff and earning more money. The very organization of the newspaper industry has been greatly influenced by the business practices of a successful industry. This age of media empires, marketing strategies and communication advancements has made monopolistic practices possible. Mini Murdochs have already appeared in the Indian media scene dictating terms to the PCI and justifying their moneymaking propositions. This new trend has erased even the traces of 'service before the self mantra'. The success of a newspaper in the modern

India is determined by its circulation and not by its promotion of what is truthful, essential and beneficial to the society.

The need for 'pluses' in daily newspapers started with the introduction of 'Delhi Times' pullout of The Times of India. The newspaper management thought that there was a void for Entertainment News. And there was no space in the main newspaper for such news. What started as a 'fill-in' for entertainment news later on has gone to become a major revenue earner, even though it continues to become an entertainment and event management supplement. Seeing its success, Hindustan Times also ventured into it through a separate daily pullout on entertainment and event management by the name of 'The Delhi City'. Both the pullouts have become a daily part of the two newspapers and are in fact supposed to be the 'papers' to be read first by the GenNext, which according to various studies, prefer these supplements as their first paper. Hindustan Times group's latest addition in its list of supplements – HT Next – has been an instant hit with the youth especially the school children. The supplement offers everything that the youth ever wanted from its newspaper, right from sports news, nuggets on celebs, career tips, humour, world news, fashion, coverage of political and national issues etc. To make the supplement interactive, columns like 'My Space' and 'Ask the Expert' have also been included.

Other newspapers followed suit, though not necessarily targeting entertainment or event management. The Indian Express came out with 'Delhi Express' supplement with the daily. The target audience was the news specific of Delhi. The Statesman followed suit with Delhi news. All other newspapers including The Hindu then came out with such supplements. Even outside Delhi, newspapers like The Tribune, Deccan Herald, Deccan Chronicle, The Asian Age had to come out with the Delhi pages of their newspapers although these newspapers were not based in Delhi. Newspaper managements have found that even though somebody may be in the habit of reading The Tribune, which is a Chandigarh-based newspaper, with emphasis on news of North India including Punjab, Haryana, Himachal Pradesh, Chandigarh and Jammu and Kashmir, unless separate Delhi pages were provided with the Delhi edition, the end consumer should get the Delhi news as an additional benefit.

Such success of pullouts prompted all newspapers in the country to bring out specific pullouts or supplements, as one would like to say. The pullouts or supplements are today specific to art, culture, agriculture, education, jobs, region-specific or may be even district specific. The Hindi newspaper industry got a real fillip from this exercise. Today all newspapers in Hindi, which were known as vernacular press, have gained from this experiment. All major Hindi dailies today have supplements or pullouts of separate districts. This vernacular press has now become a force to be reckoned with.

The best part of the whole exercise has been that today all the pluses have become money-spinners for the newspapers. There are instances where the advertisement rates for such pullouts are more than those of the main newspaper. All that a newspaper has to do to bring out such a pullout, if it is region specific, is to hire a press in the local area and keep three-four reporters who also double as sub-editors and bring out any number of pages ranging from two pages to six pages. They provide the local touch to the main newspaper and, being region-specific, sell like hot cakes. Any newspaper which has to survive today has to be region-specific and it ultimately becomes a money-earner for the newspaper.

While supplement journalism was an offshoot of the trend of market driven journalism, it had the fallout of splintering the mass audience into its heterogeneous groups, thereby taking a step in the direction of individuation of mass communication. As the introduction of supplement journalism was actuated by market considerations, its content was structured differently from that of the main broadsheet to which it was appended.

I.5.3. ***Mapping the Content of Supplements***

Chambers' Dictionary defines supplement as a separate part that comes with the newspaper, especially on Sunday. According to Readers' Digest Great Illustrated Dictionary, supplement is a separate section devoted to a special subject inserted into a newspaper, especially a coloured magazine. Most newspapers, these days, carry supplements day after day. These supplements usually carry the area's own news, features and other talks of the towns, including food, health, education, fitness, new electronic and beauty products etc. Right from Monday to Sunday, we have at least one independent supplement besides the main paper. They provide readers with all the information and gossip in profusion to meet their readers' every conceivable informational need.

Supplements are of two types: mixed and subject-specific. Mixed supplements cover various subjects. They have material for everyone and therefore, become magazines in themselves. Saturday and Sunday supplements are examples of mixed supplements. Subject-specific supplements extensively deal with different aspects of a single subject. These could be on lifestyle, science & technology, automobiles, careers, jobs and placement, property, education and so on and so forth. For example, there are investment supplements to guide you to choose shares, mutual funds of trustworthy leasing companies. If one plans to buy a car, TV, fridge, house etc, one will get ready advice from this supplement which enables one to plan funds. Sometimes there are supplements purely based on advertisements.

Supplements on the classified open up the entire world of work, nationally and globally. There are newspaper supplements devoted to art, culture, book reviews, films, drama, theatre and a lot of such writings. Education supplements discuss in detail various courses, their placement prospects and institutes offering them. Likewise, lifestyle supplements help keep their readers abreast of the latest trends, dos and don'ts of interior decoration, latest designer outfits, the most happening pubs and discotheques and eating joints etc. Saturday and Sunday supplements offer their readers a treat of reading material enough to enable them to spend the weekend enjoying these.

Though supplements provide information in printed form, these are undoubtedly different from newspapers in terms of content, layout and design, size, page make up, advertisement space, headlines and visuals etc. Supplements are more localized.

I.5.4. *Theoretical Underpinnings of Supplement Journalism*

Supplement journalism marks a shift in the usual content of newspapers, which for the most part have been busy more with the surveillance function of mass communication. As a part of that surveillance, the main newspapers have focused on hard news dealing with developments in the political and business world as impinging on the lives of the members of the society/nation and the collective whole of the society/nation itself. Supplements seek to break away from this concern to fulfill the other gratifications citizens seek from newspapers in particular and mass media in general. They also tend to de-stress the weary minds of their readers by providing them the necessary cathartic outlet. The following theories of mass communication, therefore, seem to structure and underpin the popular reception of the supplements.

I.5.4.a. *Commercial Theory*

Mass media today plan, produce and disseminate their messages taking into consideration the commercial aspects also. For, it has been found by researchers that even developmental messages, if covered in an entertaining manner, go a long way in appealing to the tastes of the readers. This theory, therefore, considers consumers as primary targets and avers that mass media produce programmes, serials and entertainment shows keeping in view the tastes, needs, wishes and status of the audience. This theory is also known as the *laissez faire theory*.

According to this theory, mass media are operated by big business houses, monopolies and MNCs. These lead to intense competition among programme producers and mass media exercise tremendous manipulative powers. Also, there comes about a large variety and diversity of information, opinions and viewpoints reducing the chances of manipulation and lowering professional standards.

Supplement journalism fulfils this need of the advertisers for capturing and holding the attention of the readers. The glossy paper used and the salacious content featurised along with colourful pictures attract the attention of the readers and pass it on to the advertisers for pushing their messages across. In the attention economy, supplements, therefore, become the tools of grabbing maximum eyeballs for the advertisers.

I.5.4.b. *Play Theory*

Media impacts have been interpreted in a variety of theories and models. Generally, media is believed to be exercising corrupting effect on masses. Several communication scholars have highlighted media's harmful influences on the audience. Yet another view is that media provides audience only with a 'play experience.' William Stephenson has opined that media is there to provide pleasure. Newspapers are read not for news or information but for pleasure and entertainment. Stephenson thus concludes that entertainment is the primary function of mass media. He brands media as 'buffer against conditions which would otherwise be anxiety producing.' He interprets the impact in these terms because he feels that mass media protect people from worries by deliberately focusing on the higher aspects of life. This, he feels, lightens the burdens of the audience. He believes social responsibilities and several other obligations of people diminish pleasure of life for them. The function of mass media should be to help reduce pressures on the people and provide such communication as enhances their pleasures.

Supplements perform this role to perfection. Their pleasing layout, glossy paper, uninhibited riot of colours, and interesting content helps to distress the readers. At times, it goes to the extent of pandering to the tastes of the readers. Thus, supplements, more than any other part of a newspaper, help the readers to release their pent up tension of the day and recreate an element of joy within them.

I.5.4.c. *Uses and Gratifications Theory*

As opposed to the Play theory, this theory propounds that "media serves a variety of needs stemming from the personal and social situations of the individual." As John Fiske puts it, "This approach takes as its basis the belief that the audience has a complex set of needs which it seeks to satisfy in the mass media.... This model of communication assumes an audience that is at least as active as the sender. It also implies that a message is what the audience makes of it, not what the sender intends, and thus has some similarity with the semiotic method."[22]

The theory is based on the assumptions that the audience is active and it is not a passive receiver of whatever the media broadcast. It selects and uses programme content. Also, audience members freely select the media and the programmes that they can best use to gratify their needs. The media producer may not be aware of the uses to which the programme may be put, and different audience members may use the same programme to gratify their various needs.[23]

As Stanley J. Baran and Dennis K. Davis say, "One of the first mass communication text books, The Process and Effects of Mass Communication, offered an early active-audience conceptualization. Author Wilbur Schramm (1954, p. 19) asked the question, 'What determines which offerings of mass communication will be selected by a given individual?' The answer he offered is called the fraction of selection, and it looks like this:

$$\frac{\text{Expectation of Reward}}{\text{Effort Required}}$$

His point was that people weigh the level of reward (gratification) they expect from a given medium or message against how much effort they must make to secure that reward."[24]

Researchers have sought to interpret the motives for content, choice and the satisfaction looked for and derived from media. Generally, audience use mass media in two ways: compensatory and supplementary. While compensatory use refers to using media for education deficiency, need for social success or raising one's status, media is also used for extending existing knowledge parameters and tackling social conundrums. With their wide variety of editorial content, supplements fulfill all these needs of the readers. So, any study of supplements cannot afford to ignore the motivations underpinning the use of supplements by readers.

I.5.4.d *Agenda Setting Theory*

The term 'agenda-setting' was coined by McCombs and Shaw.[25] It describes a very powerful influence of the media – the ability to tell us what issues are important. Agenda-setting is the creation of public awareness and concern of salient issues by the news media. The theory states that two assumptions underlie most research on agenda-setting: the press and the media do not reflect reality; they filter and shape it; and secondly, media concentration on a few issues and subjects leads the public to perceive those issues as more important than other issues. One of the most critical aspects in the concept of an agenda-setting role of mass communication is the time frame for this phenomenon. In addition, different media have different agenda-setting potential.

Bernard Cohen (1963) states: "The press may not be successful much of the time in telling people what to think, but it is stunningly successful in telling its readers what to think about."[26] Echoing him, Bernard Cohen writes, "The press is significantly more than a purveyor of information and opinion. It may not be successful much of the time in telling people what to think, but it is stunningly successful in telling its readers what to think about. And it follows from this that the world looks different to different people, depending not only on their personal interests, but also on the map that is drawn for them by the writers, editors, and publishers of the papers they read."[27]

Ghorparde puts it more succinctly when he observes, "Agenda setting is a relational concept that specifies a transfer of salience from agenda primers (media) to agenda adopters (consumers)." Agenda setting research has shown that there is a correlation between what the media deems important and what the public prioritizes. In simpler terms, agenda setting claims that what the media finds important will eventually be mirrored in what people think are important. It is important to note that the notion of agenda setting is positive association between the media and the audience. From agenda setting stems the formation of public opinions and the distribution of pros and cons of a particular issue. The notion of agenda setting relies on the transfer of issues from the media to the public.

With its wide variety of content, particularly the non-political one, supplement journalism should open the flood gates of issues seeking public/media attention. In other words, it should help to broaden the agenda of public debate and discussion. As has been seen in Indian print media, the mainstream newspapers have been almost exclusively focussed on the political aspect of Indian public life. Supplements have brought under public glare issues as diverse as lifestyle and religion. It remains to be seen, however, as to what is the level and quality of engagement of the media when it covers these subjects.

I.5.4.e. *Theory of Social Differentiation*

The Theory of Social Differentiation traces the origin of differences in their institutionalized form within the society. While the agrarian society too was fraught with differences between the landed gentry and the peasantry, the industrial society has been a far more complex whole of differences based on class, caste, race, colour and gender. The social differences in the agrarian society were based more on the social and economic roles played by individual members. But these differences were often buffered by the strong 'communal' interpersonal links between them on account of age old shared values and beliefs. The industrial society has none of these 'communalising' features.

As a result, it is an atomized society where individual goals and aspirations take a natural precedence over communal, rather societal, goals and aspirations. So, when industrialization threw people belonging to different cultural, social and economic backgrounds into a shared geographical space, the modern city/town, the differences of race, colour, caste, class and gender assumed an unmitigated divisive proposition. Ferdinand Tonnies, the German sociologist, distinguished these two different kinds of social groupings, born out of the evolutionary cycle of society, as *gemeinschaft* and *gesellschaft*. As Stanley J. Baran and Dennis K. Davis remark, "He(Ferdinand Tonnies) proposed a simple dichotomy—**Gemeinschaft** or folk society and **Gesellschaft** or modern, industrial society. In folk society, people were bound together by strong ties of family, tradition, rigid social roles—basic social institutions were very powerful. .... In Gesellschaft, people are bound together by relatively weak social institutions based upon rational choices rather than tradition."[28]

In his book by the same title, published in 1887, he dwelt at length over the characteristics of these two societies. *Gemeinschaft,* often translated as community, is a social grouping in which individuals are oriented to the goals of the community as much as, if not more, to their own self-interest. Furthermore, individuals in *gemeinschaft* are regulated by common mores and beliefs about the appropriate behaviour and responsibility of every member of the community. In other words, the *gemeinschaft* was a natural extension of the family.

In contrast, *gesellschaft,* often translated as social or civil society, describes social groupings in which the individual members place their individual self-interests over and above the interests of the society and lack any sense of shared mores evolved over the ages. The members of such a society often act in their own self-interest and are, therefore, susceptible to class conflicts as well as racial and ethnic conflicts. Besides, members of such societies are appropriate targets for advertisers as each of them strives to climb the higher rung in the socio-economic hierarchy.

India, as the cliché goes, is a land of contrasts. The bullock cart and the Mercedes jostle for the same driving space. Even as India enters the twenty-first century (and by implication the post-modern information age), it continues to retain living and vibrant vestiges of the pre-industrialised past.

Incidentally, Gurgaon and Hisar happen to represent these two stages of social evolution. While Gurgaon, by and large, is representative of a *gesellschaft* society where cosmopolitanism rules the roost, Hisar is, more or less, representative of a *gemeinschaft* community where social binding is much more compared to Gurgaon. The Theory of Social Differentiation has, therefore, been used to understand the differences and similarities of readers' perception about the supplement content.

I.6. Objectives of the Study

This study attempts to analyse and compare the supplements of The Times of India, as circulated in Gurgaon, a modern urban centre of Haryana state of India and Dainik Bhaskar, as circulated in Hisar, a traditional urban centre of Haryana state of India and readers' perception of each of the two, with the objective of mapping the semantic and structural categories of content in the respective supplements of The Times of India and Dainik Bhaskar and comparing and contrasting the two categories of content in the respective supplements. Also, the study attempts to uncover the sociological and communication theories underpinning the matrix of content in the two newspapers.

The study also attempts to map readers' perceptions about supplements in Gurgaon and Hisar cities/towns of the Haryana state of India by comparing and contrasting the supplement reading habits of the newspaper readers in both the cities with an objective of exploring the social, cultural and economic underpinnings of the comparative points of departure and similarity in the newspaper reading habits of members of a *gemeinschaft* community like Hisar and *gesellschaft* society like Gurgaon. The study also draws a comparison between the content and the readership pattern of the supplements of the two papers and aims at relating these differences to the differential development of the two cities. The study explores whether the content of supplements satisfies the supplement readers.

However, the study suffers from the limitations of time and human power. As it is a single person study and as it was time bound, it had to be restricted in scope. Nonetheless, as the nature of the content of supplements does not suffer much variation from one issue to another, this limitation does not affect the results of this study.

I.7. Review of Literature

Though newspaper supplements have been there for the last over fifty years, there has scarcely been any serious attempt to analyze them. When we take a look back in time at the various instances when supplements have attracted notice, we find that most such efforts have either been in the form of newspaper reports/reviews or articles. Here again, the focus of study for the most part has been commercial. Furthermore, even these analysis have been mostly carried out in the USA. Besides, some of these studies were based on magazines instead of newspaper supplements/pull outs. This section examines the efforts to analyze newspaper supplements with a view to justify the raison d etre of carrying out this study.

The earliest study carried out by Publishers' Information Bureau (PIB) in USA reported the shooting up of ad revenue by 3.3 per cent and the decline of pages by 1.4 per cent for 1986.[29] As a group, the 147 magazines studied by PIB saw a 3.3 per cent increase in 1986 advertising revenue over 1985, for a record revenue total of $5,120,345,209. That increase came despite a 1.4 per cent decrease in ad pages for the year, to 152,643.17.

Ad pages for newspaper supplements rose by 3.8 per cent for the year; revenue remained essentially flat. The Los Angeles Times' revamped magazine supplement doubled its ad revenue (103.8%) on a similar rate of gain in ad pages, while USA Weekend revenue declined by 22 per cent. Advertising page totals declined for every magazine among PIB's 1986 top-10 page sellers compared to 1985.

Yet another study on how people used and absorbed media in UK came up with interesting findings on the use of supplements vis-à-vis other media.[30] To do this, it drew on two new, and substantial, studies conducted between September 2001 and April 2002 by NFO WorldGroup - one a qualitative research survey, the other a quantitative one. The studies were commissioned by PPA as a magazine industry contribution to the current UK media advertising debate.

According to the study, newspapers seem to be used in a rather different way from their traditional news-assimilation role because of time pressures during the week and other, more up-to-the-minute, news sources. In particular, weekend newspaper packages are regarded as a welcome alternative to the week's bite-sized news items .

Om Gupta in his write up 'Fourth Dimension of the Fourth Estate'[31] extensively talks about the need, function and evolution of supplements. He builds up the case stating that the classic role of journalism was defined to inform, to educate and to entertain. And strictly in that order. No one ever thought of utility as a separate function. But when the satellite and cable television hit the Indian middle class in their drawing and bedrooms, suddenly the newspapers realized that its traditional role was fast losing ground to the more colorful and immediate medium. Hence, first the newspapers went colour and more features were added and then came the supplements.

Supplements planners kept on adding newer and more innovative ideas like real estate, information technology and even personal and emotional problem solutions. All this caught the attention and fancy of the reader who was predominantly youthful and enterprising. The pictures in these supplements defined the new moral standard raising quite a few eyebrows. But they announced the changing times and the traditional reader had to contend with the new profile of his age old newspaper. There was a visible change even in the layout of the hard stories both in content and layout. Many a times the newspapers led with sports or even a crime story. Crispy and informal language took over from the mundane and copybook fashion of drafting stories.

According to another study[32] that was conducted to find attitudes towards advertising in various media, although many people have a negative attitude towards advertising, advertising in magazines is seen more positively than in other media. Advertising in magazines is seen as more relevant than in other media and as being more helpful as a buying guide. Advertising in magazines and television was more trusted and believed than advertising seen elsewhere.

Commercial radio and websites came out poorly in terms of these unfavourable attitudes. In contrast, the three forms of print media - magazines, newspapers and newspaper supplements - fared much better, with relatively low levels of negative comments. When the respondents were asked if they usually trust the advertisements, 23 per cent said that they believed the ads in magazines, 17 per cent believed ads in newspapers whereas 10 per cent trusted ads in newspaper supplements. According to the study, 7 per cent of the readers agreed that they were more likely to pay attention to an advertisement if it appeared in newspaper supplements. However, 9 per cent of the newspaper supplement readers found advertisements annoying.

A study[33] was conducted by the Media Research Users Council (MRUC) to provide an understanding of the nuances of readers' habits towards newspaper pullouts and sections. The survey was conducted from July-August 2003 for Mumbai with a sample size of 1920. The survey revealed that for The Times of India, the average issue readership was 55 per cent of the claimed readership. However, when one checked the pullouts, the figure shot up. For Education Times, the figure was 87 per cent whereas for Ascent it was an impressive 91 per cent.

According to Karen Robock[34] during the late 1960s and early 1970s, the weekend supplements hosted a different breed of magazine journalist: the staff writer. These intrepid and often eccentric wordsmiths introduced the country to narrative journalism. The supplements themselves, laid out on stock paper with cheap ink, and printed by a process called rotogravure, a process now generally reserved for advertisements, averaged 18 pages in length. Tossed in weekend papers across the country along with the flyers, they turned out to be diamonds in the rough, taking Canadians around their country and around the world, and introducing art to the world of art direction.

Deepti Mahajan[35] contends that supplements and weekly pull-outs are products of the advertisers' need to reach out to the consumers. Advertising needs lead to the development of new media products. Supplements and topical pull-outs are products born out of such needs. Main newspapers/supplements and newsmagazines carry a variety of features – beauty and healthcare, fashion and technology – that exist largely to support the accompanying ads. At times, pull-outs carry features and ads aimed at selling one particular brand. Tourism ministries of countries/states are increasingly using pull-outs and special features as an advertising vehicle. Interest-specific supplements like 'Education Times' (The Times of India), 'Ascent' (The Times of India), 'HT Careers' (The Hindustan Times) etc., and subsidiary publications like the 'Outlook Traveller' and 'India Today travelPLUS' allow the advertisers to narrowcast their messages.

According to Robin Parker[36] newspaper supplements may boost newspaper circulation but the main gain from it lies in the advertising revenues. Specialist glossy supplements, devoted to a single interest, are flavour of the month among weekend newspapers locked in a battle for readers.

Newspapers claimed supplements built circulation. The Observer said supplements could boost circulation by up to 20,000 copies, while The Daily Telegraph said its occasional specials generated uplifts of around 7 per cent, with modest retention in subsequent weeks. The downside was they risked advertisers moving their existing campaigns from the paper into the supplements. But glossy supplements did not come cheap. Advertisers used them to reach a broader audience than consumer magazine readers, although they admitted it was unclear what proportion of each newspaper's readers actually read them. The relatively high cost often limited frequency, yet they needed to appear regularly to generate continuity of readership. This was a dilemma for the Telegraph and others.

According to another study[37], newspaper supplements are one of the most effective ways of spreading planning and design ideas to large numbers of people and generating public debate. They are particularly useful for presenting proposals from action planning events, especially if combined with other coverage before and afterwards.

The advantages of newspaper supplements are numerous:

- Cheap. Inexpensive as compared to producing and distributing a special report.
- Coverage. Reaches a very high proportion of the population (in most areas).
- Credibility. Has greater credibility than a report produced by consultants.
- Familiarity. Feels less threatening than most specially produced planning reports.
- Format. Large format allows drawings to be published at a reasonable scale.
- Immediacy. Very quick publication and distribution. The results of one day's workshop can be distributed the next day.
- Skills. Brings expert journalistic skills to bear.

Newspaper supplements are particularly relevant in cultures where newspapers are a popular media, adapted and accessible to all layers in the population and where freedom of expression is well respected.

I.8. Research Methods

As the objectives of this research include an analysis of readers' perception of the content in newspaper supplements and a comparative mapping of the content of newspaper supplements, quantitative research design was found most suitable.

I.8.1. *Methods of Data Collection*

In quantitative research design, information is collected through surveys of media audiences or content analysis of media texts on the basis of the quantification of observations of certain pre-determined parameters/variables. For the purpose of content analysis of newspaper supplements, the researcher selected two news dailies with the maximum circulation—The Times of India and Dainik Bhaskar, taking one from each of the two languages of English and Hindi.

I.8.1.a. *Sampling*

In order that a content analysis of newspaper supplements could be undertaken, it was necessary to go in for multi-stage sampling. In the first instance, it was necessary to select the sample out of the plethora of newspapers published and registered with the Registrar of Newspapers in India (RNI). On the basis of the circulation figures released by the RNI, the researcher selected two news dailies with the maximum circulation, taking one from each of the two languages of English and Hindi.

The selection of the two languages was based on their relative cultural significance. While English has traditionally been a symbol of the upwardly mobile middle and affluent classes, Hindi has been the language of the masses in North India. As such, English represents 'the modern', while Hindi 'the traditional' in the cultural dynamics of Indian society. As newspapers are repositories of the popular culture in any country, the differentiation in the language helps one to gauge the temper of the popular culture in two different segments of the society. While English helps to map the cultural affinities of the modernized uptown segment of the society, Hindi helps in knowing the cultural mores of the still traditional hinterland of the society.

On the basis of the parameter so fixed, The Times of India (TOI) and Dainik Bhaskar (DB) were selected for the purposes of this study. The Times of India is an English daily that comes out of the stable of Bennett Coleman & Co Ltd., a media conglomerate with interests in print, electronic and online media. On the other hand, Dainik Bhaskar is brought out by the Bhaskar Group. While The Times of India has been a leading paper from its inception prior to the independence of the country, Dainik Bhaskar has established itself in recent years on the crest of an aggressive marketing strategy in the Hindi heartland of India.

Once the newspapers had been identified, the next stage was of sampling the number of issues released by each of the two dailies. As it was a study of newspaper supplements and not the main newspaper, the number of issues required for an authentic study was limited. Here, it is pertinent to note that while the news covered in the main newspaper changes on a daily basis, the subjects covered in a supplement have a greater permanence. In other words, mapping the content of a supplement is possible with a fewer number of issues. Besides, that also takes care of redundancy of data. Keeping in mind this reality, it was decided to take all the supplements issued in one month in each of the two papers.

I.8.1.b. *Coding and Tabulation of Data*

The parameters mentioned above were coded and data collected from the sample was entered on the code sheet for tabulation. Small tables were then prepared from the master table for each of the two newspapers.

I.8.1.c. *Data Analysis*

The data obtained was analysed using percentage, average and ratio methods. In the first place, the results of TOI were analysed for each of the supplements and then these were compared across the spectrum of all the supplements of TOI. A similar exercise was carried out for DB. In the second instance, the results of the two newspapers were collated to arrive at the comparisons and contrasts of cultural moorings of the two.

I.8.2. *Survey Research*

In survey research, the researcher selects a sample out of the target audience/population and then administers a questionnaire to the respondents falling in the sample. Respondents are asked a variety of questions regarding their behaviour, intentions, attitudes, awareness, motivations, and demographic and lifestyle characteristics. Data collected from the respondents is then tabulated and analysed.

The survey method has several advantages. First, the questionnaire is simple to administer. Second, the data obtained is reliable because the responses are limited to the alternatives stated. The use of fixed-response questions reduces the variability in the results that may be caused by differences in interviewers. Finally, coding, analysis, and interpretation of data is relatively simple.[38]

I.8.2.a. *Sampling*

As the purpose of this media research was to generate findings that can be of use in mapping audience behavior, representative samples were crucial for deriving such results. In view of this, a sample was drawn of adult literate citizens living in Gurgaon and Hisar.

Gurgaon is a part of Delhi NCR. By virtue of its proximity to Delhi, it is a happening place. Industrially advanced, culturally uptown and modern, it displays characteristics of a metropolitan city which is susceptible to the spectre of consumerism. The people living here are perfect feed for an advertiser. In contrast, Hisar is a relatively less advanced and tradition bound town, which displays all the characteristics of a traditional society. The comparison between the two can be best summed up in the German sociologists, Ferdinand Tonnies' concepts of *gemeinschaft* and *gesellschaft* societies.[39] By drawing a sample from these two places, the researcher attempted to delineate the comparative graph of readers' perceptions about the content of supplements.

A sample of 500 respondents was drawn from each of the two cities using the random sampling method. The district census data of Gurgaon and Hisar was used as a base for the random selection of these respondents.

I.8.2.b. *Instruments of Data Collection*

Survey research uses the instruments of structured questionnaires which are administered to the sample for getting primary data. Questionnaires can be administered either personally, through mail, telephone or through email. Each of these methods has its own advantages and disadvantages. The personally administered interviews are the best means of collecting primary data. As the investigator is personally available, the respondents can seek explanations wherever required. Most often, personally administered interviews call for the assistance of the data collectors trained for the job. Questionnaires can also be mailed to the respondents.

However, such a method of data collection is fraught with the danger of mortality of questionnaires. As the recipients of questionnaires are unaware of their source, they do not feel inclined to take the pain of filling them up. Rather, they regard all such mails as an unsolicited nuisance. Even if there is a certain Good Samaritan, he gets put off if the questionnaire is lengthy. So, such instruments of data collection have to be kept short and also some inducement has to be offered to the respondents to fill them up. The telephonically delivered questionnaires are all the more dicey. Though easy to deliver and prompt in disposal, such questionnaires have to be extremely brief and racy. But this method of data collection is again problematic as it amounts to intrusion in the privacy of the respondents. Of all these methods, the most convenient and suitable are the ones delivered personally or through email. Both the methods enjoy instantaneousness of communication apart from affording a detailed question answer session.

In view of the comparative merit of the personally administered questionnaire, the researcher went in for this method of data collection. Accordingly, a detailed bilingual questionnaire was prepared to ascertain the readers' supplement reading behaviour and to know their views about the content of newspaper supplements.

I.8.2.c. *Coding and Tabulation of Data*

Questionnaires once administered generate data which is quantifiable. The next stage entails tabulation of the information. A master table serves as the basis of the preparation of the smaller tables pertaining to the different aspects of the problem. Accordingly, all the parameters were coded for easy tabulation of data collected. From the master table, smaller tables were prepared for ease of statistical analysis.

I.9.2.d. *Analysis of Data*

After tabulation, data can be processed at two levels; one descriptive and the other inferential. Descriptive analysis of data involves use of the descriptive statistical tools of measures of central tendencies and dispersion. Inferential analysis uses the statistical tools of correlation and regression. If the purpose of the research undertaken is prediction, then modeling and simulation techniques with the help of computer softwares can be utilized.

For the purposes of this study, only descriptive analysis was undertaken. The statistical tool used for analysis was percentage method.

REFERENCES

[1] Stanley J. Baran & Dennis K. Davis (2000), Mass Communication Theory: Foundations, Ferment, and Future, Second edition, Singapore: Thomson Wadsworth, p.7.

[2] http://www.indianetzone.com/6/indian_media.htm (in an article 'Indian Media') Indianetzone Web portal on Indian Culture and Lifestyle.

[3] Denis McQuail (2000) McQuail's Mass Communication Theory, 4th Edition, London: Sage Publications, p. 20.

[4] Navneet Anand (2008) *Media Globalisation and Mcdonalisation of Consumers*, Mass Communicator, 2 (2), pp.8-9.

[5] The Times of India (TOI) was one of the first newspapers to launch this strategy to counter the influence of HT in English print media markets. (Interview with K.K. Sharma, former News Editor, Times of India).

[6] Denis McQuail (2000) McQuail's Mass Communication Theory, 4th Edition, London: Sage Publications, p. 20.

[7] R.K. Dhar, (2008), *The Communication Epiphany: New Media and the Redemption of the Other*, Proceedings of the IAMCR 2008 Congress, Media and Global Divides, Stockholm.

[8] http://www.indianetzone.com/6/indian_media.htm (in an article 'Indian Media') Indianetzone Web portal on Indian Culture and Lifestyle.

[9] Ibid.

[10]Ibid.

[11] Om Gupta, (2002) Media Rewind: Fourth Dimension of the Fourth Estate, Vidura Volume 37, Issue 2.

[12] http://books.google.co.in

[13] Ibid.

[14] http://www.comminit.com/en/node/1277

[15] John Fiske, (1990), Introduction to Communication Studies, Second edition, Oxford: Routledge, first published, 1982, Reprint, 2006, p. 2.

[16] In Gabriel Garcia Marquez' 100 years of solitude the village community in Latin America is fed on the romanticized tales of India by the gypsies.

[17] Fiske, J (1990) Introduction to Communication Studies second edition, Oxford: Routledge, first published, 1982, Reprint, 2006, pp. 30-31.

[18] Ibid, p. 9.

[19] Ibid, p. 6.

[20] Ibid, p. 9.

[21] R.K. Dhar, 2008, *The Communication Epiphany: New Media and the Redemption of the Other,* Proceedings of the IAMCR 2008 Congress, Stockholm.

[22]Fiske, J (1990) op. cit., p.151.

[23] Ibid, p. 155.

[24] Stanley J. Baran & Dennis K. Davis (2000), op. cit., p. 248.

[25] Denis McQuail (2000) op. cit., p. 455.

[26]http://www.tcw.utwente.nl/theorieenoverzicht/Theory%20clusters/Mass%20Media/Agenda-Setting_Theory.doc/

[27] Stanley J. Baran & Dennis K. Davis (2000), op. cit., p. 300.

[28] Ibid, p. 56.

[29] 1987 http://findarticles.com/p/articles/mi_m3065/is_v16/ai_4788477

[30] Absorbing Media, http://www.magazinescanada.ca/files/Absorbing% 20Media %20Booklet.pdf

[31] Om Gupta, (2002) op. cit.

[32] http://www.ppamarketing.net/cgi-bin/wms.pl/714

[33] Indiantelevision.com's Breaking News, Posted on Dec 02, 2003 at 8.00 pm on http://us.indiantelevision.com/headlines/y2k3/dec/dec20.htm

[34] *A look back at "a brief and shining moment that will never come again." How the freebie inserts changed Canadian journalism* http://www.rrj.ca/issue/2004/spring/423/

[35] *Advertorials: blurring the dividing line,* Available at URL:

http://209.85.175.104/search?q=cache:ONFOkOEo5YYJ:www.indiatogether.org/2004/aug/med-advert.htm+effect+of+advertising+on+newspaper+supplements&hl=en&ct= clnk&cd=39&gl=in&client=firefox-a

[36] *Newspaper Supplements - Papers take on mags for ad share,* Media Week Media Week 25-Jul-06

http://www.brandrepublic.com/News/571459/Newspaper-Supplements---Papers-mags-ad-share/

[37] Strategic Principles-Participation-Methods, Available at: http://www.ilo.org/ciaris/pages/english/tos/strprinc/particip/methodes/fiche_5.htm

[38] Lawrence A. Crosby, Sheree L. Johnson, and Richard T. Quinn, "Is Survey Research Dead?" Marketing Management, page 861, Ch 63

[39] http://en.wikipedia.org/wiki/Gemeinschaft_and_Gesellschaft

CHAPTER II

CONTENT ANALYSIS OF THE TIMES OF INDIA SUPPLEMENTS

This chapter analyses the results obtained from the content analysis of India's most widely read English daily, The Times of India (TOI), Delhi edition, as circulated in Gurgaon, a modern urban centre in the National Capital Region.

By virtue of its pre-eminent position in terms of circulation, TOI could be considered as the mirror image of the socio-cultural manners and morals of people living in Delhi NCR. An analysis of the content of its supplements could, therefore, throw up interesting insights into the social and cultural life of people in a modern urban society. To this end, this chapter has been divided into two sections: Section 1 discusses the findings of the content analysis of individual TOI supplements, while the second section discusses the comparative analysis of the content of all TOI supplements.

II.1. General Parameters

TOI comes out with seven supplements over a week. The distribution of these supplements is, however, not even over all the week days. On the first day of the week, TOI comes out with 2 supplements, one each of Delhi Times (DT) and Education Times; on the second day it comes out with only Delhi Times; on the third day it comes out with 3 supplements again, one each of DT, Times Ascent (TA) and Gurgaon Plus (GP); on the fourth day it comes out with only one supplement i.e. DT; on the fifth day, with 2 supplements, one each of DT and What's Hot; on the sixth day again with three supplements, one each of DT, Times Property (TP) and GP; and on the last day of the week, it comes out with as many as 2 supplements which are DT and Times Life (TL). From the preceding discussion, it is obvious that only DT comes out on all the days of the week while the others with the exception of GP come out on only one day in a week; GP comes out on two days.

Despite the regularity of the scheme of issue of the 7 supplements of TOI over the week days, the supplements happen to be non-uniform in terms of their pagination and size. For instance, DT tends to vary the number of its pages and size most frequently, even though the supplement continues to be brought out as a broadsheet. Following sub-sections deal with the content analysis of each of these supplements.

II.1.a. *Delhi Times (DT)*

DT is the only supplement of TOI which comes out everyday with the main newspaper. It is issued as a broadsheet using newsprint as its paper. The sampled issues of DT were seen to have 288 pages in all in a month's time, which averaged out to 9.3 pages per day, showing the non-uniform nature of the number of pages that the supplement carries on different days.

II.1.a.i. *Space Distribution in DT*

Table II.1

Sl. No.	Parameters	Total	Average	Percentage
1	Edit	317472	10241	59.63
2	Ad	214968	6934.4	40.37

59.63 per cent of the total space of this supplement is devoted to the editorial matter while 40.37 per cent is occupied by advertisements, which works out roughly to the ratio of 3:2. Obviously, advertisements occupy a significant portion of the total space indicating thereby the marketing function of this supplement. Viewed in this perspective, one can well understand the variation in the number of pages of the supplement. In other words, whenever the number of advertisements increases more pages are added to the supplement to accommodate them. In an interview with the researcher, an editor of a news daily admitted that supplements often vary the number of their pages in accordance with the variation in the space requirement of the advertisements.

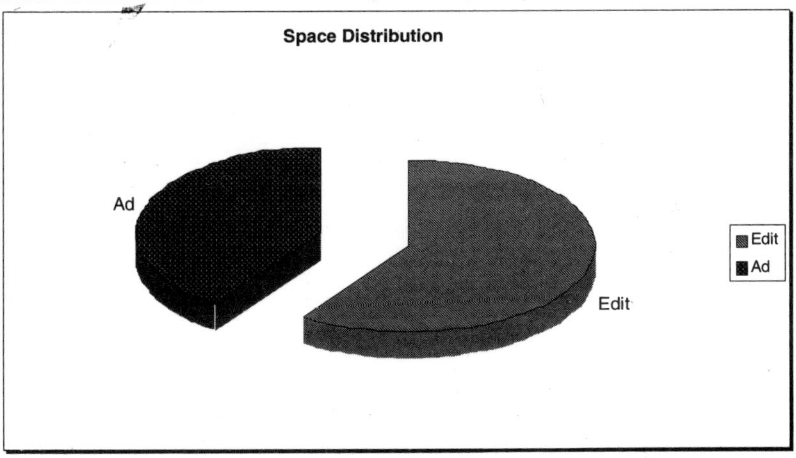

Figure II.1

II.1.a.ii. *Edit Space Distribution Between Text and Visuals*

Table II.2

Sl. No.	Parameters	Total	Average	Percentage
1	Text	235094	7583.6	74.05
2	Visual	82378	2657.3	25.95

Table II.2 depicts the edit space distribution between text and visuals in the supplement. The table shows that the edit space distribution between the text and the visuals is understandably tilted in favour of text, which takes up 74.05 per cent of the total edit space. In comparison, visuals occupy 25.95 per cent of the total edit space. In ratio terms, the edit space distribution works out roughly to 3:1 between the text and the visuals.

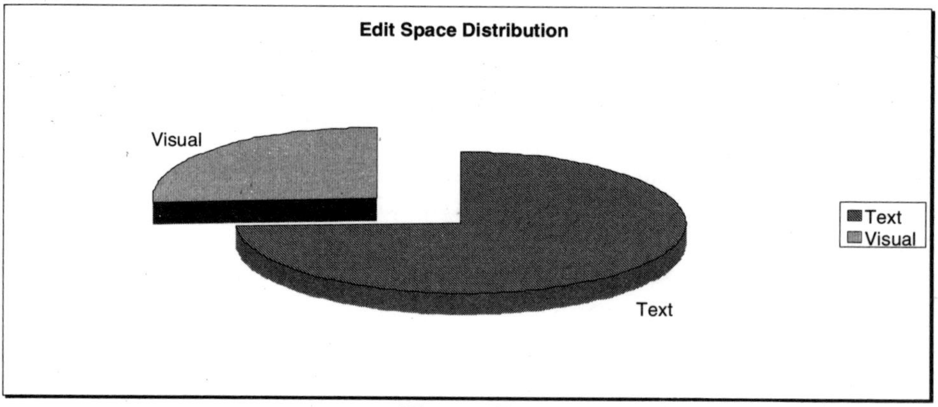

Figure II.2

II.1.a.iii. *Edit Space Distribution among Formal Categories*

Table II.3

Sl. No.	Parameters	Total	Average	Percentage
1	Interviews	29533.5	952.7	9.3
2	Soft Stories	86524	2791.1	27.25
3	Features	38680	1247.7	12.18
4	Memoirs	1216	39.2	0.38
5	Miscellanies	161518.5	5210.3	50.89

DT distributes its edit space over 5 kinds of formal categories which are interviews, soft stories, features, memoirs and miscellanies. On an average, each issue of DT carries miscellanies, which include zodiac, vaastu, fengshui, snippets, anecdotes, puzzles, jokes, comic strips, schedules, utility tips, readers' opinion etc., over a space of 5210.3 sq cm, soft stories over a space of 2791.1 sq cm, features 1247.7sq cm and interviews 952.7 sq cm; the least space being taken up by memoirs (39.2 sq cm). In percentage terms, miscellanies occupy 50.88 per cent of the total edit space, soft stories 27.25 per cent, features 12.18 per cent, whereas interviews and memoirs occupy 9.3 per cent and 3.83 per cent respectively. From the formal distribution of edit space, it is clear that the supplement lacks focus. With a little over 40 per cent of the total supplement space going to advertisements and more than 50 per cent of the edit space being accorded to miscellanies, the supplement shows its flippant character. However, the situation is somewhat redeemed by the soft stories and features which together occupy 39.43 per cent of the edit space. So, DT comes off as a superficial supplement meant only to attract attention to its variety but not to hold it for long. This accounts for the primacy of the marketing function, so succinctly brought out in the interview with the editor of the news daily. The intent is clear: DT is there to attract eye balls to deflect them to the advertisements in it and not to amuse or inform the reader with interesting human interest stories, which could in fact eat into the reading, or should it be said, viewing time of the reader/viewer.

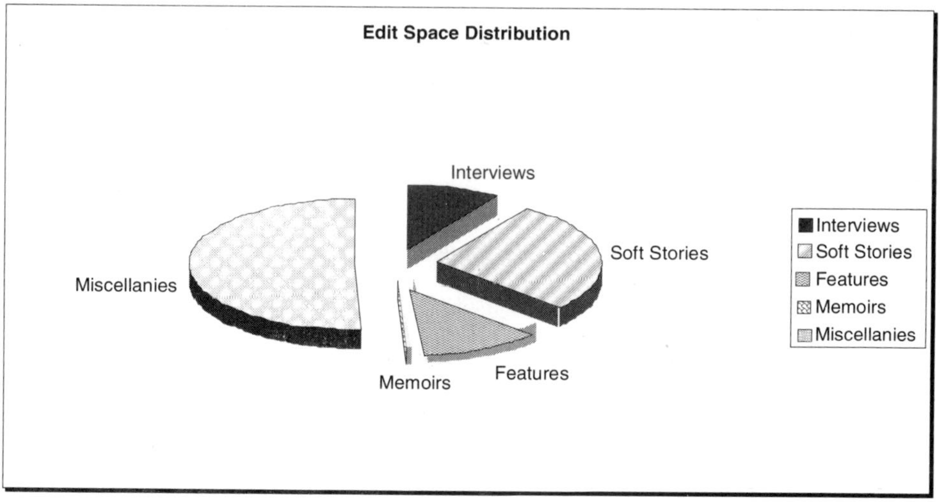

Figure II.3

II.1.a.iv. *Feature Space Distribution*

Table II.4

Sl. No.	Parameter	Total	Average	Percentage
1	Well Being	1234	39.8	3.19
2	Photo	3080	99.3	7.96
3	Celebrity	6948	224	17.96

4	Beauty	4142	133	10.71
5	Culinary	3608	116	9.33
6	Lifestyle	6470	208	16.73
7	Crime	3126	100	8.08
8	Politics	2428	78.3	6.28
9	Relationship	2982	96.2	7.71
10	Children	843	27.2	2.18
11	Bollywood	3819	123	9.87

The sample revealed that feature space is distributed over eleven subjects in different degrees of importance. The maximum space was occupied by celebrities (17.96%), followed by lifestyle features (16.73%), beauty (10.71%), Bollywood features (9.87%), culinary (9.33%), crime (8.08%), photo features (7.96%), relationship (7.71%), political features (6.28%), well being (3.19%), and children-related (2.18%). From the subject-based distribution of feature space, it is clear that high percentage space is given to beauty and glamour. It is understandable as these happen to attract attention, which is extremely vital for the advertisers. Once again, the marketing function gets highlighted in the subject-based distribution of feature space.

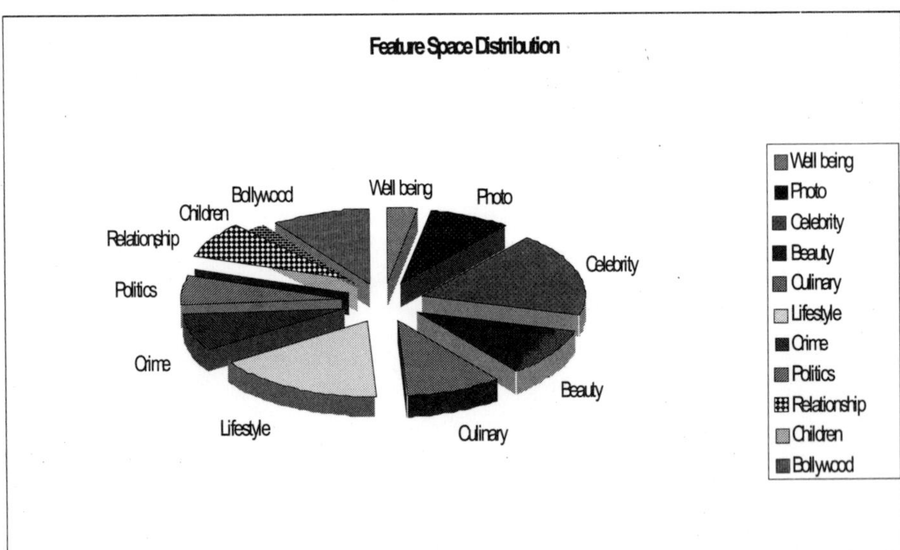

Figure II.4

II.1.a.v. *Relationship Feature Space Distribution*

Table II.5

Sl. No.	Parameters	Total	Average	Percentage
1	Formal	0	0	0.00
2	Informal	1248	40.3	41.89
3	Intimate	1734	55.9	58.11

An analysis of the feature space accorded to relationships shows that space devoted to intimate relationships is as large as 58.11 per cent compared to 41.88 per cent to informal relationships, while none is given to formal relationships. The high percentage of space given to intimate relationships is obviously meant to titillate and pander to the baser passions of the readers in order to attract them.

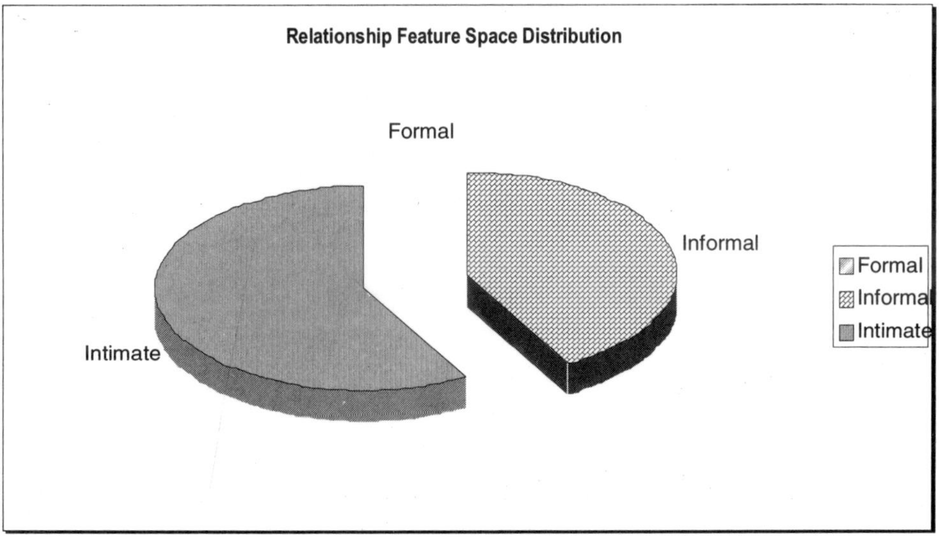

Figure II.5

II.1.a.vi. *Distribution of Visuals*

Table II.6

Sl. No.	Parameters	Total	Average	Percentage
1	Human Visuals	1852	59.7	93.72
2	Non-human Visuals	124	4	6.28

Of the total number of visuals (1976), the maximum number of visuals are of human beings (1852) and only 124 non-human. In percentage terms, human visuals are 93.72 per cent in number, while the non-human visuals are 6.28 per cent. The preponderance of human visuals is understandable as these can arrest attention for more than non-human visuals can.

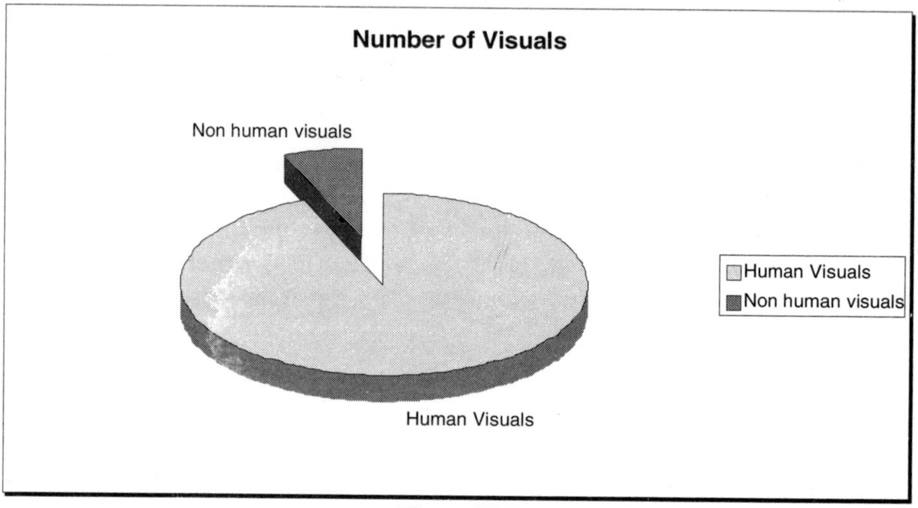

Figure II.6

II.1.a.vii. *Distribution of Human Visuals on the Basis of Societal Roles*

Table II.7

Sl. No.	Parameters	Number	Average	Percentage
1	P-3	460	14.8	24.83
2	TV and Films	1024	33	55.37
3	Political	32	1	1.68
4	Sports	56	1.8	3.02
5	Others	280	9	15.10

Further, the supplement depicts human beings in the societal roles of Page 3 personalities, TV & film personalities, political, sports and other personalities. Of these, the maximum number of visuals are those of TV & film personalities (55.37%), followed by those of Page 3 (24.83%), sports (3.02%), and political (1.68%); others number 15.10 per cent. The data shows a wide variation between the first two, on the one hand and the last three, on the other hand. The message is clear that DT highlights beauty and glamour as opposed to any other societal role. This is in keeping with the results deduced so far and further goes to prove that the supplement strives to attract eye balls and not to engage the reader in any meaningful dialogue.

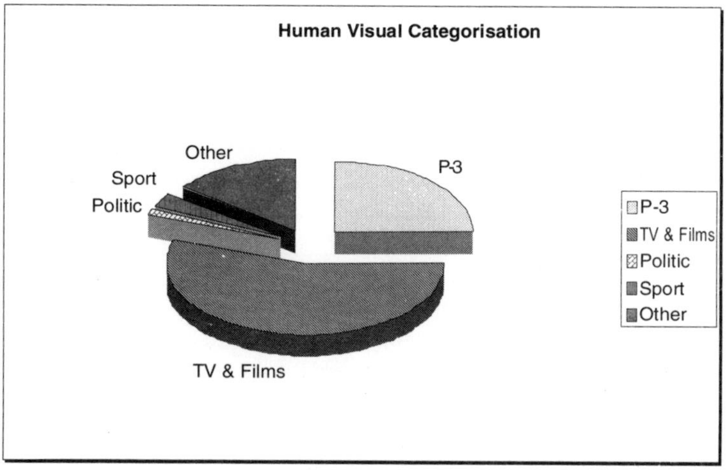

Figure II.7

II.1.a.viii. *Gender-Based Distribution of Human Visuals*

Table II.8

Sl. No.	Parameters	Number	Average	Percentage
1	Male	740	23.9	49.79
2	Female	748	24.1	50.21

A look at the table shows that the gender-based distribution of human visuals is slightly skewed in favour of the female visuals. While men account for 49.79 per cent of the human visuals, women account for 50.21 per cent. This preponderance of female visuals needs to be compared with the abysmally low percentage of working women in Indian public life. Obviously, the supplement realizes the potential of female visuals to attract readers' attention.

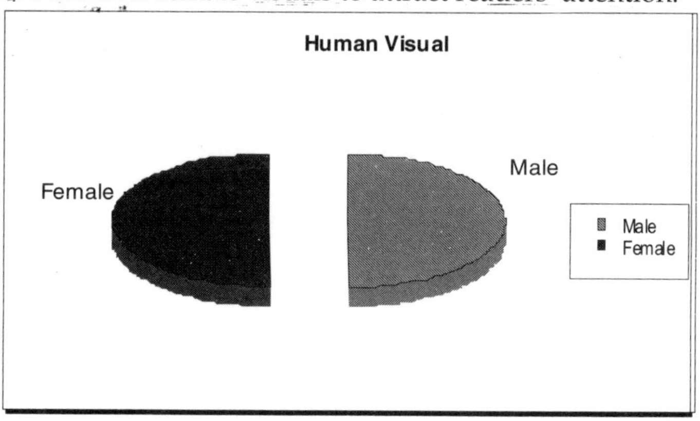

Figure II.8

II.1.a.ix. *Sartorial-Based Distribution of Human Visuals*

Table II.9

Sl. No.	Parameters	Total	Average	Percentage
1	Minimally Exposed	1424	45.9	76.88
2	Moderately Exposed	288	9.3	15.58
3	Maximally Exposed	140	4.5	7.54

The table shows that in the sample issues of the supplement, the maximally exposed human visuals were the least; these were only 7.54 per cent of the total number of human visuals, while the moderately exposed visuals were 15.58 per cent and minimally exposed human visuals were 76.88 per cent. This result needs to be understood in the context of the increasing tendency to expose among the male and female celebrities in the Indian media. Interestingly, this finding contradicts this general trend and perception.

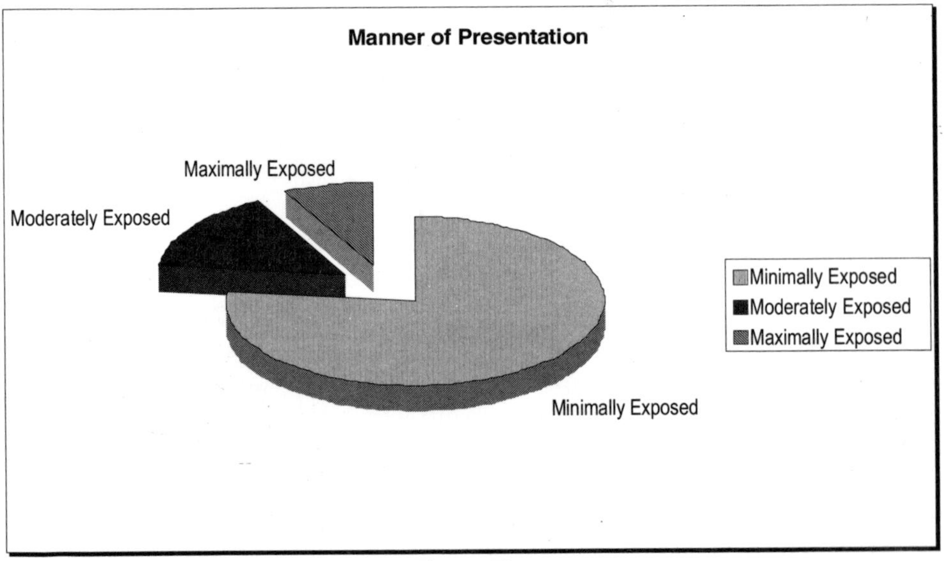

Figure II.9

II.1.a.x. *Presentation-Based Distribution of Visuals*

Table II.10

Sl. No.	Parameters	Total	Average	Percentage
1	Bordered Visuals	1648	53.2	83.39
2	Borderless Visuals	328	10.6	16.61

The table shows that 83.39 per cent of the visuals were presented within frames, while 16.61 per cent of the visuals were borderless. The presentation-based distribution of visuals shows that the layout of visuals continues to be formal and very few visuals break the stylistic constraints of presentation. In this respect, the presentation of visuals in DT is conservative.

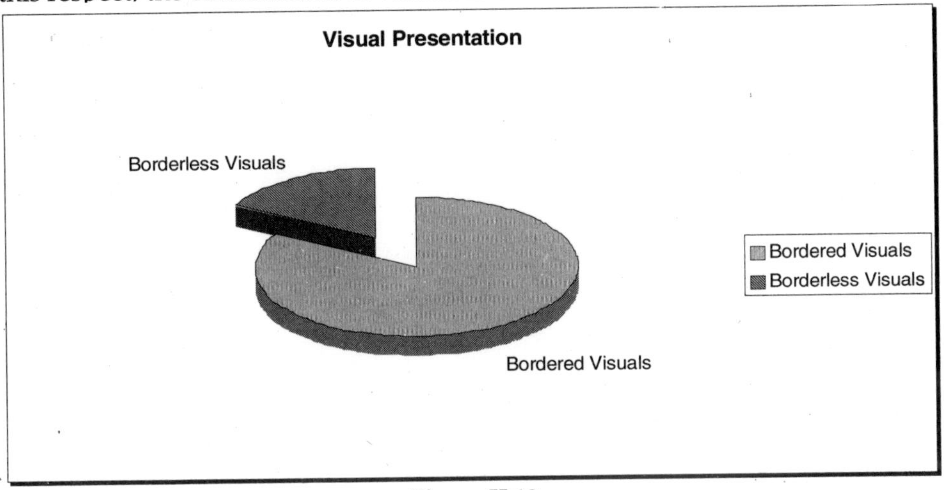

Figure II.10

II.1.b. *What's Hot*

As already mentioned, What's Hot comes as a pull out with DT every Friday of the week. The pull-out covers a wide range of subjects such as zodiac, monuments, fashion, utility tips, beauty, lifestyle, new gadgets, heritage, food, tourism, music, recreation, fengshui, vaastu, events, TV and event schedule, relationships, counseling, agony aunt, cinema, TV, well being, spirituality, celebrities, jokes, golden words, entertainment and the creative arts. The pull out is printed on newsprint and is published on a tabloid size paper. On an average, every single issue of this pull out has 40 pages.

II.1.b.i. *Edit-Ad Distribution of Space*

Table II.11

Sl. No.	Parameters	Total	Average	Percentage
1	Edit	96972	24243	66.02
2	Ad	49908	12477	33.98

Of the total sample pull out space of 146880 sq cm, the edit space occupies 96972 sq cm while advertisements are spread out over 49908 sq cm. In percentage terms, the editorial space constitutes 66.02 per cent of the total pull out space, whereas advertisements constitute 33.98 per cent space. As this pull out is information-based, the editorial space happens to be much larger than the advertising space. Besides, the use of newsprint too is explainable on account of the primary function of this pull out which is to inform the readers about what is where and/or when.

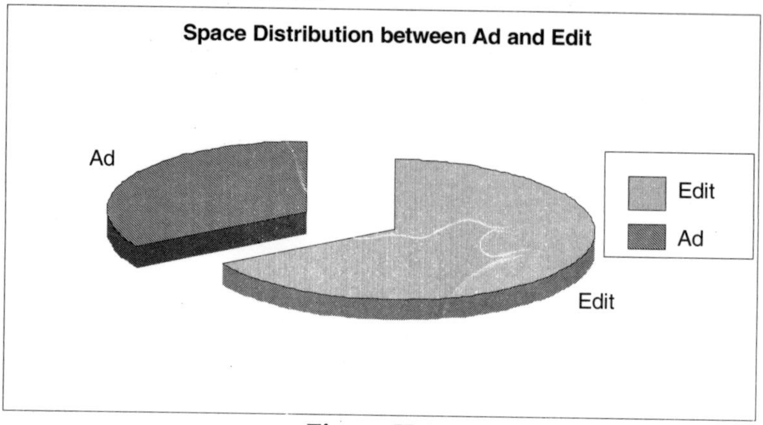

Figure II.11

II.1.b.ii. *Text-Visual Distribution of Edit Space*

Table II.12

Sl. No.	Parameters	Total	Average	Percentage
1	Text	68664	17166	70.81
2	Visuals	28308	7077	29.19

The table shows that the text in this pull out occupies 70.81 per cent of the total edit space compared to visuals which take up 29.19 per cent of the total edit space. The preponderance of the text in this pull out is understandable in view of its mandate to provide miscellaneous information.

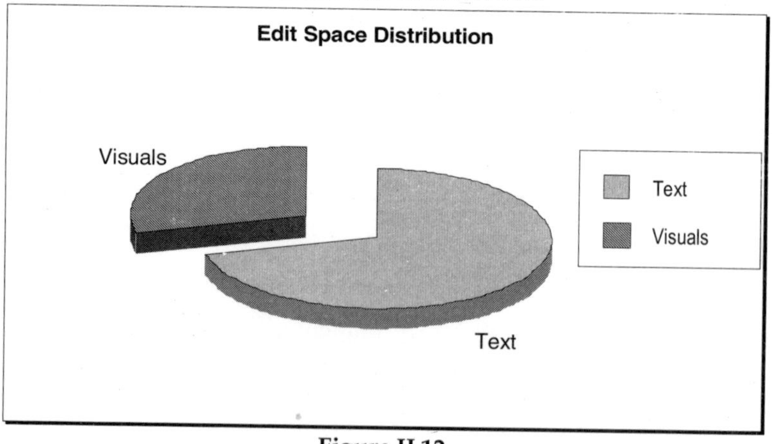

Figure II.12

II.1.b.iii. *Form-Based Distribution of Edit Space*

Table II.13

Sl. No.	Parameters	Total	Average	Percentage
1	Memoirs	378	94.5	0.39
2	Review	12950	3237.5	13.35
3	Feature	33732	8433	34.79
4	Tech news	3136	784	3.23
5	Print promos	6001	1500.25	6.19
6	Miscellanies	40775	10193.75	42.05

The edit space of this pullout is distributed over six different types of forms. These are memoirs, reviews, features, technology news, print promo and miscellanies. Here, the miscellanies also include weekend planner, weekday planner, and latest books and music dvds. As the table shows, there are wide variations in the distribution of space among them. Most of the edit space, which is 42.05 per cent, is taken up the miscellanies followed by features (34.79 %), reviews (13.35%), print promos (6.19%), technology news (3.23%) and lastly, memoirs (0.39%). The edit space distribution explains the large gap observed between the text and the visual space as shown in the previous table.

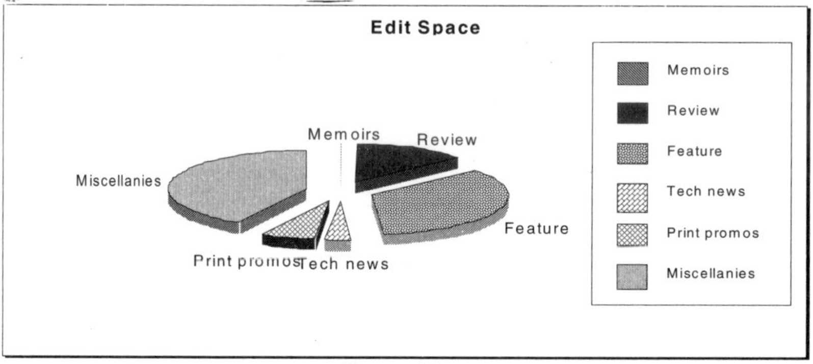

Figure II.13

II.1.b.iv. *Review Space Distribution*

Table II.14

Sl. No.	Parameters	Total	Average	Percentage
1	Book Review	1330	332.5	10.27
2	Movie review	3150	787.5	24.32
3	Music Review	1898	474.5	14.66
4	Theater Review	5076	1269	39.20
5	Art review	1496	374	11.55

The table shows that the review space is distributed over book reviews, movie reviews, music reviews, theatre reviews and art reviews unequally. The maximum space is devoted to theatre reviews (39.20%) followed by movie reviews (24.32%), music reviews (14.66%), art reviews (11.55%) and finally, book reviews (10.27%). As it is a weekend and weekday planner, reviews constitute an important element of this pull out.

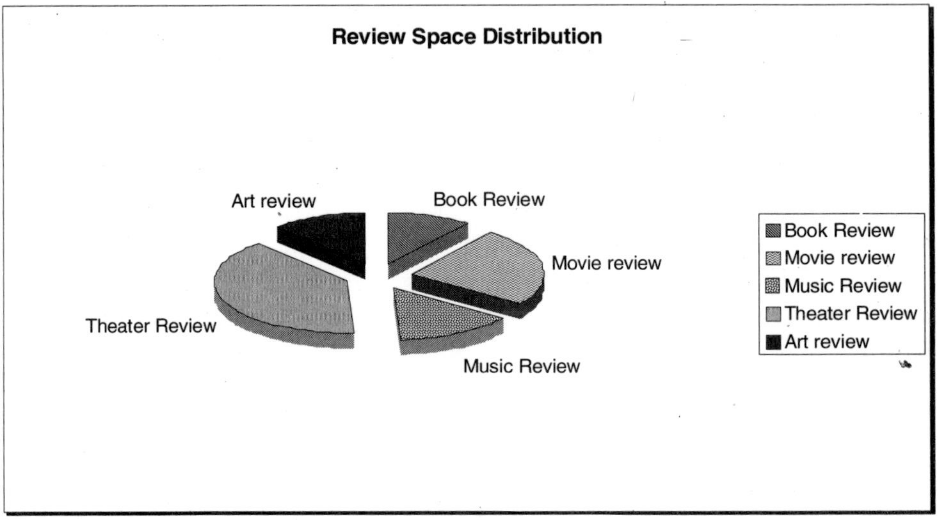

Figure II.14

II.1.b.v. *Subject-Based Feature Space Distribution*

Table II.15

Sl. No.	Parameters	Total	Average	Percentage
1	Well Being feature	3496	874	10.11
2	Celebrity Feature	2646	661.5	7.66
3	Beauty Feature	4796	1199	13.88
4	Culinary Feature	7582	1895.5	21.94
5	Travel Feature	4978	1244.5	14.40
6	Life style Feature	6064	1516	17.54
7	Relationship Feature	4170	1042.5	12.06
8	Art Feature	832	208	2.41

The feature space is distributed over as many as nine different types of subjects. These are well being, celebrity, beauty, culinary, travel, lifestyle, relationship and art. Of all the subjects covered by the features in this pullout, culinary features engage the greatest percentage of space (21.94%), followed by lifestyle features (17.54%), travel features (14.40%), beauty features (13.88%), relationship features (12.06%), well being (10.11%), celebrity (7.66%), and art features (2.41%). The nature of the subject of each of these subject-based features is such that it can hold the attention of the readers. As it is a part of the package of DT, it keeps the interest alive for readers to access DT and view the advertisements therein.

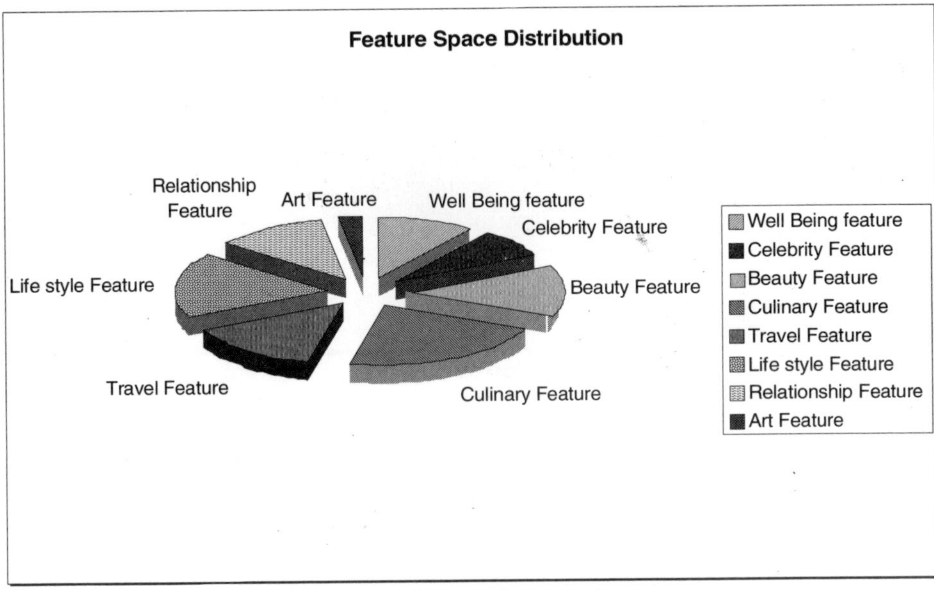

Figure II.15

II.1.b.vi. *Relationship Feature Space Distribution*

Table II.16

Sl. No.	Parameters	Total	Average	Percentage
1	Formal	0	0	0.00
2	Informal	0	0	0.00
3	Intimate	4120	1030	100.00

The table shows that none of the sample issues of WH carried any formal or informal relationship-based feature. All the relationship features in the sample issues discussed intimate relationships.

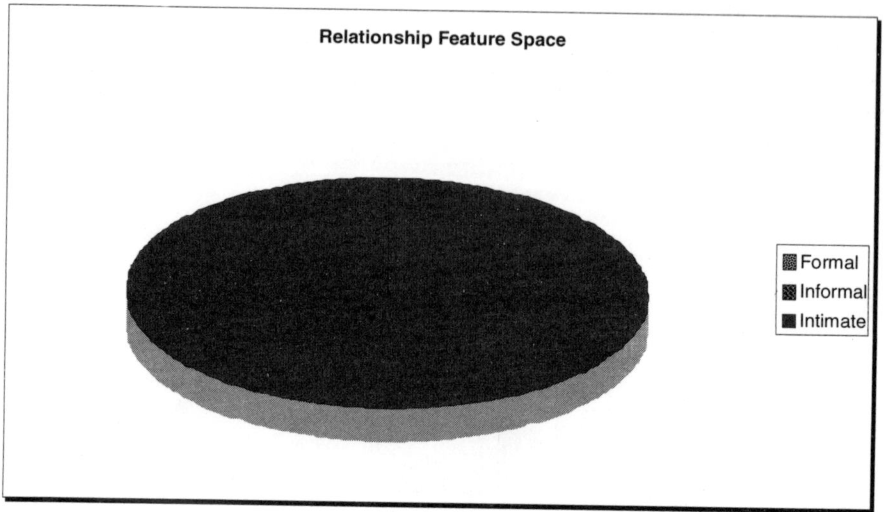

Figure II.16

II.1.b.vii. *Distribution of Visuals*

Table II.17

Sl. No.	Parameters	Total	Average	Percentage
1	Human Visuals	288	72	51.06
2	Non-human Visuals	276	69	48.94

What's Hot, on an average, contains 564 visuals per issue. Out of these 564 visuals, 72 (51.06%) are human visuals whereas 69 (48.94%) are the non-human visuals. Interestingly, there is no marked difference in the number of human and non-human visuals carried in any issue of WH. This can be explained in the light of the fact that this pull out substantially talks about latest beauty, fashion and lifestyle products along with gizmos and cuisine, and the best buys etc.

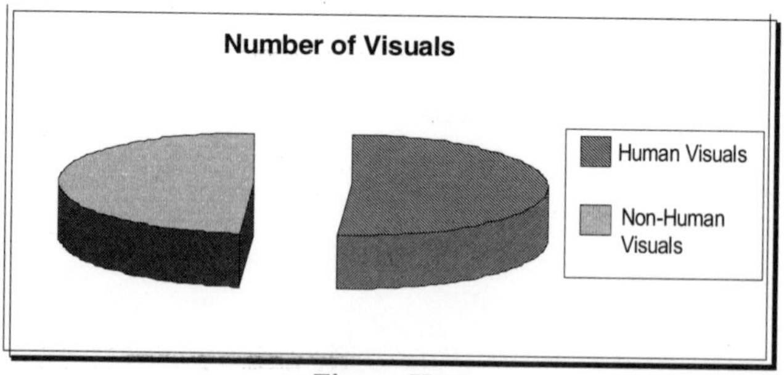

Figure II.17

II.1.b.viii. *Human Visual Categorisation*

Table II.18

Sl. No.	Parameters	Number	Average	Percentage
1	P-3	0	0	0.00
2	TV and Films	144	36	50.00
3	Political	0	0	0.00
4	Sports	0	0	0.00
5	Others	144	36	50.00

Equally interestingly, each issue of WH, on an average, has equal number of human visuals falling in two categories—TV and film personalities and non-descript human visuals. On an average, 36 visuals (50%) each of TV & film-related people and non-descript people feature in WH. It was seen that this pull out doesn't contain visuals of Page-3 celebrities, political leaders or sports stars.

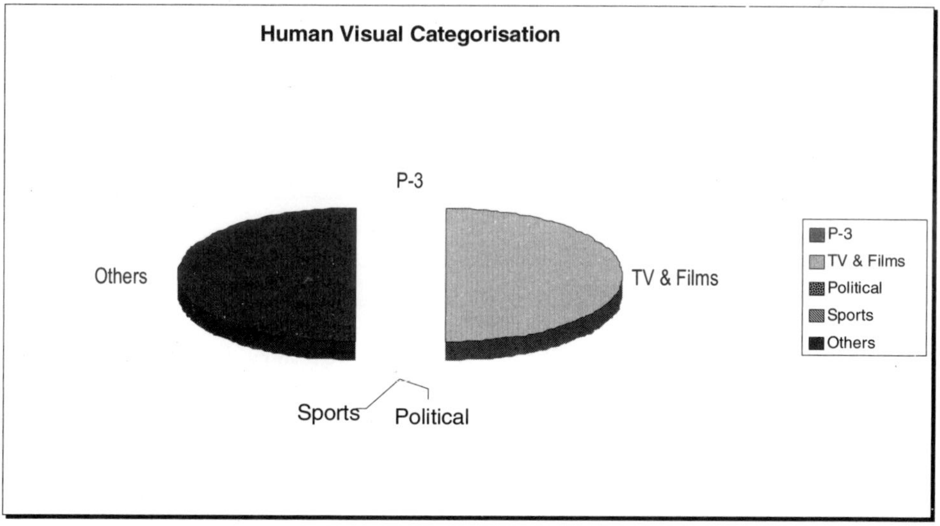

Figure II.18

II.1.b.ix. *Gender-Based Human Visual Categorisation*

Table II.19

Sl. No.	Parameters	Number	Average	Percentage
1	Male	68	17	42.50
2	Female	92	23	57.50

A look at the table depicts that the gender-based distribution of the human visuals is tilted towards female visuals. In the sample issues of the pull out, there were 17 male visuals (42.50%) in comparison with 23 (57.50%) female visuals per issue. The tilt can be justified in the wake of the broad subjects covered in WH.

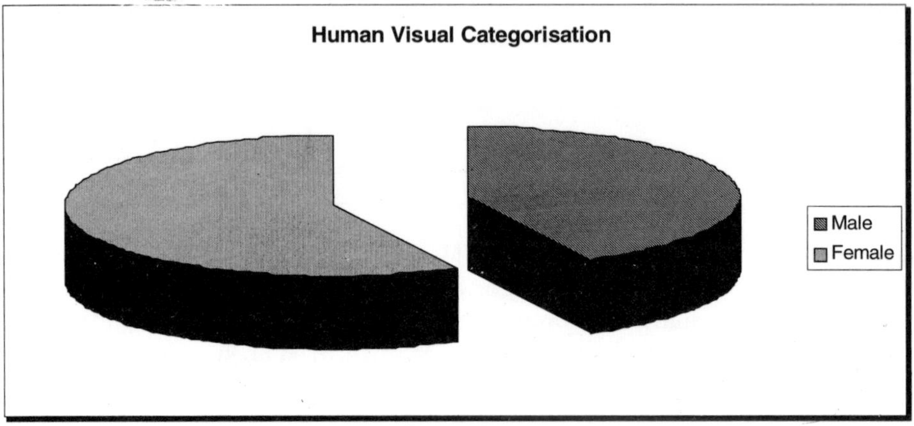

Figure II.19

II.1.b.x. *Sartorial-Based Distribution of Human Visuals*

Table II.20

Sl. No.	Parameters	Total	Average	Percentage
1	Minimally Exposed	196	49	68.06
2	Moderately Exposed	72	18	25.00
3	Maximally Exposed	20	5	6.94

The findings depicted in the above table give out very interesting findings which are quite in contrast with the general perception that TOI supplements are full of scantily-clad female visuals. The table shows that the sartorial-based distribution of human visuals is skewed in favour of minimally exposed human visuals as compared to moderately and maximally exposed human visuals. On an average, most of the human visuals fall in the category of minimally exposed visuals (68.06%), followed by moderately exposed visuals (25%). Only 6.94 per cent of the human visuals fall in the category of maximally exposed visuals. The difference between minimally exposed and moderately exposed visuals is also quite substantial.

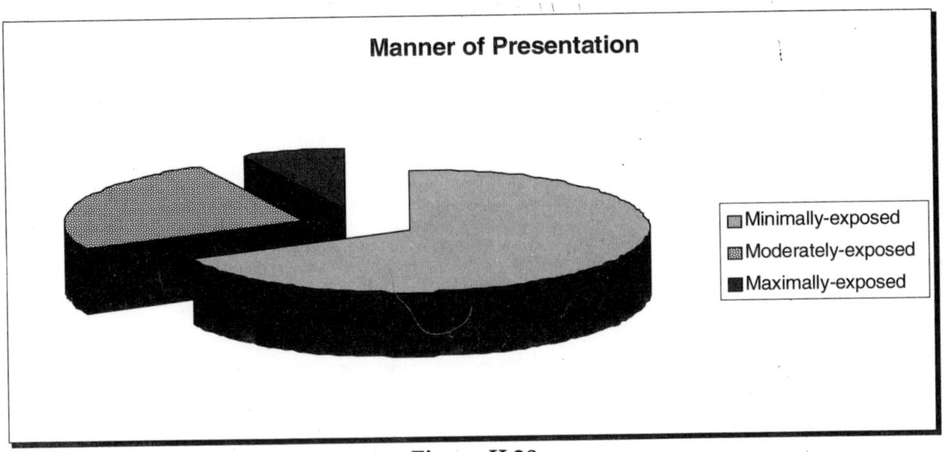

Figure II.20

II.1.b.xi. *Manner of Visual Presentation*

Table II.21

Sl. No.	Parameters	Total	Average	Percentage
1	Bordered Visuals	276	69	48.94
2	Borderless Visuals	288	72	51.06

The findings reflect that almost same number of visuals is presented as bordered and borderless in WH. The table shows that 51.06 per cent of the visuals merge with the text whereas 48.94 per cent of the visuals appear within frames

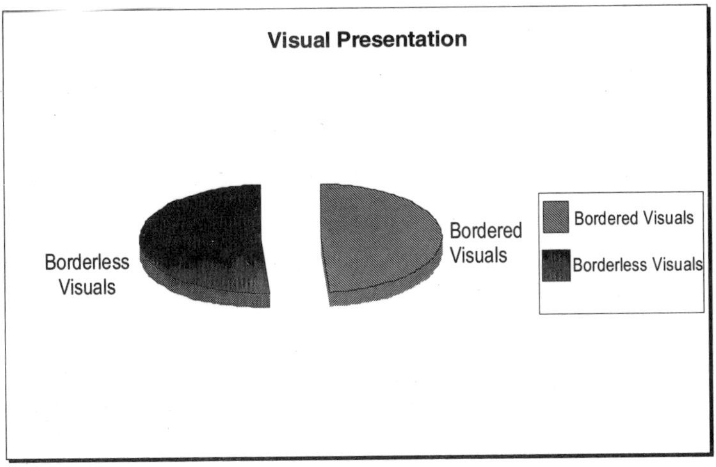

Figure II.21

II.1.c. *Times Life*

As has already been said earlier, Times Life comes out once a week on every Sunday. The supplement covers the subjects of grooming, relationships, well being, entertainment, technology, lifestyle, spirituality and social issues. Going by the nature of its content, the supplement is designed to appeal largely to readers' craving for glamour and beauty and in a few cases for graver matters like spirituality. Keeping in mind the thrust of the supplement, it is clear that it is meant to attract the attention of the largest number of readers. Not surprisingly, the supplement, unlike DT, comes on glossy paper. It gives the supplement the semblance of a magazine and makes advertisements highly alluring. This supplement too comes as a broadsheet, affording the advertisers the largest possible space. On an average, the supplement carries eight pages per issue.

II.1.c.i. *Edit-Ad Space Distribution*

Table II.22

Sl. No.	Parameters	Total	Average	Percentage
1	Edit	36506	9126.5	59.26
2	Ad	25098	6274.5	40.74

The table shows that the editorial matter occupies 59.26 per cent as opposed to 40.74 per cent of advertisements in the total supplement space. The result obtained here is in sharp contrast with that obtained in DT, where the reverse is true. But keeping in mind the high cost of advertisements in Times Life, the advertising revenue generated here is much larger than that in DT. This explains the comparatively lower percentage of advertising space.

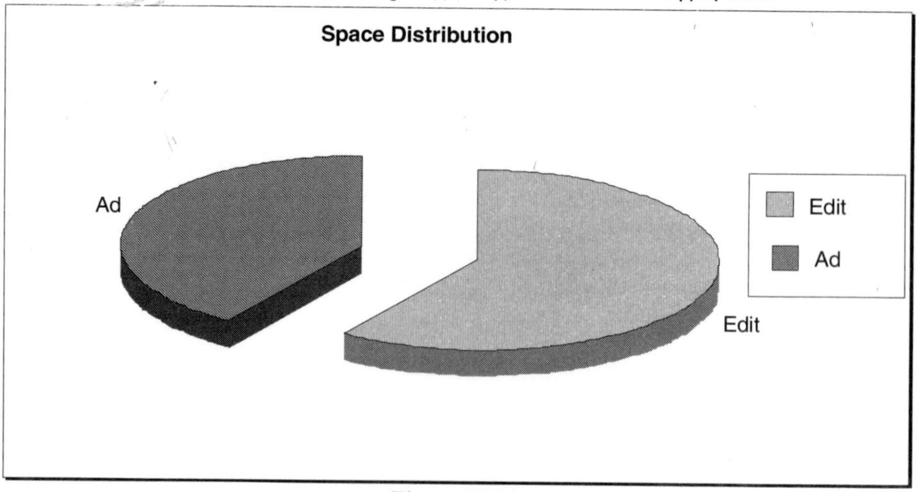

Figure II.22

II.1.c.ii. *Text-Visual Edit Space Distribution*

Table II.23

Sl. No.	Parameters	Total	Average	Percentage
1	Text	26281	6570.25	71.99
2	Visuals	10225	2556.25	28.01

The table shows that the edit space is distributed unevenly between the text and the visuals. While the text occupies 71.99 per cent of the total edit space, visuals occupy 28.01 per cent. As is obvious, there is a huge gap between the space apportioned to text and that to visuals.

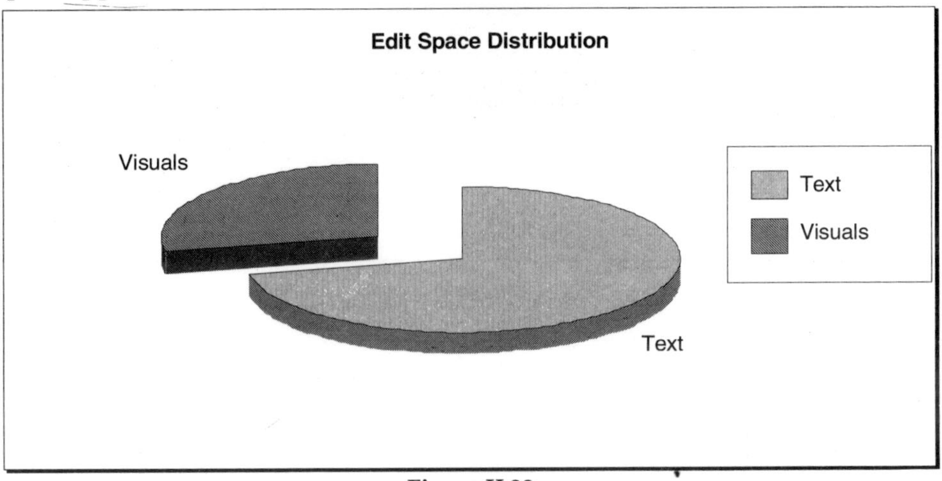

Figure II.23

II.1.c.iii. *Form-Based Edit Space Distribution*

Table II.24

Sl. No.	Parameters	Total	Average	Percentage
1	Interviews	2574	643.5	7.07
2	New Gadgets	2350	587.5	6.45
3	Features	22024	5506	60.50
4	Miscellanies	9458	2364.5	25.98

The TL issues content analysed used the four forms of interviews, technology news, features and miscellanies. There are wide variations in the edit space distribution over these forms. Features take up the chunk of edit space, occupying 60.50 per cent of the edit space. Next in order comes the category of Miscellanies. It consumes 25.98 per cent of the edit space, which is roughly a quarter. Interviews and Technology news garner as little as 7.07 per cent and 6.45 per cent respectively of the edit space. Clearly, features are the most important form in TL.

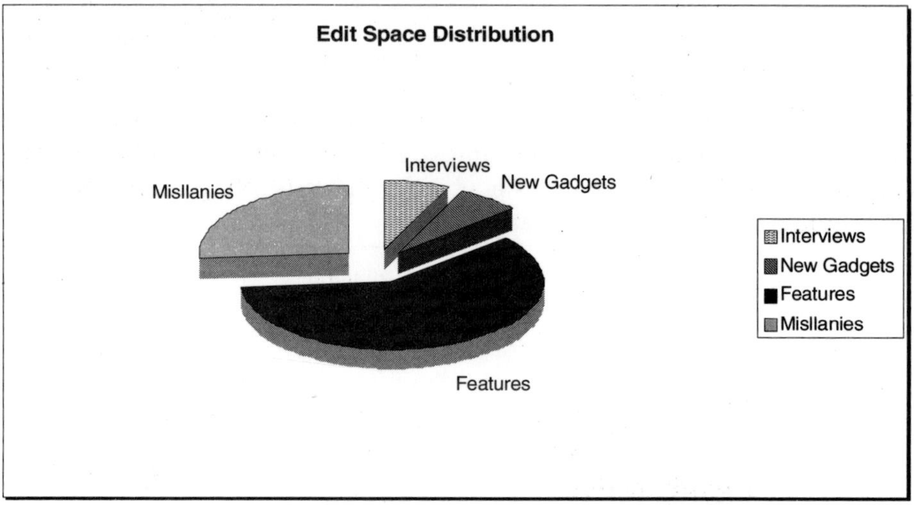

Figure II.24

II.1.c.iv. *Subject-Based Feature Space Distribution*

Table II.25

Sl. No.	Parameters	Total	Average	Percentage
1	Well being	2046	511.5	9.29
2	Celebrity	3364	841	15.27
3	Lifestyle	3552	888	16.13
4	Social Issues	5052	1263	22.94
5	Spirituality	1750	437.5	7.95
6	Relationship	6260	1565	28.42

The table shows that the feature space is distributed over six different types of subjects. These are: well being, celebrity, lifestyle, social issues, spirituality, and relationships. Of these, the maximum space is captured by relationships (28.42%), social issues (22.94%), lifestyle (16.13%), celebrity (15.27%), well being (9.29%), and spirituality (7.95%).

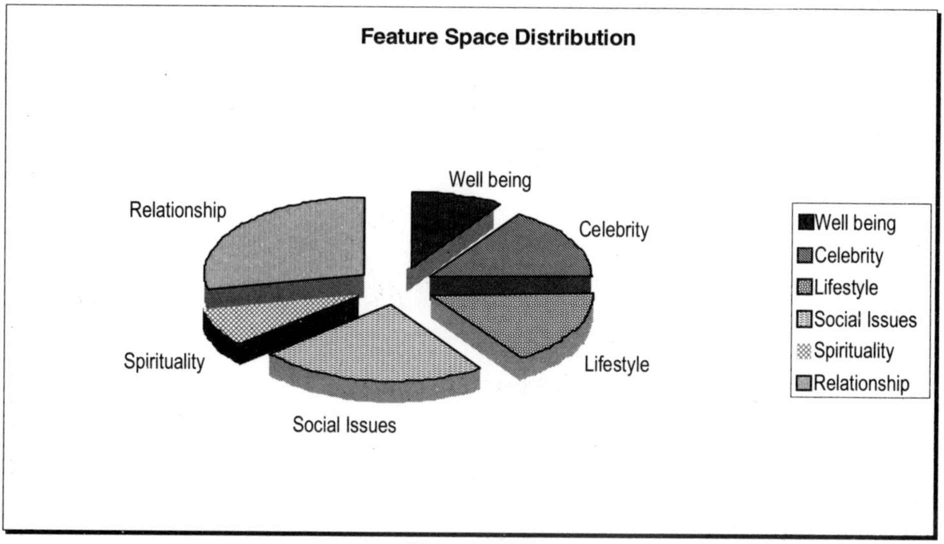

Figure II.25

II.1.c.v. *Relationship-Based Feature Space Distribution*

Table II.26

Sl. No.	Parameters	Total	Average	Percentage
1	Formal	0	0	0.00
2	Informal	2066	516.5	33.00
3	Intimate	4194	1048.5	67.00

The significance of the preceding table becomes clear from the feature space distribution among the various types of relationships. The table shows that intimate relationships occupy the lion's share of relationship space, followed by informal relations and formal relationships. While intimate relationships engage 67 per cent of the relationship feature space, informal relationships take up 33 per cent of that space. The heavy preponderance of intimate relationship features in TL points to the interest such features generate in a metro suburb like Gurgaon, where human relationships have come under the greatest pressure from hectic work and home life schedules. Interestingly enough, there were no formal features in the sample issues of TL, further bolstering our argument that TL attempts to attract the attention of readers by focusing on intimate and informal relationship features.

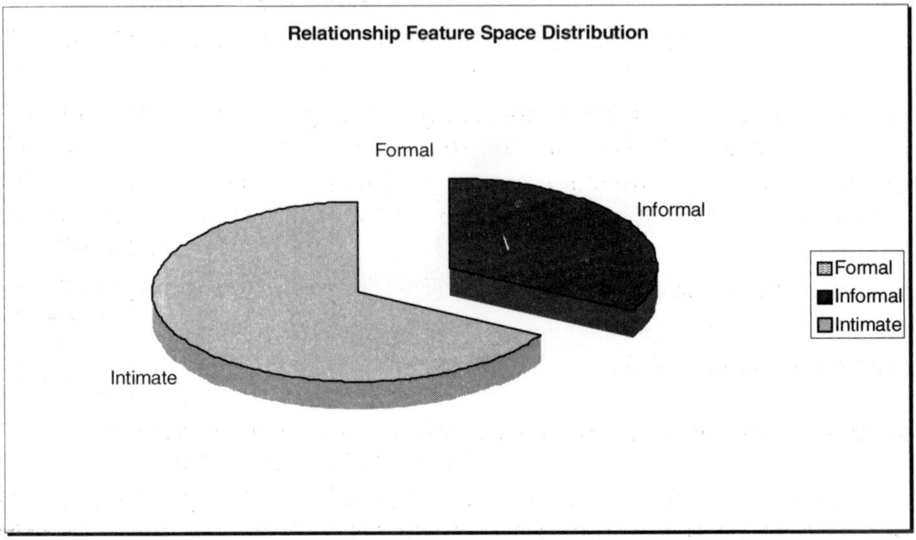

Figure II.26

II.1.c.vi. *Distribution of Visuals*

Table II.27

Sl. No.	Parameters	Total	Average	Percentage
1	Human Visuals	64	16	88.89
2	Non-human visuals	8	2	11.11

Of the 72 visuals in the sample issues of TL, a majority are human (64); non-human being a meager 8. In percentage terms, human visuals constitute 88.89 per cent of the total number of visuals, while non-human visuals are a slender 11.11 per cent.

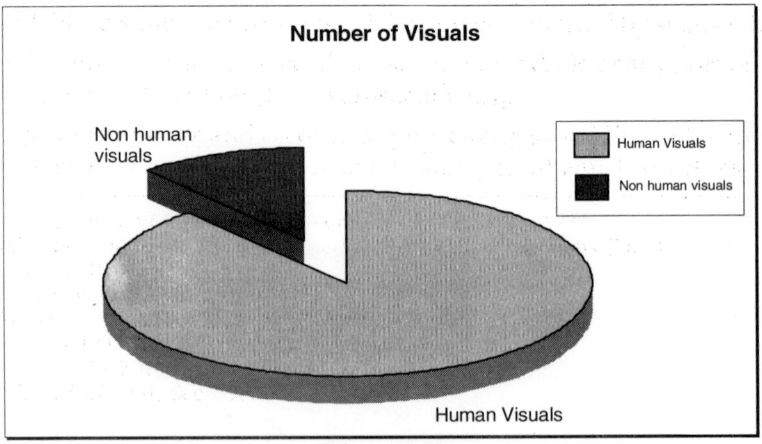

Figure II.27

II.1.c.vii. *Role-Based Distribution of Human Visuals*

Table II.28

Sl. No.	Parameters	Number	Average	Percentage
1	P-3	3	0.7	4.40
2	TV & Films	11	2.7	16.98
3	Political	0	0	0.00
4	Sports	0	0	0.00
5	Non-celebrity	50	12.5	78.62

The table shows that of the 64 human visuals, 50 visuals are of non-celebrities, followed by 11 of TV & film personalities, and 3 of Page-3 personalities. In percentage terms, non-celebrity visuals account for 78.62 per cent of the human visuals, TV & film personality visuals for 16.98 per cent and Page 3 celebrity visuals for 4.40 per cent. The distribution of role-based human visuals shows the tendency to have as many visuals as possible in the supplement and to fill up the shortfall in celebrity and celluloid personality visuals with non-celebrity visuals.

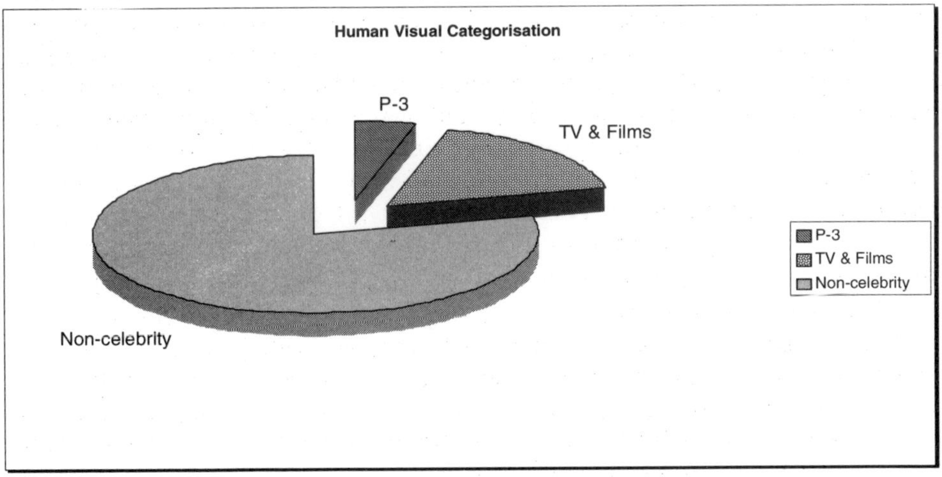

Figure II.28

II.1.c.viii. *Gender-Based Distribution of Human Visuals*

Table II.29

Sl. No.	Parameters	Number	Average	Percentage
1	Male	20	5	38.46
2	Female	32	8	61.54

Of the 64 human visuals, 12 are mixed visuals while the remaining 52 human visuals are either all female or all male. Thirty-two visuals are all female and 20 are all male. In percentage terms, female visuals account for 61.54 per cent of human visuals, male visuals for only 38.46 per cent. The distribution is obviously tilted in favour of female visuals. This finding coupled with that pertaining to relationships shows that the supplement is designed to attract eye balls for the expensive colour advertisements in it.

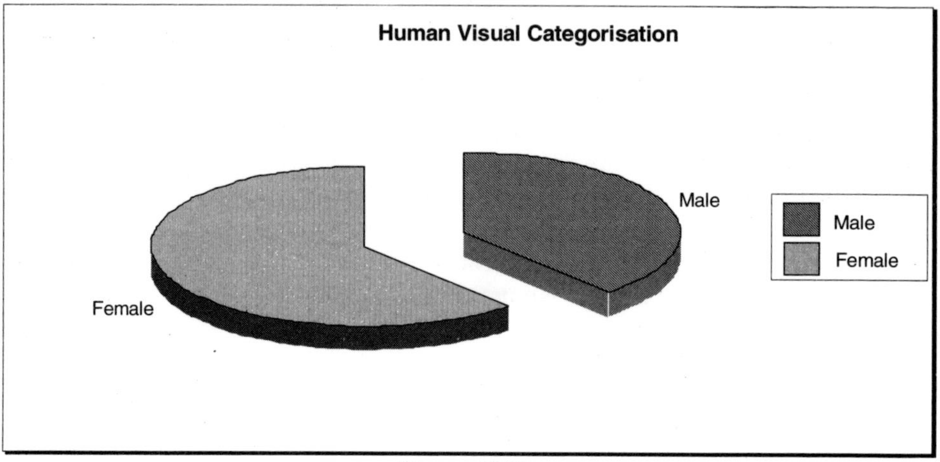

Figure II.29

II.1.c.ix. *Exposure-Based Distribution of human visuals*

Table II.30

Sl. No.	Parameters	Total	Average	Percentage
1	Minimally Exposed	40	10	62.50
2	Moderately Exposed	16	4	25.00
3	Maximally Exposed	8	2	12.50

The table shows that the maximum number of human visuals is minimally exposed, followed by the moderately exposed ones and maximally exposed ones. Of the 64 human visuals, 40 are minimally exposed and 16 moderately exposed whereas only 8 are maximally exposed. In percentage terms, the minimally exposed human visuals are 62.50 per cent of the total number of human visuals, while the moderately exposed visuals are 25 per cent and maximally exposed 12.50 per cent. Taken together, the moderately exposed and minimally exposed human visuals account for 37.50 per cent, which means that the exposed human visuals comprise more than one-third of the total human visuals. This figure may look insignificant statistically, but viewed against the backdrop of the significance that the Indian culture has over the ages attached with sobriety and moderation, this figure looks ominous and alarming. It is understandable when viewed from the perspective of the marketing function of supplement journalism.

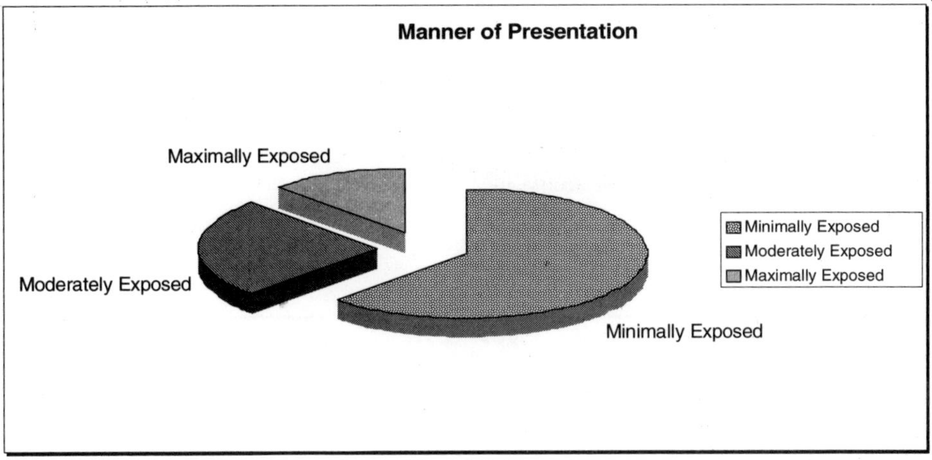

Figure II.30

II.1.c.x. *Layout-Based Distribution of Visuals*

Table II.31

Sl. No.	Parameters	Total	Average	Percentage
1	Bordered Visuals	16	4	22.22
2	Borderless Visuals	56	14	77.78

Of the total 72 visuals in the issues of this supplement that were content analysed, 16 are bordered visuals, while 56 are borderless. In terms of percentage, the bordered visuals constitute as much as 22.22 per cent of the total number of visuals, while the borderless visuals are 77.78 per cent.

The bordering of visuals in TL runs counter to the pattern observed so far in other supplements of TOI. The heightened emphasis on borderless visuals is in keeping with the liberal and avant-garde nature of the content of this supplement. By breaking the conventional norms of designing, the supplement underscores the boldness of the content reflected in relationship features, most of which harbour on intimate relationships.

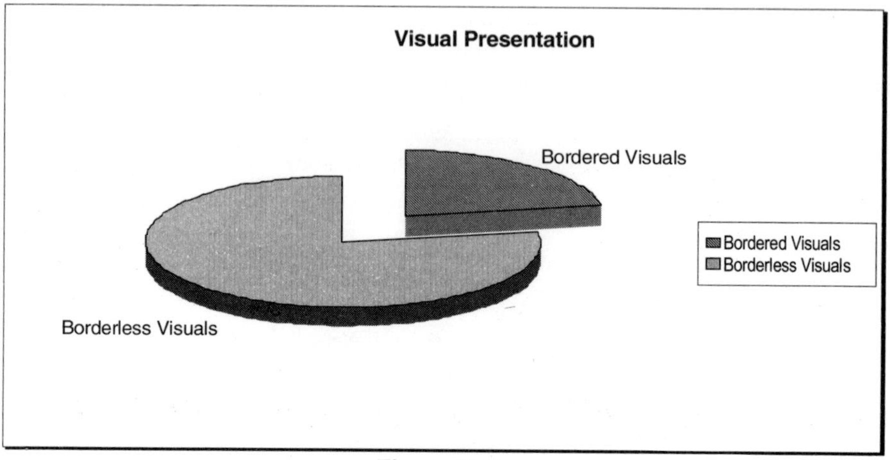

Figure II.31

II.1.d. *Education Times*

This supplement of TOI comes out every Monday. As is evident from the name itself, this supplement extensively covers the broad subject of education and its related areas of placements, admission details of various professional and vocational courses, youth, scholarly achievements, career counseling, book reviews, events, celebrity talk, readers' participation and golden words etc. The supplement targets one very important section of its readers i.e. students and aspiring professionals. This broadsheet supplement is brought out on newsprint and on an average consists of 16 pages per copy per issue. As the topics covered by the supplement require non-flippant approach, ET is understandably sober in its content and layout.

II.1.d.i. *Edit-Ad Space Distribution*

Table II.32

Sl. No.	Parameters	Total	Average	Percentage
1	Edit	45568	11392	37.33
2	Ad	76512	19128	62.67

The Table II.32 representing edit-ad space distribution shows that in ET, advertisements occupy much larger space than the editorial matter. The advertisements occupy 62.67 per cent as opposed to a meager 37.33 per cent of editorial space in the total supplement space. The preponderance of advertisements owes to the purpose of its publication. This supplement seeks to carry advertisements of academic nature which target the huge student population in the country.

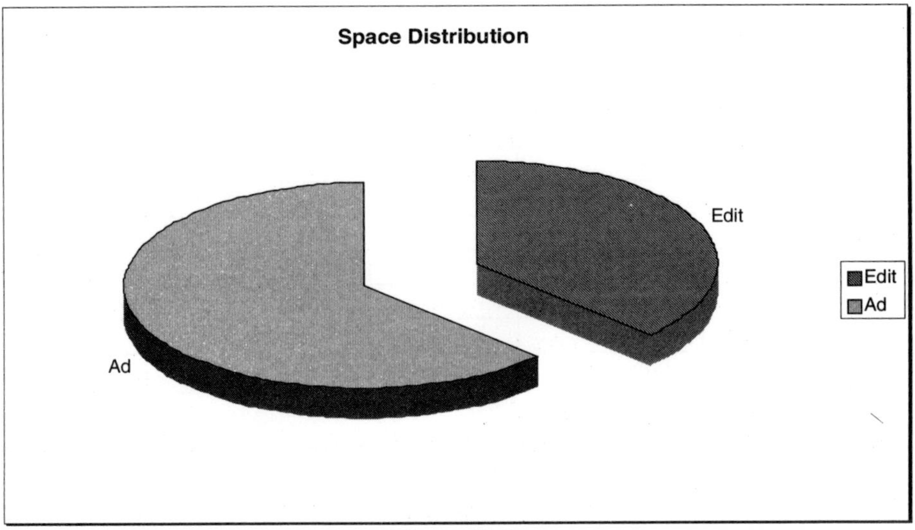

Figure II.32

II.1.d.ii. *Text-Visual Based Edit Space Distribution*

Table II.33

Sl. No.	Parameters	Total	Average	Percentage
1	Text	39915	9978.75	87.59
2	Visuals	5653	1413.25	12.41

An analysis of the sample issues of ET shows that the space devoted to text in the editorial section happens to be far more than that allotted to visuals. In the sample issues, the text took up 87.59 per cent of the space compared to 12.41 per cent taken up by visuals.

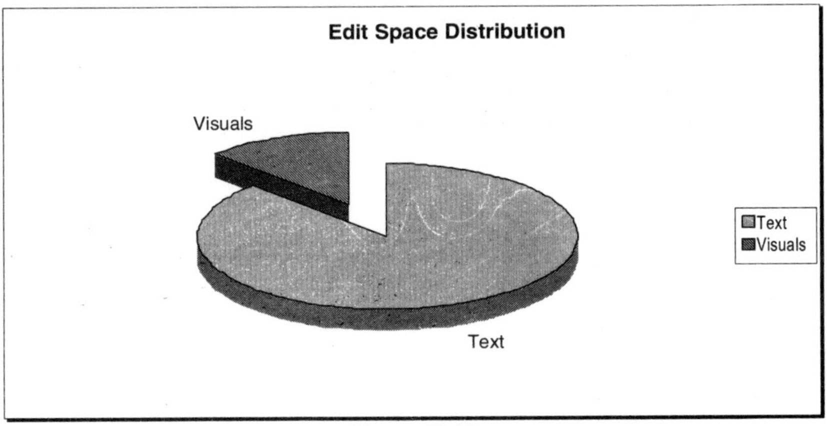

Figure II.33

II.1.d.iii. *Form-Based Edit Space Distribution*

Table II.34

Sl. No.	Parameters	Total	Average	Percentage
1	Interviews	2140	535	4.7
2	Memoirs	3104	776	6.81
3	Reviews	600	150	1.32
4	Features	8914	2228.5	19.56
5	Hard News	10380	2595	22.78
6	Soft News	3468	867	7.61
7	Miscellanies	16962	4240.5	37.22

ET carries editorial matter in six different forms. Each of these forms takes up varying percentages of edit space. But, the form which takes the lion's share in the sample issues is the wide assortment of events, admission and job vacancy details, career counseling etc. summed up under the label, miscellanies. These take up around 37.22 per cent of the share followed by hard news (22.78%), features (19.56%), soft news (7.61%), memoirs (6.81%), interviews (4.70%), and reviews (1.32%). Contrary to general perception about the space given to news in supplements, hard news gets much more space than even soft news and features. In fact, this formal category is next only to miscellanies.

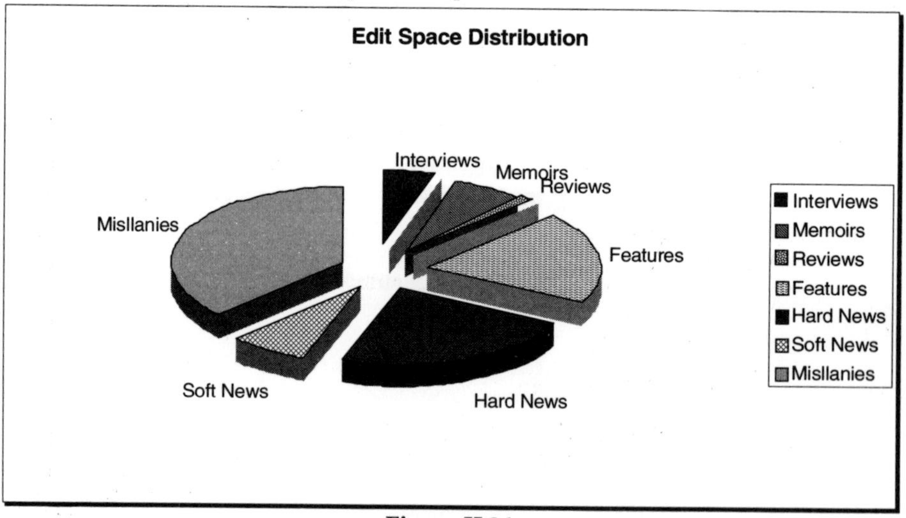

Figure II.34

II.1.d.iv. *Subject-Based Feature Space Distribution*

Table II.35

Sl. No.	Parameters	Total	Average	Percentage
1	Utility	1764	441	19.79
2	Celebrity	1150	287.5	12.90
3	Career	6000	1500	67.31

In the sample issues, features span three subject areas. These are utilities, celebrities, and careers. As is understandable, the maximum space is taken up by career-based features (67.31%). Of two other subjects covered, utilities occupy 19.79 per cent space compared to celebrities (12.90%). So, though the feature space recognizes the primacy of career based features, the overall edit space distribution is tilted in favour of hard news.

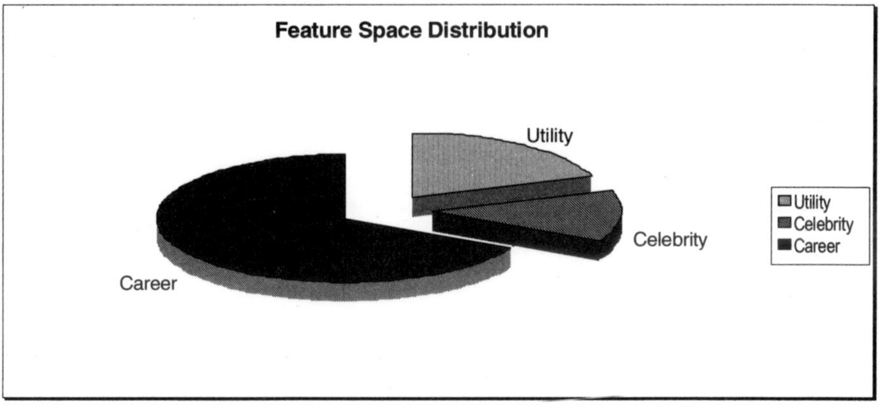

Figure II.35

II.1.d.v. *Review Space Distribution*

Table II.36

Sl. No.	Parameters	Number	Average	Percentage
1	Book	600	150	100.00
2	Film	0	0	0.00
3	Music	0	0	0.00
4	Theatre	0	0	0.00
5	Art	0	0	0.00

ET carries reviews on books exclusively. All the reviews identified in it relate to books. Obviously, it is very much in order for a supplement on education and career to devote all the space marked for reviews to books.

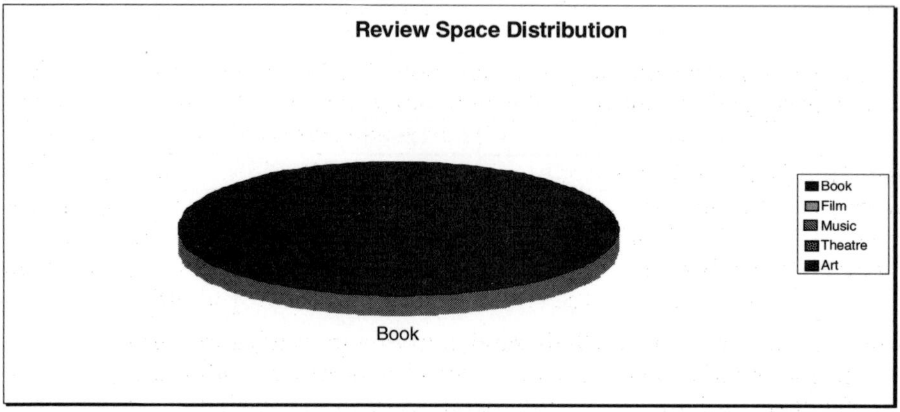

Figure II.36

II.1.d.vi. *Types of Visuals*

Table II.37

Sl. No.	Parameters	Total	Average	Percentage
1	Human Visuals	112	28	96.55
2	Non-human Visuals	4	1	3.45

Of the 116 visuals in the sample, an overbearing 112 visuals were of humans, while only 4 were of non-humans. In percentage terms, the human visuals account for 96.55 per cent of the total number of visuals, while the non-human account for a mere 3.45 per cent.

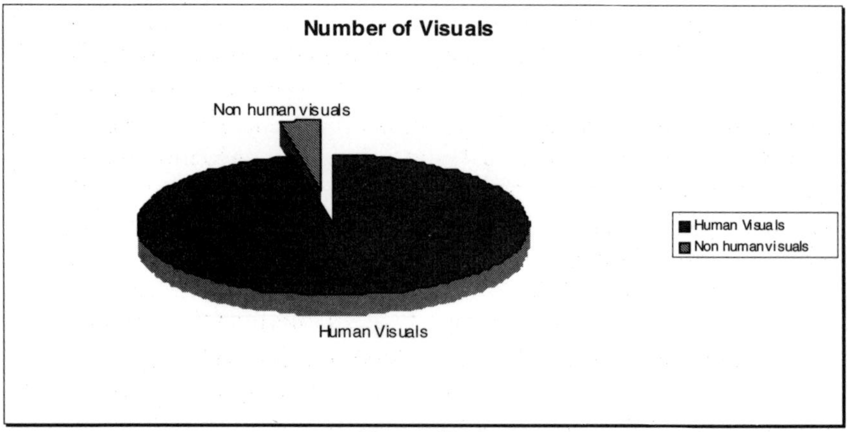

Figure II.37

II.1.d.vii. *Role-Based Human Visuals*

Table II.38

Sl. No.	Parameters	Number	Average	Percentage
1	P-3	0	0	0.00
2	TV & Films	4	1	3.57
3	Political	8	2	7.14
4	Sports	0	0	0.00
5	Others	100	25	89.29

Of the various roles highlighted in human visuals, the ones that are of nondescript personalities are the largest in number (100) and percentage (89.29%), followed by those of political personalities (7.14%) and TV and Films (3.57%). Obviously, ET does not seek to create any role models for the youth. The purpose of pictures is only to relieve the monotony induced by the text and thereby to retain the readers' interest.

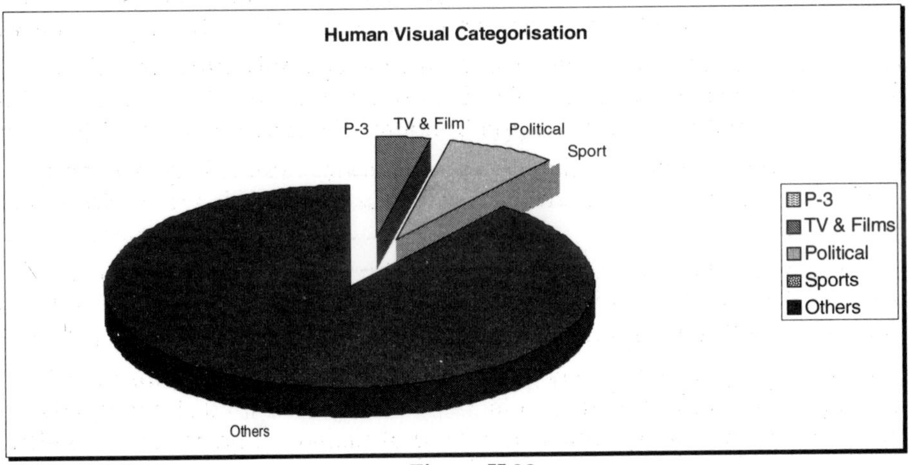

Figure II.38

II.1.d.viii. *Gender-Based Human Visuals*

Table II.39

Sl. No.	Parameters	Number	Average	Percentage
1	Male	40	10	52.63
2	Female	36	9	47.37

Of the 112 human visuals, the ones that have both male and female figures are 36. The human visuals that are either male or female are 76 in number. Of these 76 visuals, the maximum number is that of males (40), followed by that of females (36). But, the difference is too slender to be of any consequence. It shows the increasing importance women are gaining in education in modern times and in a metropolis like Delhi NCR.

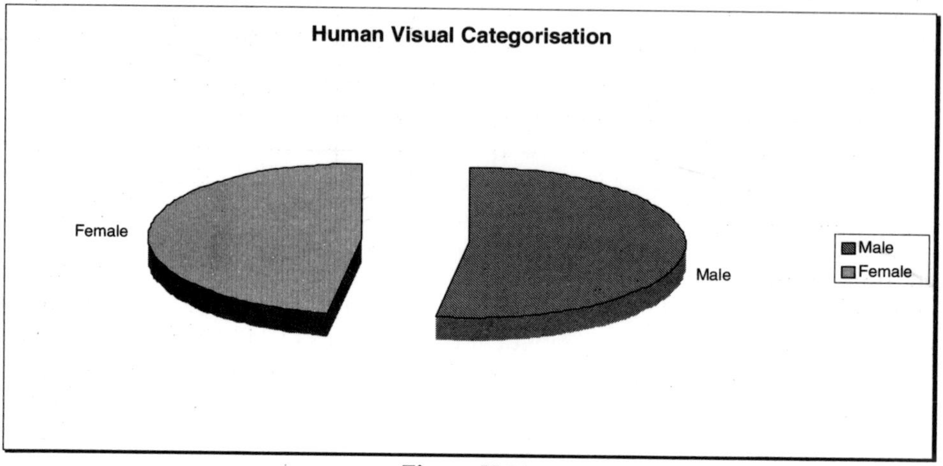

Figure II.39

II.1.d.ix. *Exposure in Human Visuals*

Table II.40

Sl. No.	Parameters	Total	Average	Percentage
1	Minimally Exposed	112	28	100.00
2	Moderately Exposed	0	0	0.00
3	Maximally Exposed	0	0	0.00

Of the 112 human visuals, none falls in the category of maximally and moderately exposed visuals. All are minimally exposed visuals. This is understandable as the visuals here are the hinges on which a highly formal subject like education has been covered.

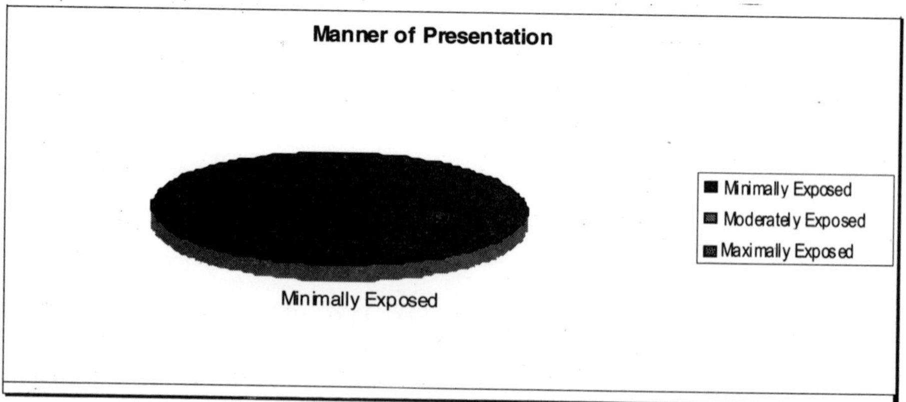

Figure II.40

II.1.d.x. *Framing of Visuals*

Table II.41

Sl. No.	Parameters	Total	Average	Percentage
1	Bordered Visuals	116	29	100.00
2	Borderless Visuals	0	0	0.00

In the visuals under review, none is borderless; all are bordered. The observance of formal rules of layout with respect to pictures underlines the formal character of the subject covered by this supplement.

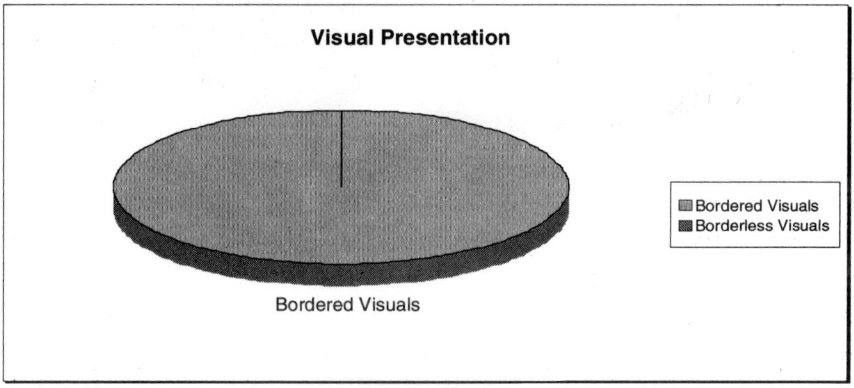

Figure II.41

II.1.e. *Gurgaon Plus*

Gurgaon Plus (GP) comes out on two days of the week. These are Wednesday and Saturday. It carries local news which the main newspaper cannot carry for want of space. The subjects mostly covered in this supplement are religion, education, home science, beauty, lifestyle, technology, entertainment, children, health, achievements, grievances, reviews and events. On an average, GP carries 8 pages per issue, which are broadsheets. The paper quality tends to change from issue to issue. At times, the paper used is glossy and at times, newsprint.

II.1.e.i. *Edit-Ad Space Distribution*

Table II.42

Sl. No.	Parameters	Total	Average	Percentage
1	Edit	46230.75	5136.75	44.17
2	Ad	58434.75	6492.75	55.83

The table shows that the space of this supplement is pretty evenly distributed between edit and advertising. In the sample issues, the editorial part occupies

44.17 per cent, while the advertisements carry 55.83 per cent of the total supplement space. The difference in the space allocation between the two is marginal compared to what we observed in DT. All the same, the preponderance of advertising space shows the use of the supplement to garner advertising revenue.

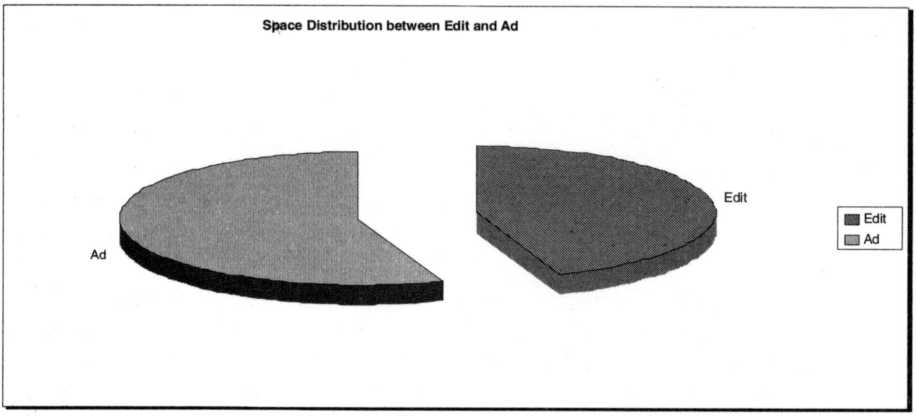

Figure II.42

II.1.e.ii. *Text-Visual Based Space Allocation*

Table II.43

Sl. No.	Parameters	Total	Average	Percentage
1	Text	26118	2902	56.49
2	Visual	20112.75	2234.75	43.51

The table shows that the text takes up more than 50 per cent of the edit space compared to the visuals. While the text is allocated 56.49 per cent of the edit space, visuals are allotted 43.51 per cent space. Though the text may have occupied such a large space, the space occupied by the visuals is a substantial 43.51 per cent, giving the space a very reader friendly visual look.

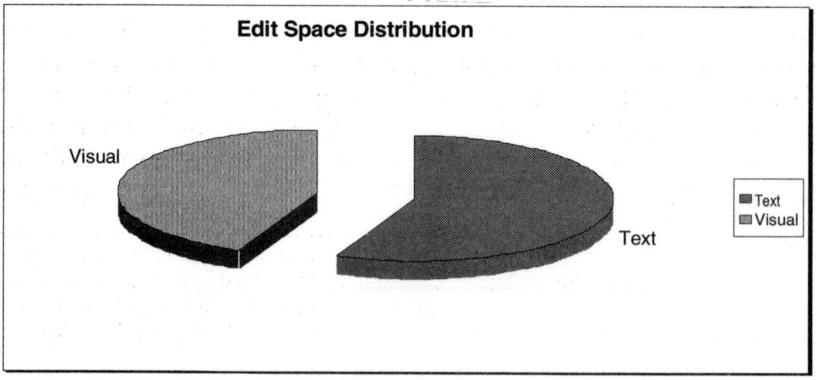

Figure II.43

II.1.e.iii. *Form-Based Edit Space Distribution*

Table II.44

Sl. No.	Parameters	Total	Average	Percentage
1	Soft Stories	4529	1131.5	22.03
2	Features	13156	3289	64.03
3	Hard News	484	121	2.35
4	Miscellanies	2381	595.25	11.59

In Gurgaon Plus, there are four form-based categories—soft stories, hard stories, features and miscellanies—share the editorial space. On an average, each issue of GP devotes a whopping 3289 sq cm of the editorial space to different types of features followed by 1131.5 sq cm of editorial space to soft stories. Miscellanies occupy the third-largest editorial space (595.25 sq cm) followed by just 121 sq cm being occupied by hard news. In percentage terms, features occupy 64.03 per cent of the total edit space, soft stories 22.03 per cent, and miscellanies 11.59 per cent while hard stories occupy a meager percentage of 2.35. Since it is a kind of a 'know your neighbourhood' supplement targeting the newspaper's readers in Gurgaon, it is but apt that 86.06 per cent of the total edit space goes to features and soft stories primarily showcasing Gurgaon as the new 'millennium city' (read developed and modern) but at the same time also raking up issues that directly or indirectly affect the Gurgaonites.

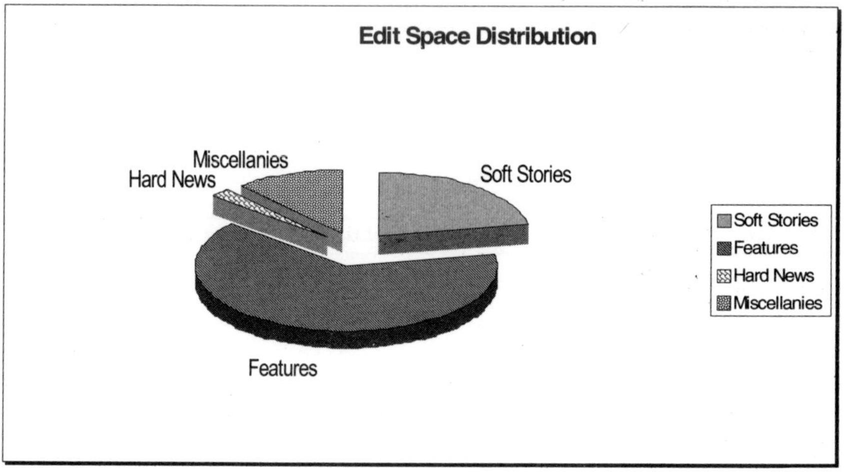

Figure II.44

II.1.e.iv. *Form-Based Feature Space Distribution*

Table II.45

Sl. No.	Parameters	Total	Average	Percentage
1	Well being	1761	440.25	13.38
2	Development	4455	1113.75	33.86
3	Technology	1222	305.5	9.28
4	Beauty	480	120	3.65
5	Culinary	1577	394.25	11.99
6	Lifestyle	231	57.75	1.76
7	Crime	596	149	4.53
8	Education	580	145	4.41
9	Grievances	1536	384	11.68
10	Recreation	718	179.5	5.46

The form-based feature space distribution in the supplement as represented in the Table II.45 reveals that feature space is distributed over ten subjects in different degrees of importance. The maximum feature space in the supplement is occupied by development features (33.86%), followed by well being (13.39%), culinary (11.99%), grievances (11.68%), technology features (9.29%), recreation (5.46%), crime-related features (4.53%), education (4.41%), beauty features (3.65%) and lifestyle (1.76%). Instead of emphasizing general topics like beauty and lifestyle, which in any case are covered in DT and TL, this supplement concentrates on place-specific issues.

II.1.e.v. *Distribution of Visuals*

Table II.46

Sl. No.	Parameters	Total	Average	Percentage
1	Human Visuals	144	16	51.61
2	Non-human Visuals	135	15	48.39

GP has almost the same number of human and non-human visuals. Of the total number of visuals in the sample (279), 144 (51.61%) are human visuals while 135 (48.39%) are non-human visuals.

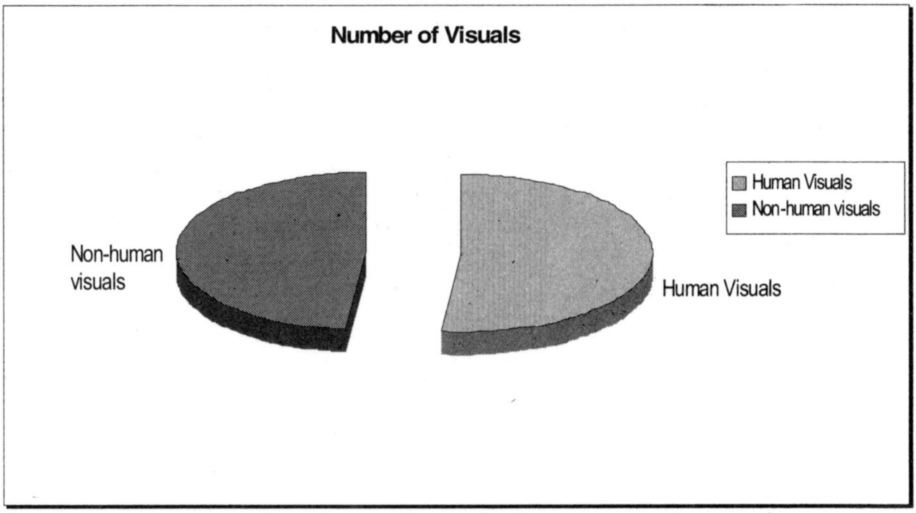

Figure II.45

II.1.e.vi. *Societal Role- Based Human Visual Distribution*

Table II.47

Sl. No.	Parameters	Number	Average	Percentage
1	P-3	17	1.89	11.81
2	Sports	8	0.89	5.55
3	Political	8	0.89	5.55
4	Artist	22	2.44	15.28
5	Achiever	26	2.89	18.06
6	Others	63	7.00	43.75

GP may be using 43.51 per cent of the total edit space for visuals but most of the visuals are of non-celebrities. The table shows that of the total number of human visuals, a large number of visuals (63) are of non-celebrities followed by visuals of achievers (26), and then that of artists (22). Visuals of Page-3 celebrities (17) come at the fourth place, followed by an equal number of visuals (8) of people from the sports and political worlds.

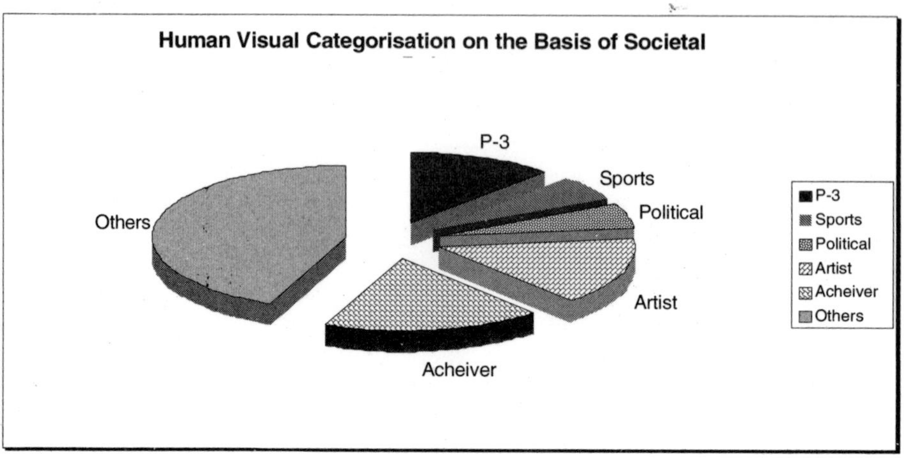

Figure II.46

II.1.e.vii. *Gender-Based Distribution of Visuals*

Table II.48

Sl. No.	Parameters	Number	Average	Percentage
1	Male	18	2	22.22
2	Female	63	7	77.78

Of the 144 visuals, 81 are mixed visuals. Rest of the visuals (63) are either all/solo male or all/solo female. According to the table, exactly the same number of human visuals (63) is female whereas 18 human visuals are that of men. Percentage wise, female visuals take a lion's share (77.78%) of the total number of human visuals whereas only 22.22 per cent of the human visuals are of men. The wide gap between the number of male and female visuals seem to be based on the notion that female visuals attract more attention as compared to male visuals.

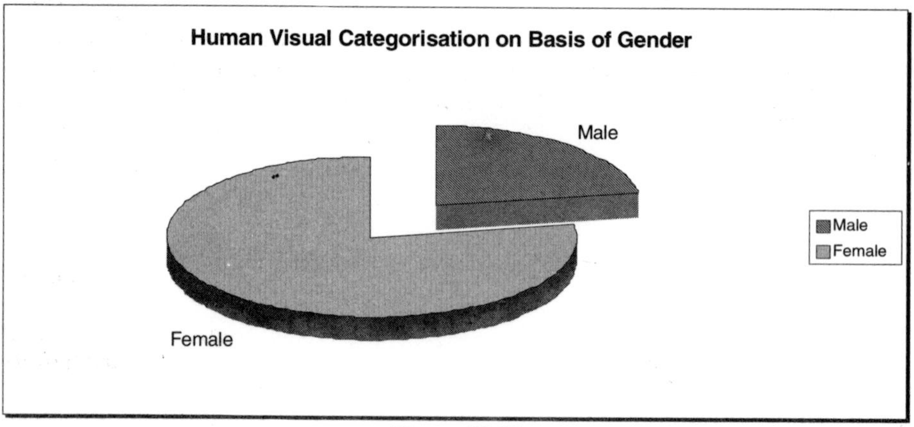

Figure II.47

II.1.e.viii. *Sartorial-Based Presentation of Visuals*

Table II.49

Sl. No.	Parameters	Total	Average	Percentage
1	Minimally Exposed	117	13	81.25
2	Moderately Exposed	27	3	18.75
3	Maximally Exposed	0	0	0.00

Of the total of 144 visuals, the number of minimally exposed visuals is the highest followed by moderately exposed. There are, however, no visuals falling in the category of maximally exposed. Again, this is against the general perception. Even the gap between the minimally exposed and the moderately exposed is also very high. Of the sample analysed, 117 visuals (81.25%) are minimally exposed followed by 27 (18.75%) moderately exposed visuals.

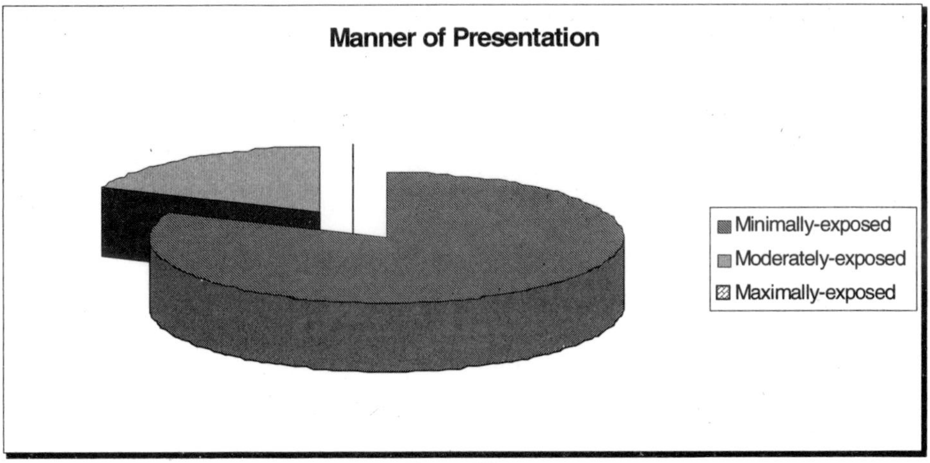

Figure II.48

II.1.e.ix. *Presentation-Based Distribution of Visuals*

Table II.50

Sl. No.	Parameters	Total	Average	Percentage
1	Bordered Visuals	108	12	38.71
2	Borderless Visuals	171	19	61.29

The supplement may adopt slightly conservative approach when it comes to sartorial presentation of visuals but it certainly does not follow the formal rules of layout. The supplement experiments with the layout by way of merging a high percentage of visuals with text; 61.29 per cent of the visuals are borderless while 38.71 per cent of the visuals are displayed within frames.

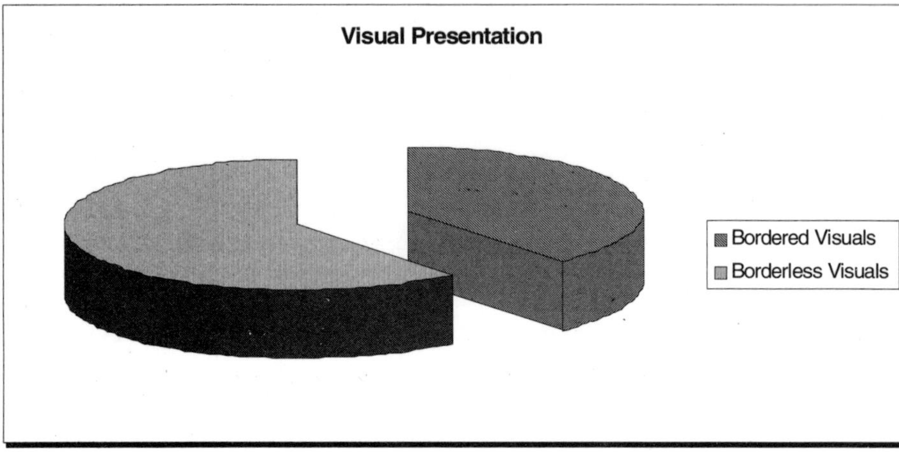

Figure II.49

II.1.f. *Times Ascent*

Times Ascent (TA) comes out in colour once a week on every Wednesday of the week. It carries information about recruitments and job opportunities in India and abroad. On an average, it carries 22 pages of broadsheet. The paper used is newsprint.

II.1.f.i. *Edit-Ad Space Allocation*

Table II.51

Sl. No.	Parameters	Total	Average	%age
1	Edit	4620	924	2.2
2	Ad	205205	41041	97.8

The table shows a wide variation between the edit and ad space. While the edit space is a slender 2.20 per cent of the total supplement space, the advertising space is a whopping 97.8 per cent. Understandably enough, this supplement is devoted to advertisements related to jobs in India and abroad.

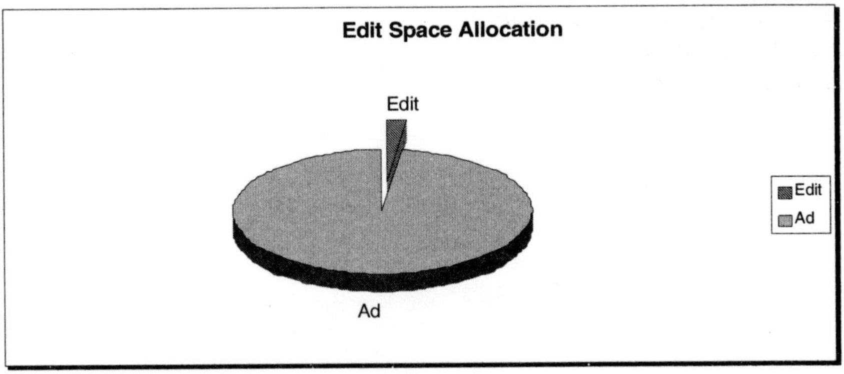

Figure II.50

II.1.f.ii. *Text-Visual Space Distribution*

Table II.52

Sl. No.	Parameters	Total	Average	%age
1	Text	3381.25	676.25	73.2
2	Visuals	1238.75	247.75	26.8

In the slender edit space, the text occupies 73.2 per cent space, while the visuals occupy 26.8 per cent space, which is roughly one-third of the total edit space.

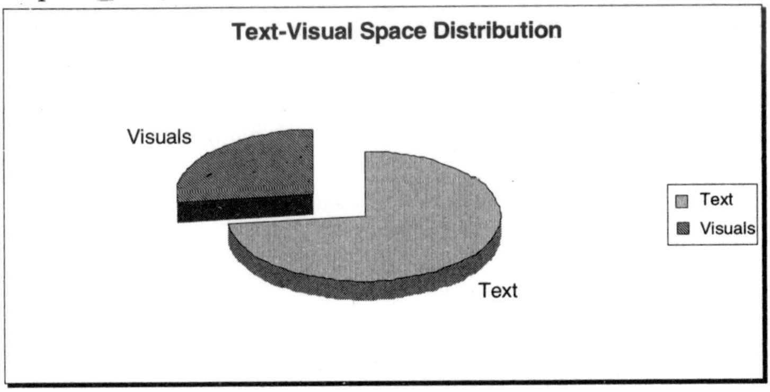

Figure II.51

II.1.f.iii. *Form and Subject-based Edit Space Distribution*

Table II.53

Sl. No.	Parameters	Total	Average	%age
1	Feature (HR)	4620	924	100

In the sample issues of TA, only one form and subject is seen to have been used. That is feature. As the table shows, 100 per cent of the edit space is used for features on HR management/development.

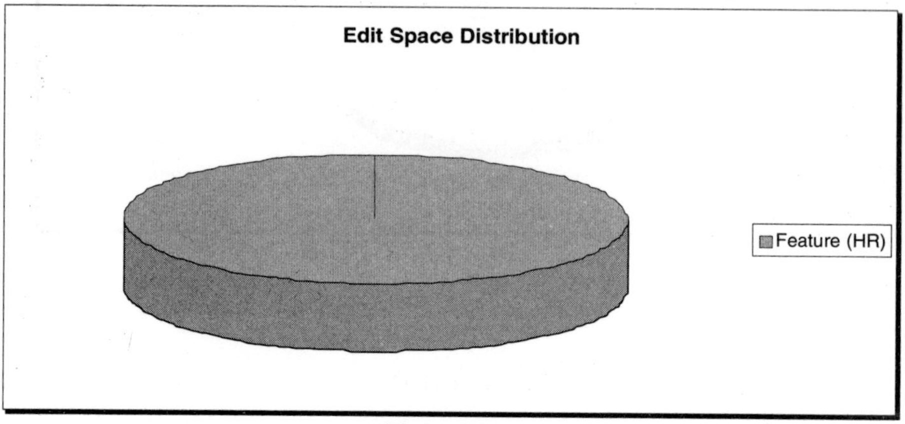

Figure II.52

II.1.f.iv. *Types of Visuals*

Table II.54

Sl. No.	Parameters	Total	Average	%age
1	Human Visuals	20	4	100
2	Non-Human Visuals	0	0	0

All the visuals in this supplement are human. This is understandable as the supplement is devoted to human resource development.

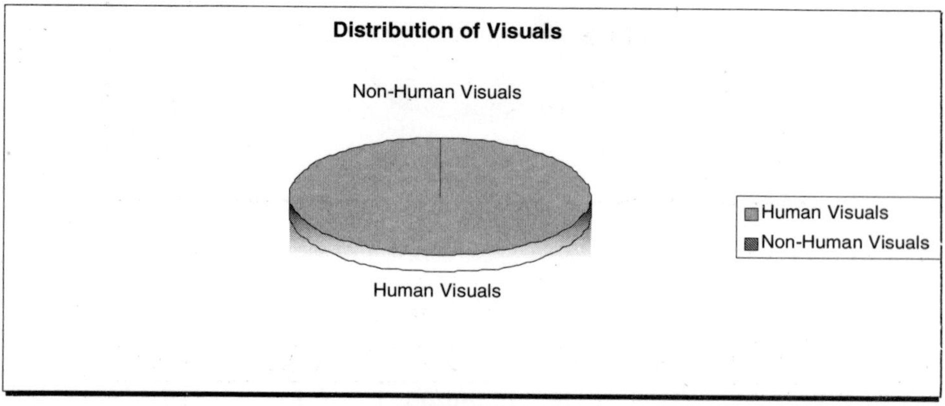

Figure II.53

II.1.f.v. *Societal Role- Based Human Visual Categorisation*

Table II.55

Sl. No.	Parameters	Total	Average	%age
1	Page-3	0	0	0
2	TV & Films	0	0	0
3	Artists	0	0	0
4	Non-Celebrity	20	4	100

All the human visuals in this supplement of TOI fall in the category of non-descript visuals.

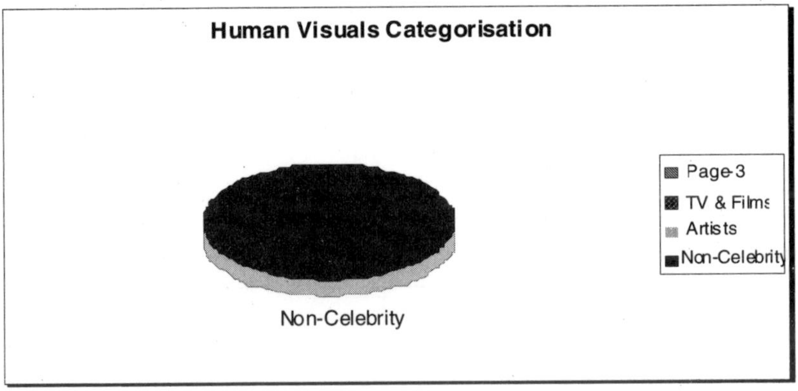

Figure II.54

II.1.f.vi. *Human Visual Categorisation on the Basis of Gender*

Table II.56

Sl. No.	Parameters	Total	Average	%age
1	Male	11	2.2	55
2	Female	9	1.8	45

On an average, each issue of TA contains 2.2 male visuals and 1.8 female visuals. In percentage terms, 55 per cent of the human visuals are of males whereas 45 per cent are of females.

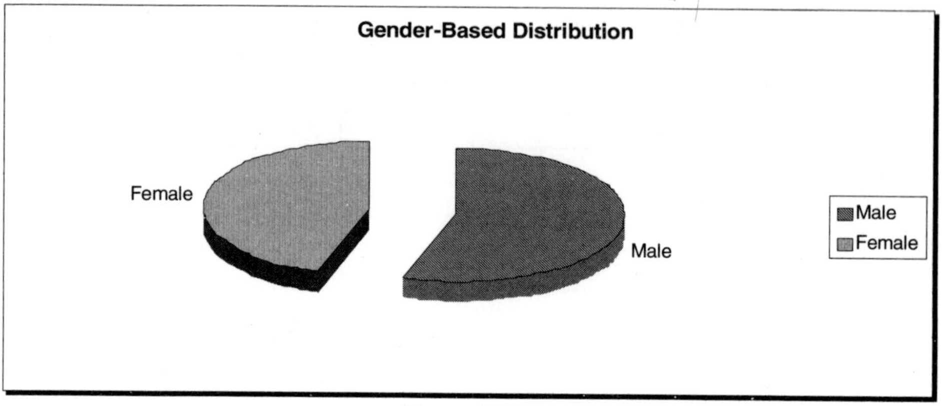

Figure II.55

II.1.f.vii. *Sartorial-Based Distribution of Human Visuals*

Table II.57

Sl. No.	Parameters	Total	Average	%age
1	Minimally Exposed	20	4	100
2	Moderately Exposed	0	0	0
3	Maximally Exposed	0	0	0

The table shows that in the sample issues of the supplement, all the human visuals fall in the category of minimally exposed. Obviously, the visuals in the supplement do not aim at attracting attention of the readers but at making features more interesting.

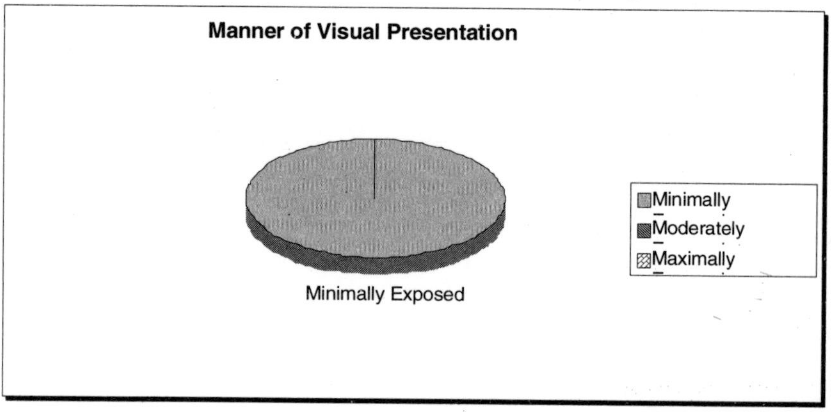

Figure II.56

II.1.f.viii. *Manner of Visual Presentation*

Table II.58

Sl. No.	Parameters	Total	Average	%age
1	Bordered	13	2.6	65
2	Borderless	7	1.4	35

The table shows that 65 per cent of the visuals are presented within frames, while 35 per cent of the visuals are borderless. On an average, 2.6 visuals are bordered whereas 1.4 visuals merge with the text. The presentation-based distribution of visuals shows that the layout of visuals is more formal than informal.

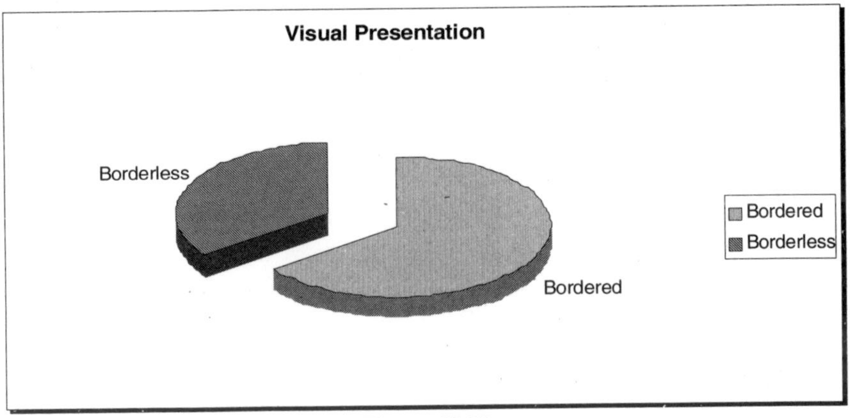

Figure II.57

II.1.g. ***Times Property***

Times Property, which comes out in colour, is published on only one day of the week i.e. Saturday. As the name itself suggests, the supplement broadly covers real estate-related information. The supplement, on an average, consists of 18 pages and uses non-glossy paper. It comes out in the size of a broadsheet. Since the supplement takes up a sober subject like investments in property, the supplement is also non-flashy in its layout.

II.1.g.i. *Edit-Ad Space Distribution*

Table II.59

Sl. No.	Parameters	Total	Average	%age
1	Edit	35332	8833	25.5
2	Ad	103260	25817	74.5

In comparison to edit space, advertisements occupy much larger space in the supplement. Only 25.5 per cent (35332 sq cm) of the total supplement space is devoted to the editorial matter whereas the rest of the space (103260 sq cm) which comes out to be 74.5 per cent of the total supplement space is occupied by advertisements. Obviously, the advertisers seem to be targeting a more specific readership which is interested in buying properties.

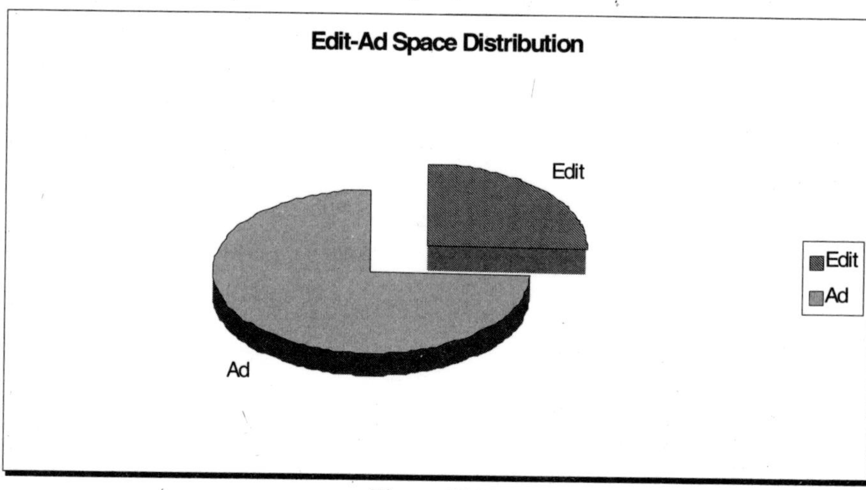

Figure II.58

II.1.g.ii. *Text-Visual Edit Space Distribution*

Table II.60

Sl. No.	Parameters	Total	Average	%age
1	Text	29061	7265.25	82.25
2	Visual	6271	1567.75	17.75

Out of the total of 35332 sq cm of edit space, a significant 29061 sq cm (82.25%) is devoted to text while the remaining edit space (17.75%) contains visuals. The difference between text and visual ratio can very well be understood in the light that TP is a sober supplement which majorly talks about latest trends and investments in real estate and other related subjects.

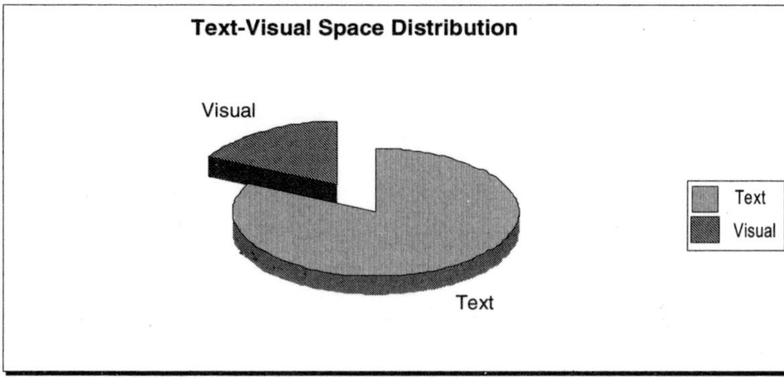

Figure II.59

II.1.g.iii. *Edit Space Distribution*

Table II.61

Sl. No.	Parameters	Total	Average	%age
1	Feature	21840	5460	61.8
2	Hard News	7488	1872	21.1
3	Miscellany	6004	1510	17.1

The table depicts that the edit space is occupied only by features, hard news and miscellanies. As much as 21840 sq cm (61.8%) of the total edit space is occupied by features whereas 1872 sq cm (21.1%) of the edit space is taken by hard news related to property and development. As much as 6004 sq cm (17.1%) is occupied by miscellany.

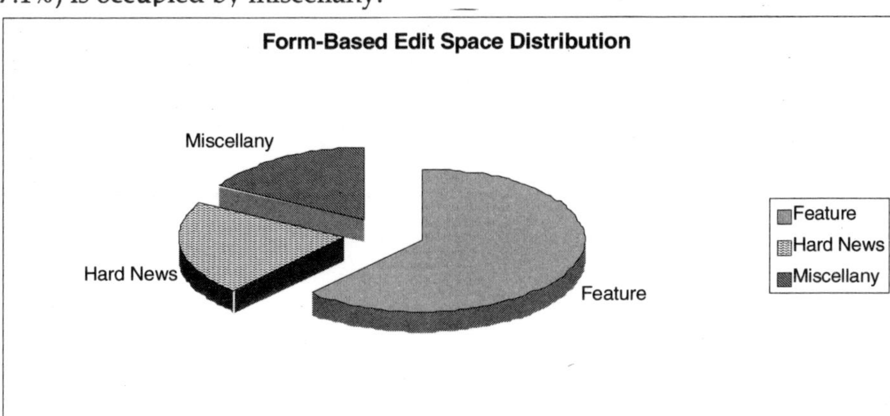

Figure II.60

II.1.g.iv. *Content-wise Feature Space Distribution*

Table II.62

Sl. No.	Parameters	Total	Average	%age
1	Lifestyle	4072	1018	18.6
2	Property	9576	2394	43.9
3	Development	8192	2048	37.5

Three subject-based categories—property, lifestyle and development—share the editorial space occupied by features. On an average, each issue of Times Property devotes 2394 sq cm of the feature space to property while 2048 sq cm of the space is occupied by development features. Lifestyle features occupy1018 sq cm of space in the supplement. In percentage terms, property features occupy 43.9 per cent of the total feature space, development features 37.5 per cent and lifestyle features 18.6 per cent. Since TP focuses on a well defined target readership, it also covers subjects that may interest or prove valuable to them.

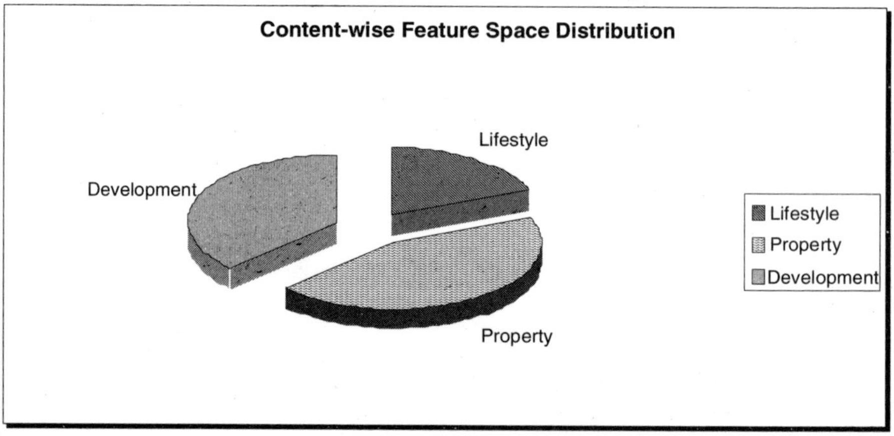

Figure II.61

II.1.g.v. *Number of Visuals*

Table II.63

Sl. No.	Parameters	Total	Average	%age
1	Human	0	0	0
2	Non-Human	36	9	100

The table shows that on an average, the supplement carries nine visuals. However, none of these visuals is human. Since the supplement focuses on property, development and other related issues, it is but understandable that all the visuals are non-human in nature.

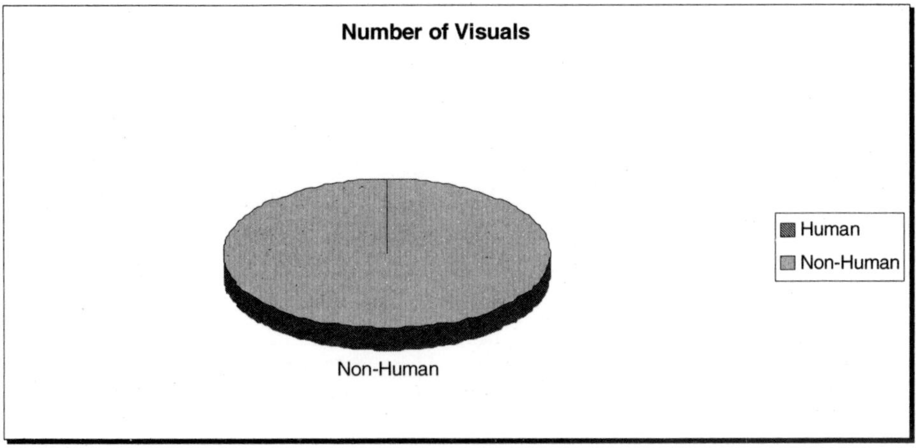

Figure II.62

II.1.g.vi. *Manner of Visual Presentation*

Table II.64

Sl. No.	Parameters	Total	Average	%age
1	Bordered	36	9	100
2	Borderless	0	0	0

The table depicts that all the visuals in Times Property are bordered. It can well be understood in the wake of the sober and serious nature of the supplement. The adherence to formal rules of visual presentation in TP underlines the formal character of the supplement.

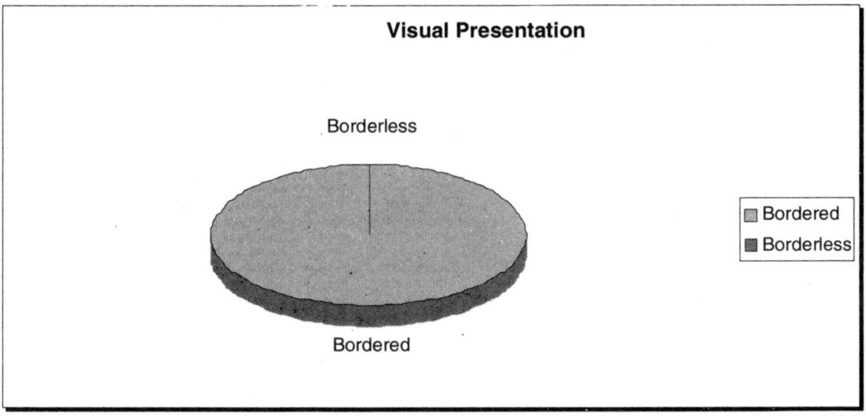

Figure II.63

II.2. Summary

The preceding discussion of the supplements of TOI throws up the following findings:

II.2.a. ***General Parameters of TOI Supplements***

Table II.65

Name of Supplement	Periodicity	Paper Quality	Paper Size
Delhi Times	Everyday	Newsprint	Broadsheet
Education Times	Weekly	Newsprint	Broadsheet
What's Hot	Weekly	Newsprint	Tabloid
Times Life	Weekly	Glossy	Broadsheet
Gurgaon Plus	Bi-weekly	Glossy/newsprint	Broadsheet
Times Ascent	Weekly	Newsprint	Broadsheet
Times Property	Weekly	Newsprint	Broadsheet

Of the seven supplements brought out by TOI, DT is the only supplement that comes out everyday with the main paper.

In terms of the general parameters of the supplements, five supplements come out on newsprint, one on glossy paper and one at times on newsprint and at times on glossy paper. While Times Life comes out on glossy paper, Gurgaon Plus, the local supplement of TOI comes out sometimes on glossy and sometimes on newsprint. The variation in the quality of paper used is prompted by the marketing concerns of the newspaper. As TL focuses on lifestyle features and products, it has to attract attention to the products advertised therein. This is possible only with glossy paper. Though Times Ascent and Times Property are advertising supplements, they do not come out on glossy paper as the products and services advertised therein do not have to be marketed aggressively.

All the supplements of TOI but for one come out on broadsheet. The only exception is What's Hot which comes out as a tabloid. As broadsheet supplements, they integrate well with the main newspaper.

II.2.b. ***Distribution of Ad-Edit Space Distribution***

Table II.66 Ad-Edit Space Distribution (in percentage terms)

Name of Supplement	Ad Space	Edit Space
Delhi Times	40.37	59.63
Education Times	62.67	37.33
What's Hot	33.98	66.02
Times Life	40.74	59.26
Gurgaon Plus	55.83	44.17
Times Ascent	97.8	2.2
Times Property	74.5	25.5

The ad-edit ratio is the highest in Times Ascent where advertisements take up 97.8 per cent of the supplement space. It is followed by Times Property (74.5% ad space), Education Times (62.67% ad space), Gurgaon Plus (55.83% ad space), Times Life (40.74%), Delhi Times (40.37%) and finally What's Hot (33.98%). The scaling down of the advertising space in each of these supplements is indicative of the overall purpose of publication of these supplements. As Times Ascent and Times Property are primarily advertising supplements, the high percentage of advertising space in each of them is understandable.

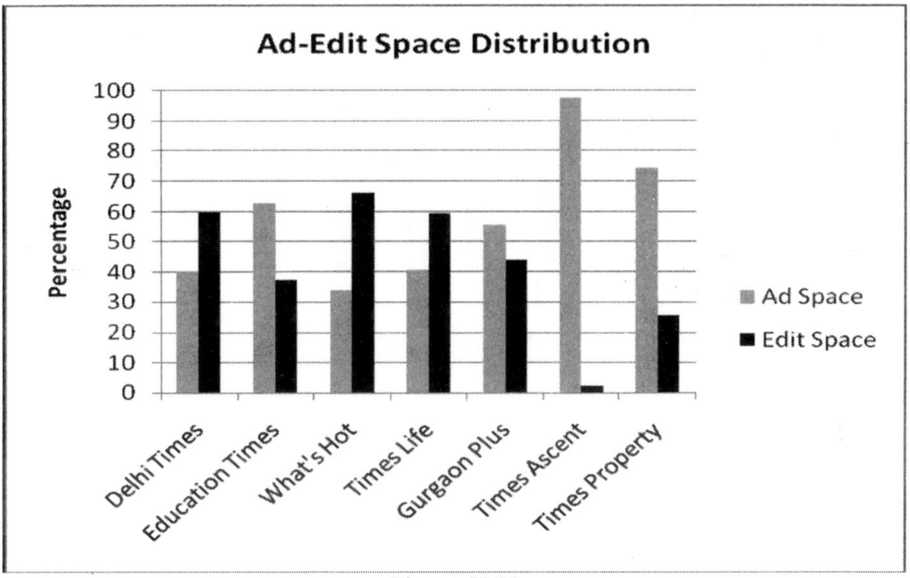

Figure II.64

II.2.c. *Distribution of Text-Visual Space*

Table II.67: Text-Visual Space Distribution (in percentage terms)

Name of Supplement	Text Space	Visual Space
Delhi Times	73.84	26.16
Education Times	87.59	12.41
What's Hot	70.81	29.19
Times Life	71.99	28.01
Gurgaon Plus	56.49	43.51
Times Ascent	73.18	26.82
Times Property	82.25	17.75

Text-visual space distribution ratio among the various supplements of TOI is again non-uniform. While the text-visual ratio (T/V ratio) is the highest in

Education Times (7.06:1), it is the lowest in Gurgaon Plus (1.3:1). Between these two extremities, the T/V ratio descends from Education Times to Times Property, then to Delhi Times, later to Times Ascent, still later to Times Life and penultimately What's Hot. The preponderance of visuals in Gurgaon Plus followed by What's Hot and Times Life owes to the rise of page-3 journalism which relies on people and lifestyle.

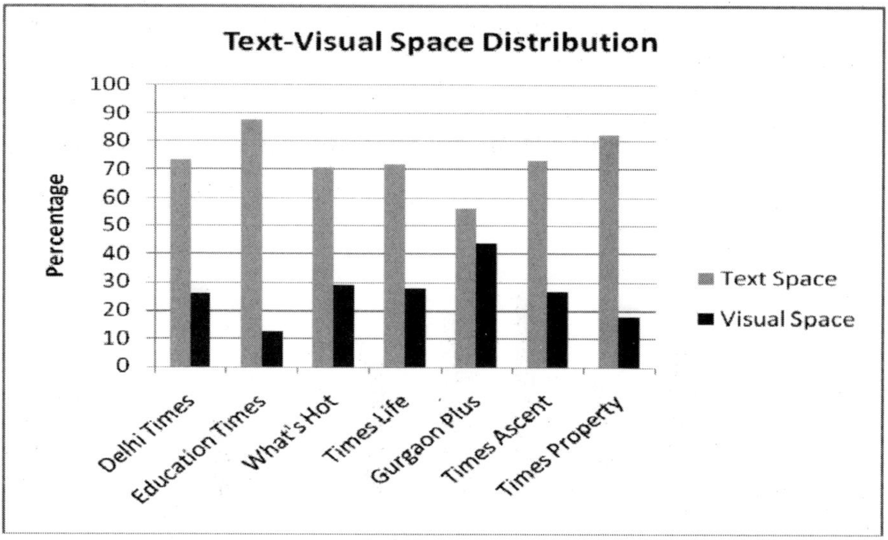

Figure II.65

II.2.d. *Distribution of Edit Space in TOI Supplements*

Table II.68 Edit Space Distribution (in percentage terms)

Parameters	DT	ET	WH	TL	GP	TA	TP
Interviews	9.3	4.7	0	7.07	0	0	0
Soft Stories	27.25	0	0	0	0	0	0
Features	12.18	19.56	34.79	60.5	64.03	100	61.8
Memoirs	0.38	6.81	0.39	0	0	0	0
Review	0	1.32	13.35	0	0	0	0
Tech News	0	0	3.23	6.45	0	0	0
Print Promos	0	0	6.19	0	0	0	0
Hard News	0	22.78	0	0	2.36	0	21.1
Soft News	0	7.61	0	0	22.03	0	0
Miscellany	50.89	37.22	42.05	25.98	11.58	0	17.1

The edit space distribution in each of the supplements of TOI tends to be more or less skewed in favour of features, if one were to leave out the sundry items of jokes, cartoons, zodiac, handy tips, snippets etc from our comparison. While features occupy 34.79 per cent of the editorial space in What's Hot, they occupy 60.5 per cent of the space in Times Life, 64.03 per cent space in Gurgaon Plus, 19.56 per cent space in Education Times, 61.8 per cent space in Times Property and 100 per cent of the total edit space in Times Ascent. Only in DT and Education Times do features not take up maximum space. The high priority accorded to features in the editorial space of most of the supplements of TOI shows the need for leisure reading among the TOI supplement readers.

II.2.e. *Feature Space Distribution in TOI Supplements*

Table II.69: Feature Space Distribution (in percentage terms)

Feature Type	DT	ET	WH	TL	GP	TA	TP
Wellbeing	3.19	0	10.11	9.29	13.38	0	0
Photo	7.96	0	0	0	3.65	0	0
Celebrity	17.96	12.9	7.66	15.27	0	0	0
Beauty	10.71	0	13.88	0	0	0	0
Culinary	9.33	0	21.94	0	11.99	0	0
Lifestyle	16.73	0	17.54	16.13	1.76	0	18.6
Crime	8.08	0	0	0	4.53	0	0
Politics	6.28	0	0	0	0	0	0
Relationships	7.71	0	12.06	28.42	0	0	0
Children	2.18	0	0	0	0	0	0
B'wood	9.87	0	0	0	0	0	0
Travel	0	0	14.4	0	0	0	0
Art	0	0	2.41	0	0	0	0
Social Issues	0	0	0	22.94	0	0	0
Spirituality	0	0	0	7.95	0	0	0
Utility	0	19.79	0	0	0	0	0
Career	0	67.31	0	0	0	0	0
Development	0	0	0	0	33.86	0	37.5
Technology	0	0	0	0	9.28	0	0
Education	0	0	0	0	4.41	0	0
Grievances	0	0	0	0	11.68	0	0
Recreation	0	0	0	0	5.46	0	0
HRD	0	0	0	0	0	100	0
Property	0	0	0	0	0	0	43.9

The feature space distribution in each of the supplements of TOI shows a variegated fare. While in DT, the top three slots are taken up by celebrity, lifestyle and beauty features in a descending order, in What's Hot culinary, lifestyle and travel features occupy the maximum feature space in the descending order. In Times Life, relationships, social issues and lifestyle occupy the maximum feature space, while in Education Times career, utility and celebrity features occupy most of the feature space in a descending order. In GP development, well being and culinary features occupy the maximum feature space while in Times Property property, development and lifestyle features occupy the maximum feature space in a descending order. In Times Ascent, only HR development features figure, thereby taking up 100 per cent feature space. The wide variety of the subjects features focus on in each of the supplements of TOI shows a general preference for lifestyle, relationship, culinary, celebrity, beauty and Bollywood features. The inference is obvious: the TOI supplements highlight the pleasing and beautiful aspect of life with a view to relieve the stress and the boredom of a harried metropolitan audience. Besides, by focusing on such subjects as attract the readers' eyeballs, the paper is able to sell the attention of its wide readership to the marketers. The paper, therefore, fulfils both the entertainment and the commercial function of mass media.

II.2.f. *Feature Space Accorded To Relationship Features*

Table II.70: Relationship Feature Space Distribution (in percentage terms)

Name of Supplement	Formal	Informal	Intimate
Delhi Times	0	41.89	58.11
Education Times	0	0	0
What's Hot	0	0	100
Times Life	0	33	67
Gurgaon Plus	0	0	0
Times Ascent	0	0	0
Times Property	0	0	0

An analysis of relationship features highlighted in TOI supplements like DT, What's Hot and Times Life shows that the paper dares to bare the nature of intimate relationships more than the informal and formal relationships obtaining in the society. While Times Life devotes 67 per cent of the relationship feature space to the discussion of intimate subjects, considered taboo in a traditional society, What's Hot apportions cent per cent of its relationship feature space to intimate subjects. Similarly, DT sets apart 58.11 per cent of the relationship feature space for the discussion of such issues. Interestingly, relationship features in none of the three supplements discussed formal relationships. Again, only DT and Times Life set apart space for informal features, but this space is far less than that given to intimate relationships. TOI, true to the popular perception, comes out as an avant-garde newspaper by stepping into the territory of the profane and the prohibited.

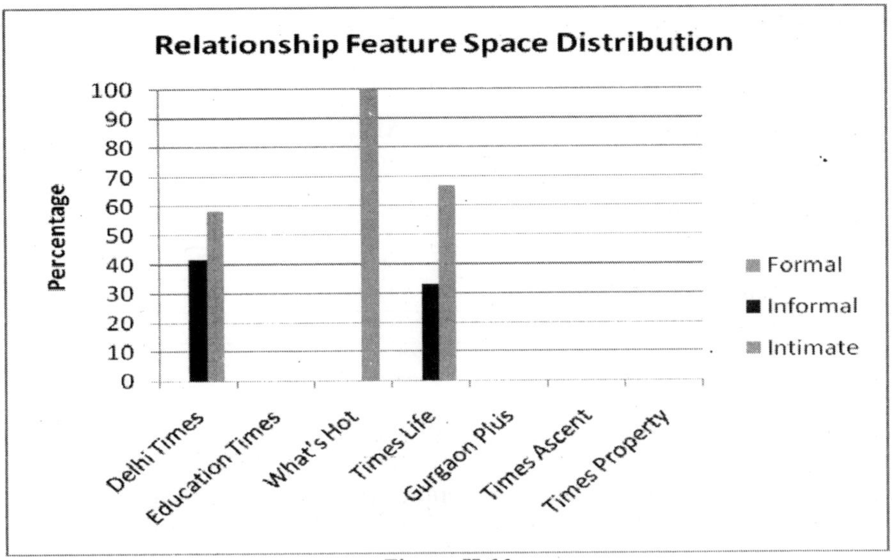

Figure II.66

II.2.g. *Societal Role-Based Human Visual Categorisation*

Table 11.71 Human Visual Categorisation (in percentage terms)

Name of Supplement	Page-3	TV & Films	Political	Sports	Non-Celebrities
Delhi Times	24.83	55.37	1.68	3.02	15.1
Education Times	0	3.57	7.14	0	89.29
What's Hot	0	50	0	0	50
Times Life	4.4	16.98	0	0	78.62
Gurgaon Plus	12.5	0	0	6.25	81.25
Times Ascent	0	0	0	0	100
Times Property	0	0	0	0	0

TOI gives a high priority to the visuals of TV and film personalities in its supplements, particularly DT.(55.3%) and What's Hot (50%). Even in Times Life, if we were to set aside the non-descript visuals of sundry roles which account for 78.62 per cent, the visuals of TV and film personalities (16.98%) are the highest among all the categories of roles.

II.2.h. *Human Visual Categorisation on the Basis of Gender*

Table II.72: Gender-Based Visual Categorisation (in percentage terms)

Name of Supplement	Male	Female
Delhi Times	49.79	50.21
Education Times	52.63	47.37
What's Hot	42.5	57.5
Times Life	38.46	61.54
Gurgaon Plus	22.22	77.78
Times Ascent	55	45
Times Property	0	0

An analysis of the visuals in the supplements of TOI reveals that all the supplements of TOI but for two accord high priority to female visuals (all female/solo). The female visual percentage in various supplements ranges from 77.78 per cent to 45 per cent. Male-female visual ratio in Gurgaon Plus is as high as ~ 2:7 followed by Times Life where the ratio is ~2:3. In What's Hot, 57.5 per cent of the human visuals are that of females followed by DT (50.21%). Interestingly, DT has almost the same number of male and female visuals with a very slight tilt towards female visuals. Education Times and Times Ascent -- the only two supplements where the male visuals are more than the female visuals also do not depict wide variation. The message is loud and clear—TOI supplements use female visuals liberally to instantly grab the attention of readers.

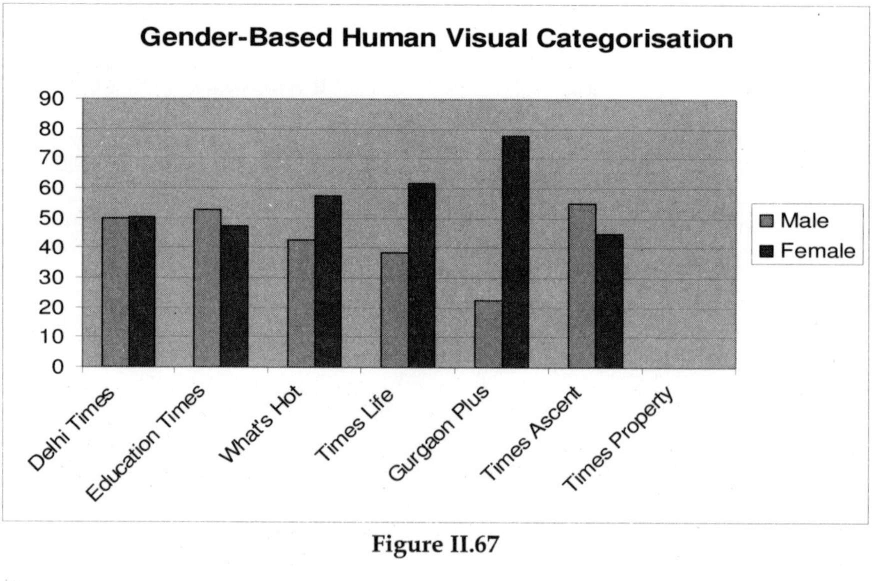

Figure II.67

II.2.i. *Human Visual Presentation*

Table II.73: Manner of Human Visual Presentation (in percentage terms)

Name of Supplement	Minimally Exposed	Moderately Exposed	Maximally Exposed
Delhi Times	76.88	15.58	7.54
Education Times	100	0	0
What's Hot	68.06	25	6.94
Times Life	62.5	25	12.5
Gurgaon Plus	81.25	18.75	0
Times Ascent	100	0	0
Times Property	0	0	0

Interestingly, the TOI supplements may highlight female visuals and even may be bold enough to talk about taboo subjects, but the maximum number of human visuals in all the TOI supplements does not highlight the contours of human body. Unlike the prevalent public image of TOI splashing explicit female visuals unscrupulously, maximum number of human visuals in all the TOI supplements fall in the category of minimally exposed visuals. Only three TOI supplements out of seven, Times Life, Delhi Times and What's Hot, carry explicit human visuals. Here also, the percentage of maximally exposed human visuals ranges from 6.94 per cent to 12.5 per cent of the human visuals.

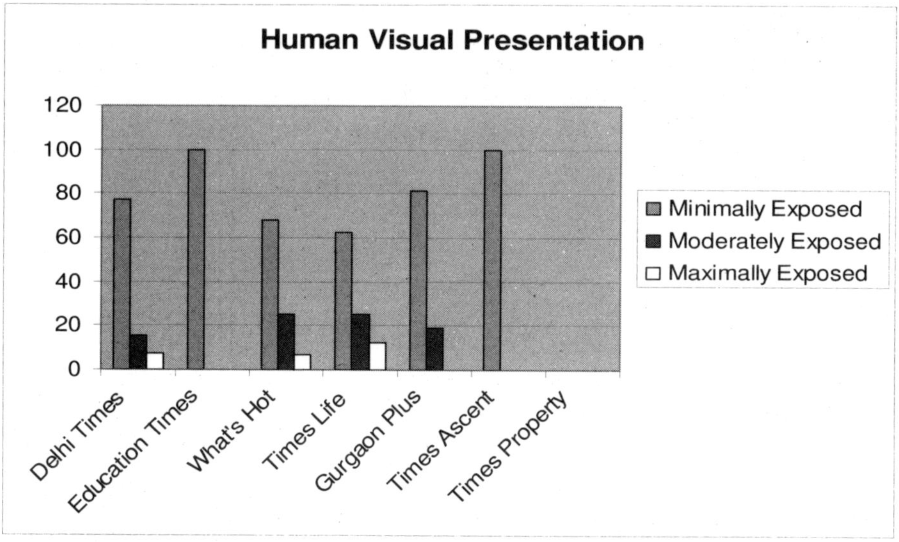

Figure II.68

II.2.j. *Layout of Visuals*

Table II.74

Name of Supplement	Bordered	Borderless
Delhi Times	83.39	16.61
Education Times	100	0
What's Hot	48.94	51.06
Times Life	22.22	77.78
Gurgaon Plus	38.71	61.29
Times Ascent	65	35
Times Property	100	0

The treatment accorded to visuals in various supplements of TOI doesn't depict any consistency. Three supplements of TOI-- What's Hot, Times Life and Gurgaon Plus—are modern in terms of visual presentation. Here, the number of visuals merging with the text is more with TL taking the lead with 77.78 per cent of the total number of visuals integrating with text. On the other hand, we have Delhi Times, Education Times, Times Ascent and Times Property which are still conservative in their visual treatment.

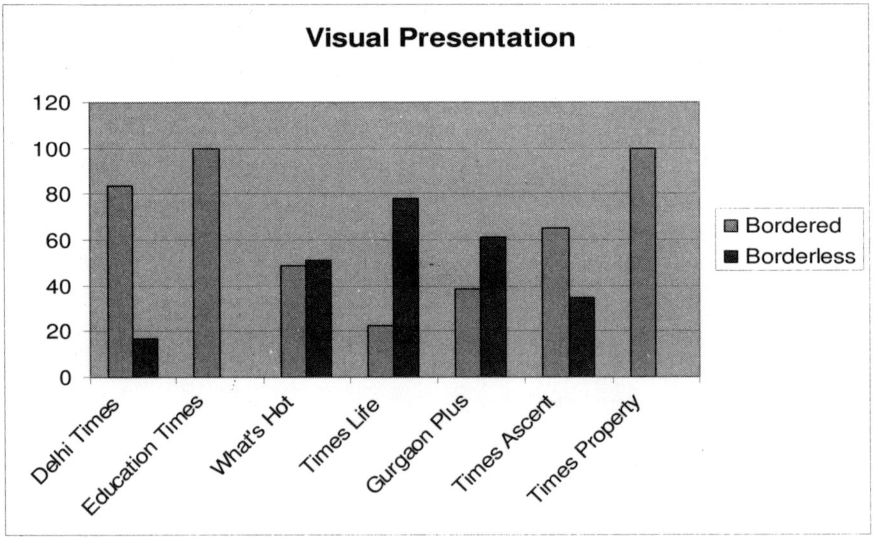

Figure II.69

CHAPTER III

CONTENT ANALYSIS OF DAINIK BHASKAR SUPPLEMENTS

Dainik Bhaskar (DB) is a Hindi newspaper that reaches out to the largely Hindi speaking areas of the Northern region of India. The supplements surveyed here belong to the Panipat edition as the main paper comes out from Jaipur in Rajasthan. The paper comes out with four supplements regularly on different days of the week. As it is a Hindi newspaper with a readership largely based in the Hindi hinterland of Haryana, its supplements present results very different from those of TOI. The following sections attempt an explication of the results thrown up by the content analysis of its supplements, which are Madhurima, Navrang, Rasrang and Bal Bhaskar. While Madhurima comes out on every Wednesday, Navrang comes out on every Saturday, Rasrang on every Sunday and Bal Bhaskar twice a month.

III.1.a. *Madhurima*

As Madhurima comes out every Wednesday, its target audience is the housewives and the school going children (Interview with Dinesh Mishr, Resident Editor, Dainik Bhaskar, Panipat edition). Madhurima covers subjects as diverse as television, recreation, relationships, counseling, films, human ethics, utility tips, social issues, literature, spirituality, human interest and culinary details. On an average, it carries 8 pages per issue, the pages being printed on newsprint having tabloid size. As the quality of the paper is not very good, this supplement is not brought out with the primary motive of earning advertising revenue. This is borne out by an analysis of the space distribution between editorial and advertising content in this supplement.

III.1.a.i. *Edit-Ad Distribution of Supplement Space*

Table III.1

Parameters	Total	Average	%age
Edit Space	27027.5	5405.5	84.46
Ad Space	4972.5	994.5	15.54

Of the total average supplement space per issue of 6400 sq cm, the edit space occupies 5405.5 sq cm, while advertising content takes up only 994.5 sq cm space. In percentage terms, edit space occupies 84.46 per cent space, whereas advertising content takes up 15.54 per cent space. So, even though advertising content gets space in the supplements, it remains way below the edit content.

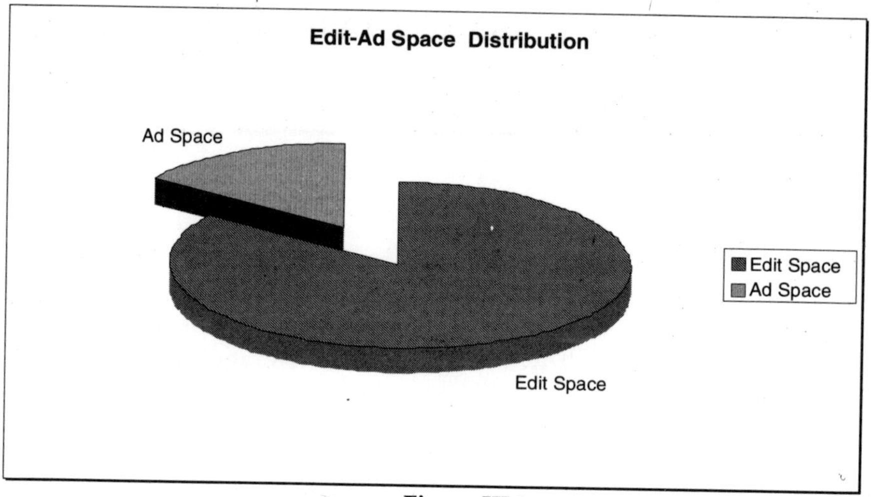

Figure III.1

III.1.a.ii. *Text-Visual Based Distribution of Edit Space*

Table III.2

Parameters	Total	Average	%age
Text	17335	3467	64.14
Visuals	9692.5	1938.5	35.86

The table shows the distribution of edit space between text and visuals. It shows that the text takes up 64.14 per cent of the editorial space whereas visuals take up 35.86 per cent space. The ratio of text space to visual space is approximately 1.7:1. All the same, having 35.86 per cent visual space gives the supplement a visual appeal that attracts and holds the attention of the readers.

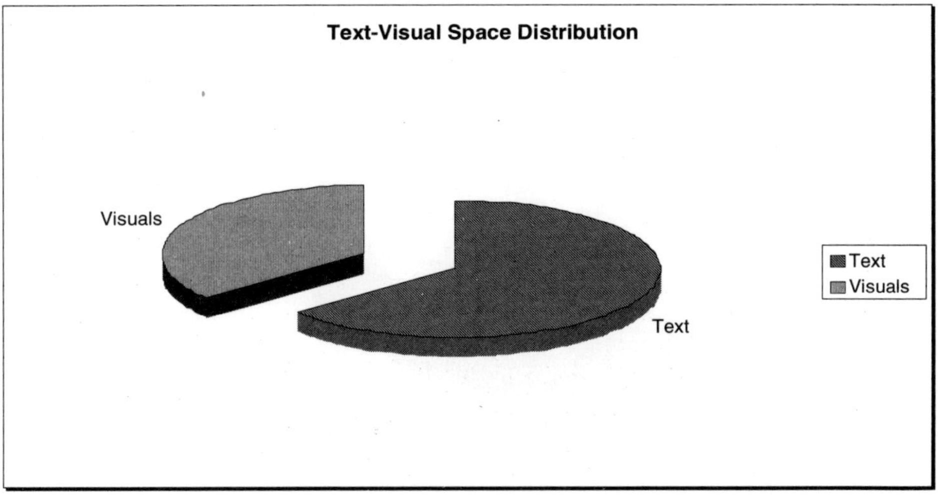

Figure III.2

III.1.a.iii. *Form-Based Edit Space Distribution*

Table III.3

Parameters	**Total**	**Average**	**%age**
Poetry	650	130	2.40
Memoirs	1200	240	4.44
Interviews	1620	324	5.99
Feature	5240	1048	19.39
Fiction	11345	2269	41.98
Miscellany	6972.5	1394.5	25.80

The editorial content of this supplement is distributed over five major journalistic forms apart from miscellaneous items. Interestingly enough, fiction occupies the maximum edit space, which is a substantial 41.98 per cent. It is followed by the miscellaneous items consuming 25.8 per cent space. The second place occupied by this category of edit content is understandable as it is an assortment of editorial items. At the third place are features, occupying 19.39 per cent edit space. Interviews, memoirs, and poetry consume the edit space marginally in the percentages of 5.99, 4.44 and 2.40 respectively.

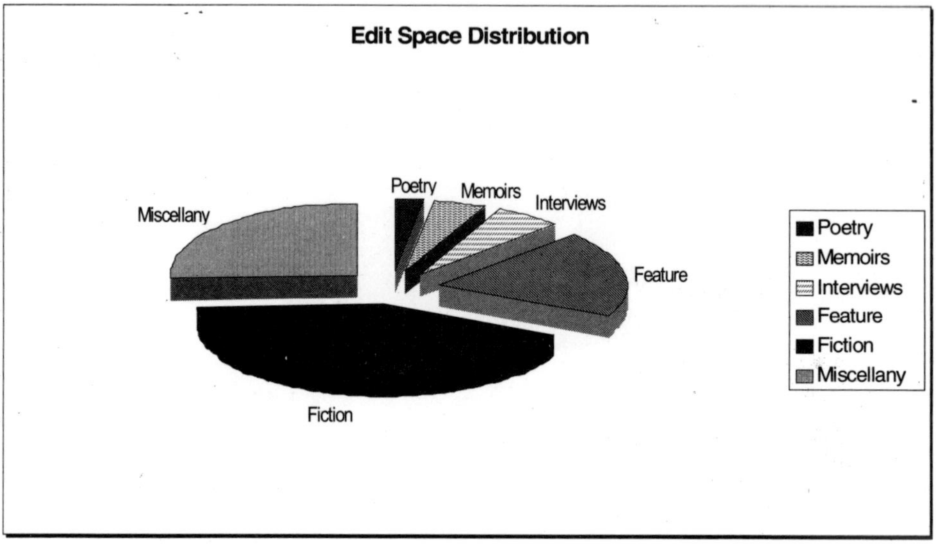

Figure III.3

III.1.a.iv. *Subject-Based Feature Space Distribution*

Table III.4

Parameters	Total	Average	%age
Children	2180	236	41.6
Women	3060	612	58.4

The subject-based feature space distribution as represented in the Table III.4 reveals that most of the features in the sample issues of this supplement are on women, followed by those on children. Women take up as much as 58.4 per cent of the feature space whereas children occupy 41.6 per cent.

The preponderance of women and children in the features shows that this supplement targets families particularly housewives and their prime concern, their children. The substantial percentage of space consumed by children could be because the sample period pertained to the month of May, which happens to be vacation time for the kids.

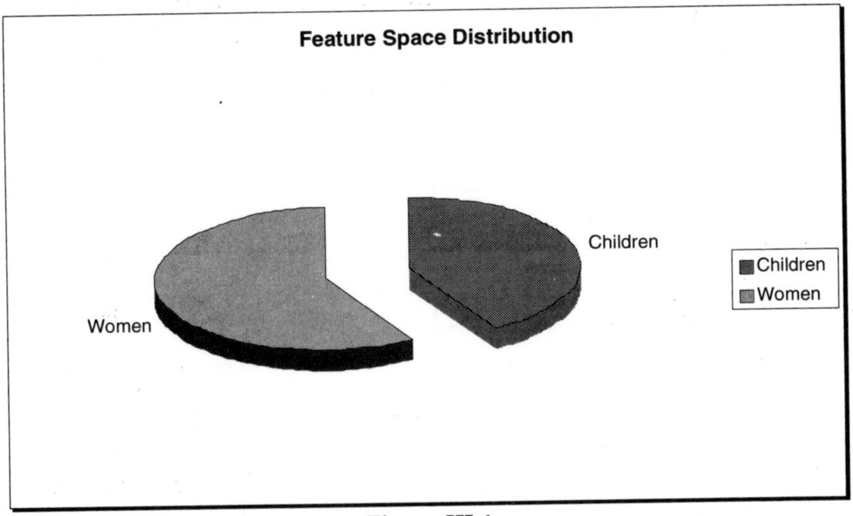

Figure III.4

III.1.a.v. *Types of Visuals*

Table III.5

Parameters	**Total**	**Average**	**%age**
Human Visuals	65	13	76.47
Non-Human Visuals	20	4	23.53

The table shows that on an average there are 13 human visuals and 4 non-human visuals in each issue of Madhurima. In percentage terms, human visuals comprise 76.47 per cent of the total number of the visuals in it, while the non-human visuals constitute 23.53 per cent.

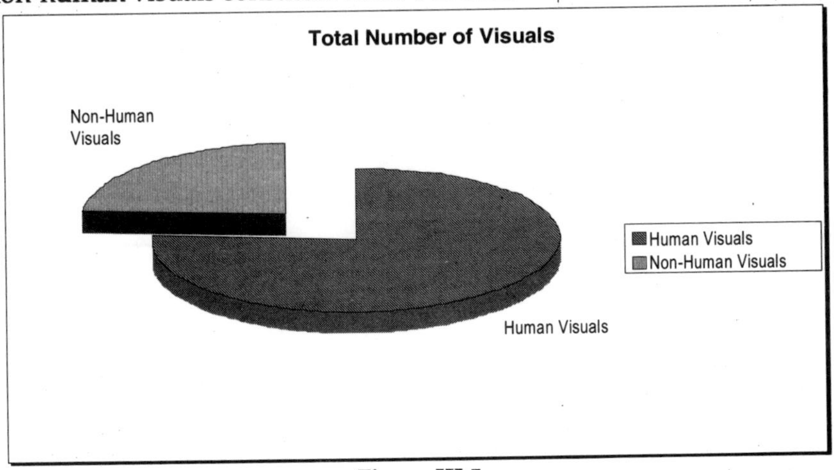

Figure III.5

III.1.a.vi. *Role-Based Human Visual Distribution*

Table III.6

Parameters	Total	Average	%age
Political	0	0	0
Sports	0	0	0
P-3	5	1	7.69
TV & Films	5	1	7.69
Performing Artists	5	1	7.69
Others	50	10	76.93

In view of the preponderance of fiction in this supplement, most of the human visuals in it are non-celebrity and commonplace. These account for 76.93 per cent of the human visuals. Human visuals from the worlds of Page 3, TV & films, and performing arts account individually for 7.69 per cent each.

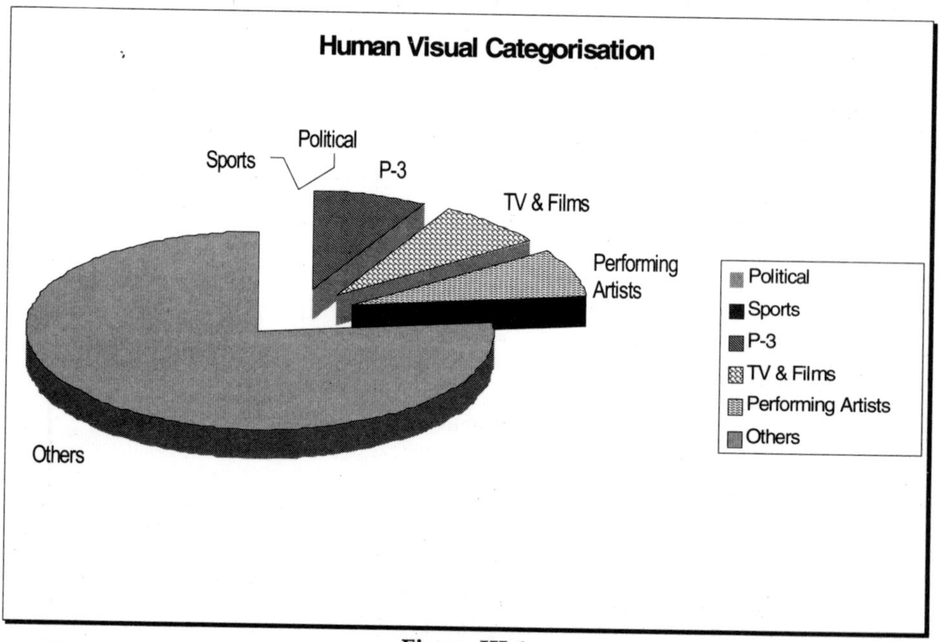

Figure III.6

III.1.a.vii. *Gender-Based Distribution of Human Visuals*

Table III.7

Parameters	Total	Average	%age
Mixed	5	1	7.69
Male	0	0	0.00
Female	60	12	92.31

Of the 65 human visuals, five are mixed. Of the remaining 60 human visuals, all are female visuals. As the supplement targets housewives and children, the tilt in favour of the women is understandable.

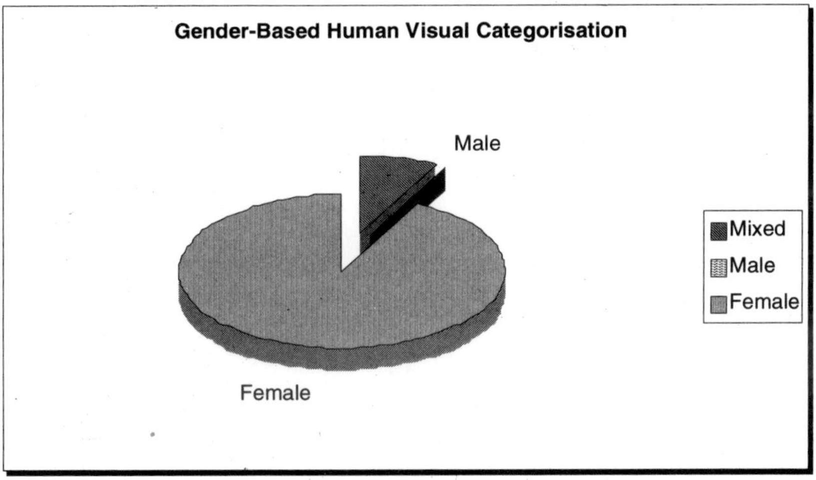

Figure III.7

III.1.a.viii. *Manner of Presentation of Human Visuals*

Table III.8

Parameters	Total	Average	%age
Minimally-exposed	65	13	100.00
Moderately-exposed	0	0	0.00
Maximally-exposed	0	0	0.00

All the human visuals in the sample supplements are minimally exposed. The minimal exposure of the human visuals shows the regard for Indian values of sobriety and moderation.

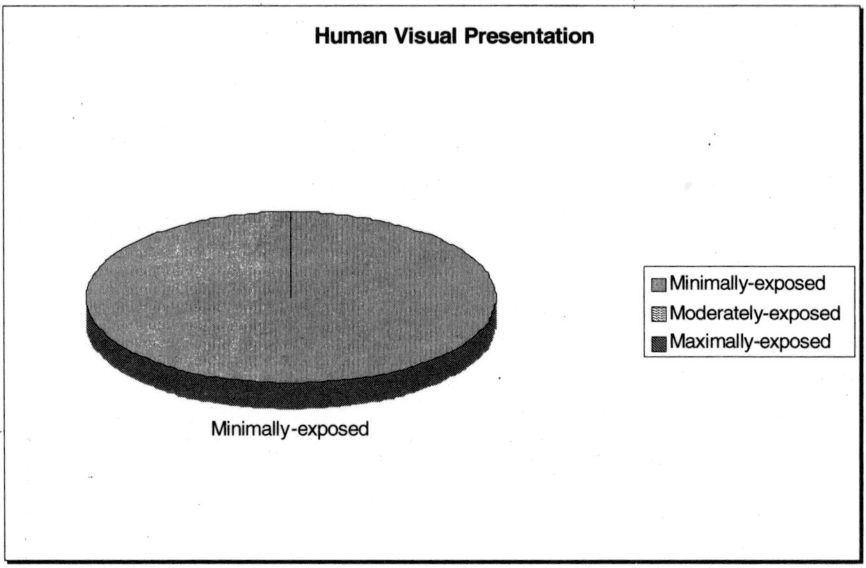

Figure III.8

III.1.a.ix. *Presentation of Visuals*

Table III.9

Parameters	Total	Average	%age
Bordered	15	3	17.65
Borderless	70	14	82.35

Table III.9 represents the presentation of visuals in the supplement. Out of the 85 visuals in the sample issues of the supplement, only 15 have a frame, the remaining 70 are frameless. In percentage terms, the borderless pictures account for 82.35 per cent of the total number of pictures, whereas the bordered ones account for a paltry 17.65 per cent. The visuals in the borderless pictures spill over the textual portion of the editorial space, creating the impression of larger than life pictures. This discarding of the formal principles of layout and design is indicative of a new liberal tendency of presentation of visuals in an otherwise conservative supplement.

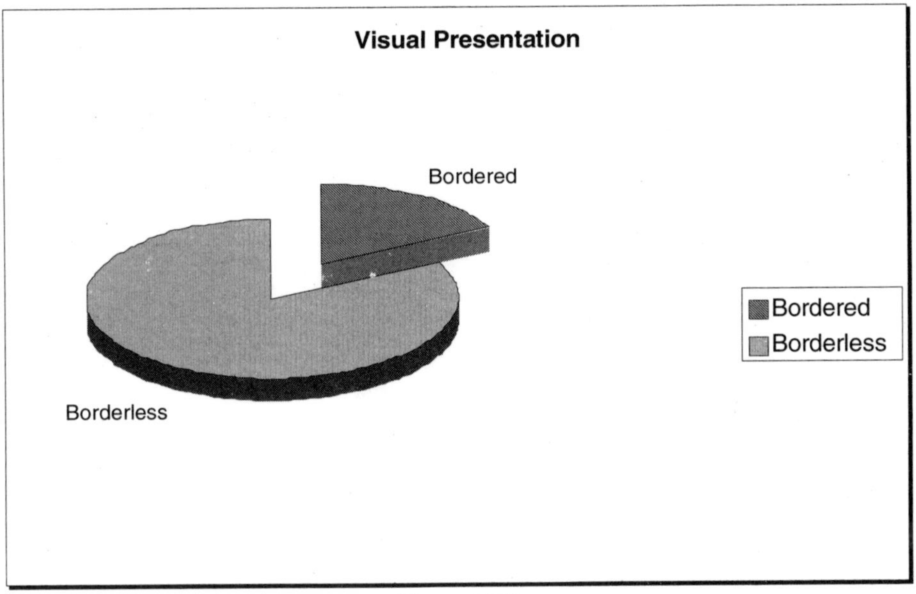

Figure III.9

III.1.b. *Navrang*

Issued on every Saturday of the week, this supplement covers the subjects of films, television, and reviews apart from regular columns. On an average, the supplement carries four pages per issue. The supplement is brought out on broadsheet-sized newsprint paper.

III.1.b.i. *Edit-Ad Space Distribution in the Supplement*

Table III.10

Parameters	Total	Average	%age
Edit Space	25052	6263	93.55
Ad Space	1728	432	6.45

The table shows that the supplement space is divided unevenly between the editorial content and advertisements. In fact, it is skewed in favour of editorial content, which comprises 93.55 per cent of the supplement space. That leaves only 6.45 per cent of the supplement space for the advertisements. Like its other counterpart, Madhurima, this supplement too allocates very little space to advertisements. Rather, the advertising content in it is far less than that in Madhurima. The consistent tendency to accord less space to advertising content owes to the absence of consumerism in the Hindi hinterland of the state.

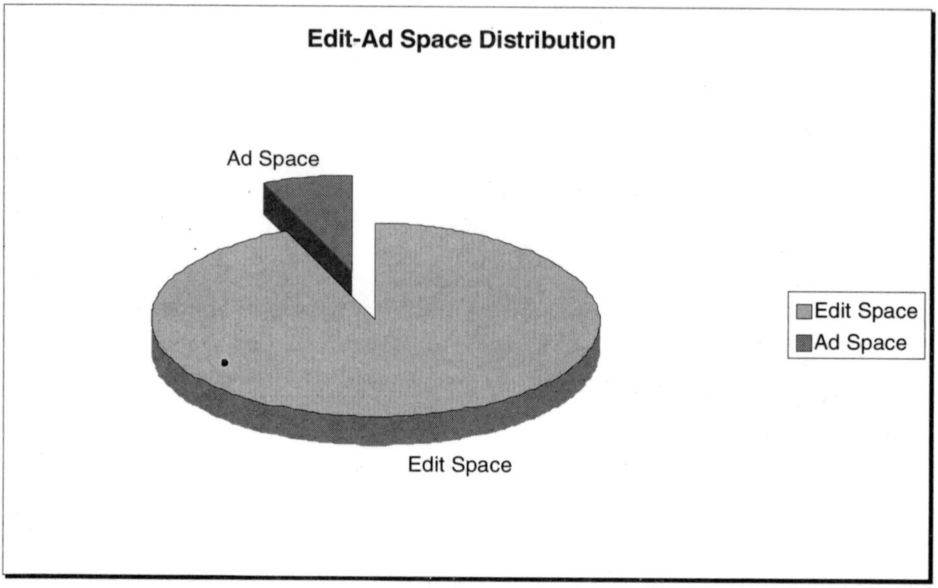

Figure III.10

III.1.b.ii. *Edit Space Distribution between Text and Visuals*

Table III.11

Parameters	Total	Average	%age
Text	12202	3050.5	48.71
Visuals	12850	3212.5	51.29

Interestingly enough, visuals account for 51.29 per cent of the edit space, while the text occupies only 48.71 per cent. The preponderance of visuals in this supplement indicates the attempt to hold the attention of the readers through a variety of visuals and thereby boost the circulation of the paper/supplement. It would be very appropriate to mention over here that as the paper is in Hindi, it has to face stiff competition from other Hindi newspapers published in the region. By using a generous sprinkling of visuals, the paper makes this supplement inviting and fascinating to read. Not surprisingly, DB has been able to secure the highest circulation among Hindi newspapers.

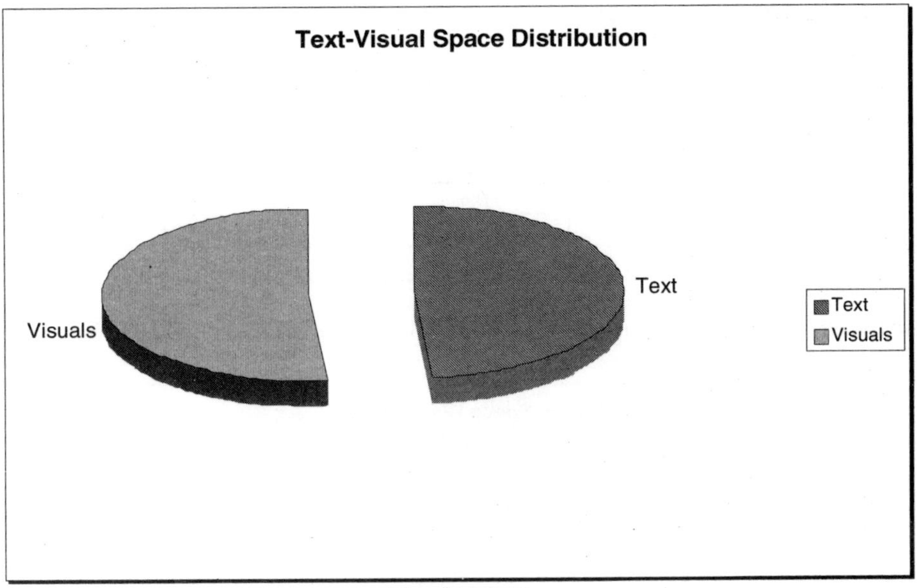

Figure III.11

III.1.b.iii. *Form-Based Edit Space Distribution*

Table III.12

Parameters	Total	Average	%age
Regular Columns	816	204	3.26
Soft News	2060.5	515.12	8.22
Review	1491.5	372.87	5.95
Interview	17987.25	4496.81	71.8
Features	1126	281.5	4.49
Memoirs	268	67	1.07
Miscellany	1302.75	325.7	5.21

Of the various forms of journalistic writing used in this supplement, interviews take the lion's share of the edit space (71.80%). The remaining space is shared between soft news (8.22%), reviews (5.95%), features (4.49%), regular columns (3.26%), memoirs (1.07%), and miscellany (5.21%).

III.1.b.iv. *Review Space Distribution*

Table III.13

Parameters	Total	Average	%age
Book	1491.5	372.87	100.00
Film	0	0	0.00
Art	0	0	0.00
Theatre	0	0	0.00

All the reviews in this supplement are of books recently released. None is of films, art or theatre.

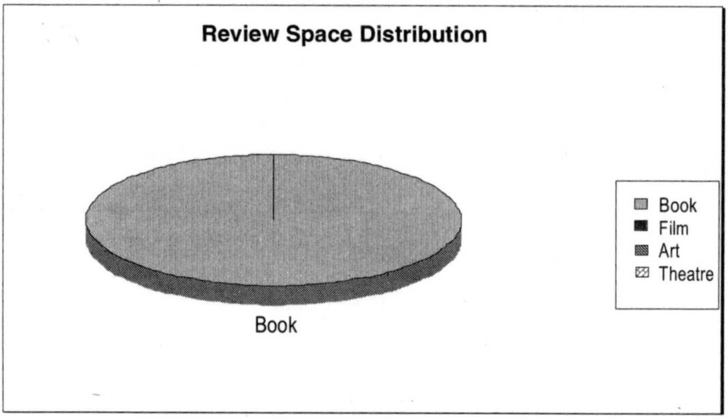

Figure III.12

III.1.b.v. *Subject-Based Feature Space Distribution*

Table III.14

Parameters	Total	Average	%age
Fashion	563	140.75	50.00
Films	563	140.75	50.00

The supplement carries features on two subjects. These subjects are fashion and films. These two subjects constitute the high points of popular culture and are therefore highly attractive subjects for readers. Interestingly enough, each of the two occupy equal space. Out of the total space occupied by the features (1126 sq cm), exactly 50 per cent (563 sq cm) is occupied by features on fashion. Exactly the same space is occupied by features on films.

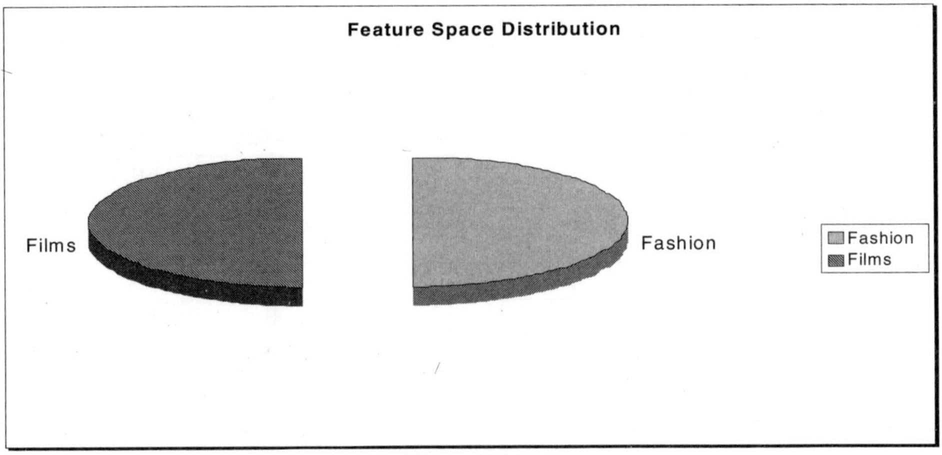

Figure III.13

III.1.b.vi. *Types of Visuals*

Table III.15

Parameters	Total	Average	%age
Human Visuals	112	28	100.00
Non-Human Visuals	0	0	0.00

As represented in the Table III.14, all the visuals in Navrang are of humans. There are no visuals which are of non-human objects. Clearly, the supplement strives to accentuate its human touch to attract readers and to boost circulation.

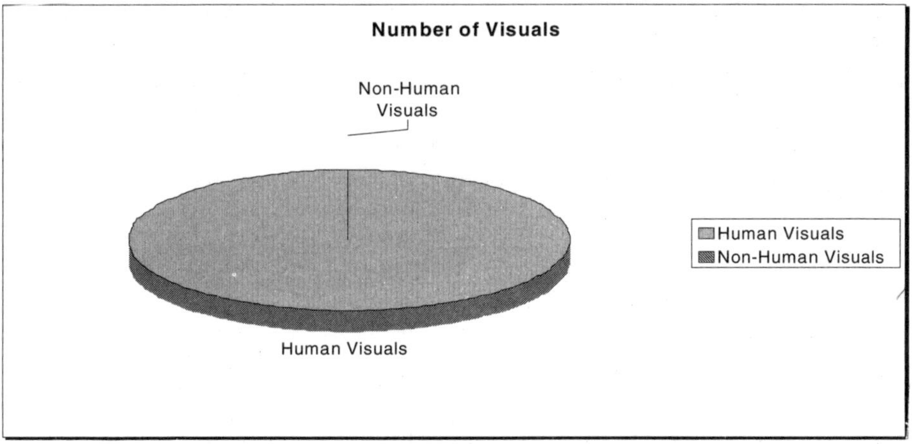

Figure III.14

III.1.b.vii. *Role-Based Human Visual Distribution*

Table III.15

Parameters	Total	Average	%age
Political	0	0	0.00
Sports	0	0	0.00
P-3	0	0	0.00
TV& Films	112	28	100.00
Performing Artists	0	0	0.00
Others	0	0	0.00

Of all the diverse roles highlighted in the other supplements, only film and television- based social roles are highlighted in Navrang. This is in keeping with the emphasis of its subject matter on films and television and fashion.

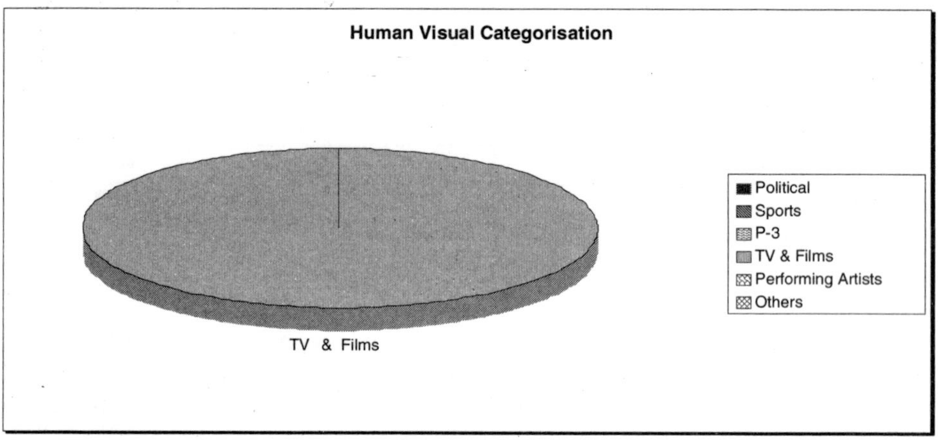

Figure III.15

III.1.b.viii. *Gender-Based Distribution of Human Visuals*

Table III.16

Parameters	Total	Average	%age
Male	44	11	45.36
Female	53	13.25	54.64

The number of female human visuals is more than that of male human visuals. While female pictures account for 54.64 per cent of the total number of human pictures in the supplement, the male pictures are 45.36 per cent. Clearly, the accent of this supplement is on celebration of glamour with a view to appealing to the aesthetic craving of the readers.

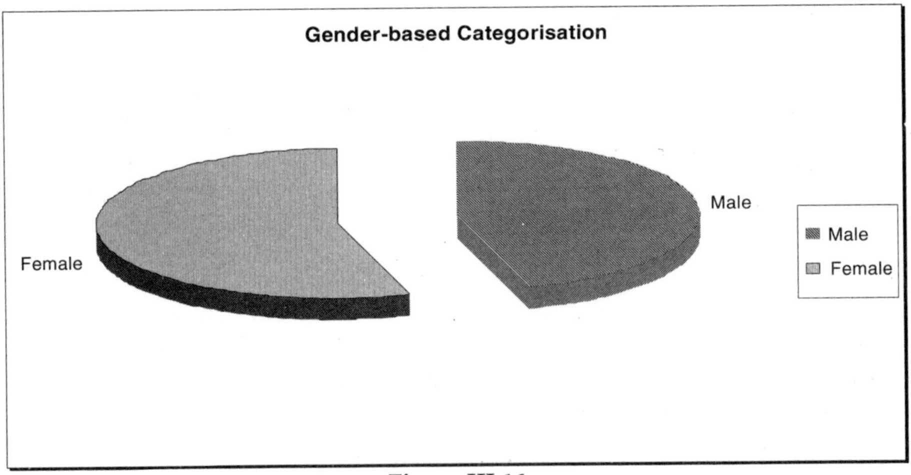

Figure III.16

III.1.b.ix. *Exposure-Based Human Visual Distribution*

Table III.18

Parameters	**Total**	**Average**	**%age**
Minimally-exposed	100	25	89.29
Moderately-exposed	12	3	10.71
Maximally-exposed	0	0	0.00

Of the 112 human visuals of film and TV celebrities, more often women than men, 100 are minimally exposed, while 12 are moderately exposed. In percentage terms, the moderately-exposed celebrities are 10.71 per cent, while minimally exposed are 89.29 per cent and maximally exposed are nil. It is clear that while, DB continues to steer clear of maximally-exposed pictures, it does give some moderately exposed ones. This could be on account of the winds of change sweeping across the cultural landscape of the Hindi hinterland of Haryana.

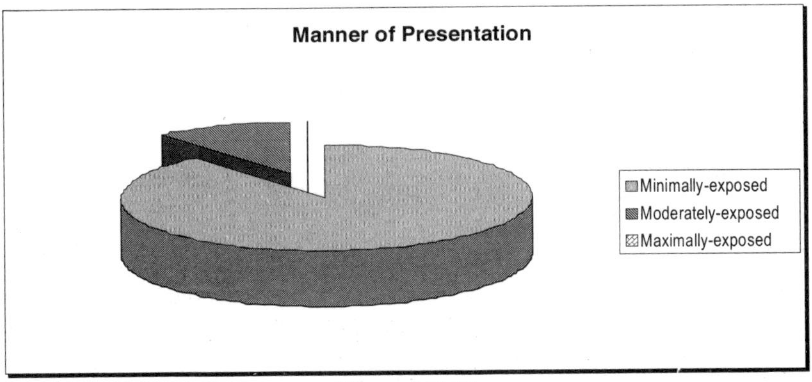

Figure III.17

III.1.b.x. *Bordering of Pictures*

Table III.19

Parameters	Total	Average	%age
Bordered	79	19.75	70.54
Borderless	33	8.25	29.46

The table shows that 70.54 per cent of the pictures are bordered as per the conservative style of layout and design, while 29.46 per cent break away from the conservative tradition and let the pictures dominate the page by running wild into the text. This gives the pictures a larger than life character, making them imposing and eye-catching.

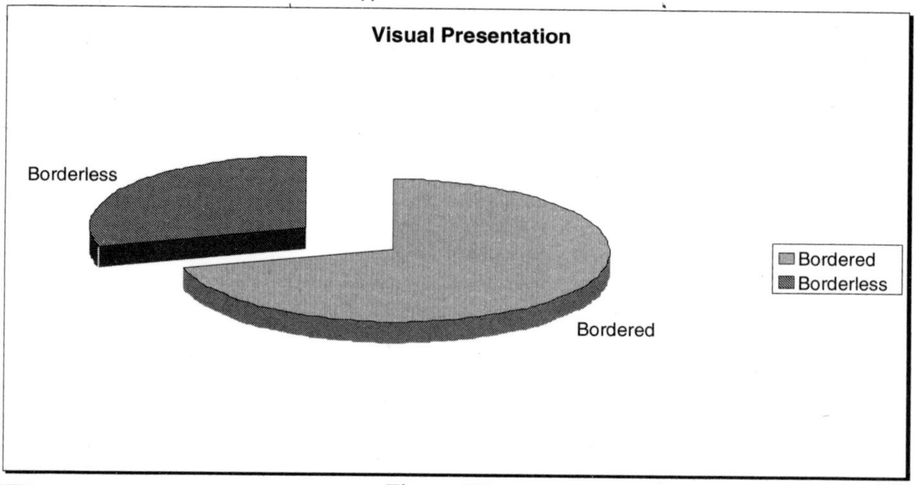

Figure III.18

III.1.c. *Rasrang*

Rasrang comes out every Sunday on newsprint quality broadsheet sized paper. It runs into four pages on an average and covers subjects as diverse as politics, literature, zodiac, social issues, fashion, human values, lifestyle, technology, nature, tourism, well being, women, celebrities, development, reviews, snippets and jokes.

III.1.c.i. *Edit-Ad Distribution of Supplement Space*

Table III.20

Parameters	Total	Average	%age
Edit Space	24861	6215.25	93.77
Ad Space	1653	413.25	6.23

The table shows that the editorial content of the supplement far exceeds the advertising part. While the edit content occupies 93.77 per cent of the total supplement space, the advertisements corner only 6.23 per cent of supplement space. Clearly, the editorial content is the mainstay of this supplement and not the advertising content. Naturally enough, the paper used is newsprint.

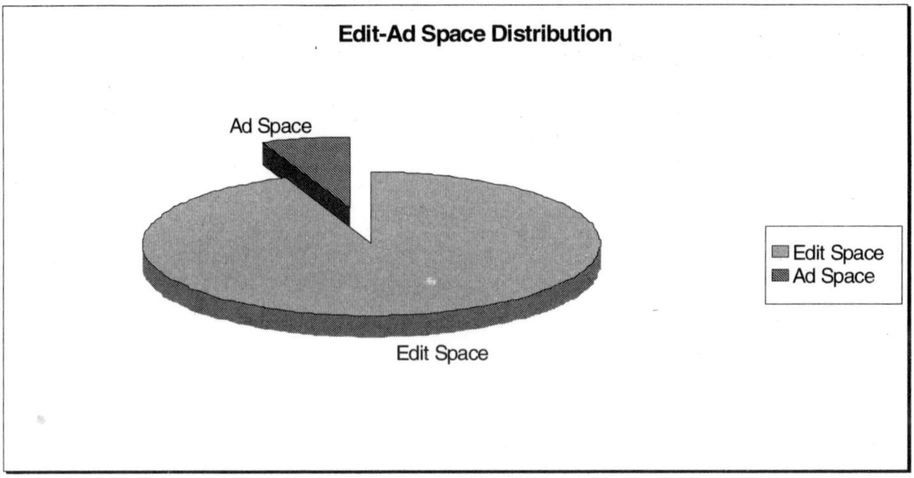

Figure III.19

III.1.c.ii. *Edit Space Distribution Between Text and Visuals*

Table III.21

Parameters	**Total**	**Average**	**%age**
Text	17132.4	4283.1	68.91
Visuals	7728.6	1932.15	31.09

The text-visual edit space distribution is skewed in favour of the text. While the text occupies 68.91 per cent of the edit space, the visuals occupy 31.09 per cent. In ratio terms, the text occupies slightly more than three-fourth of the edit space, while the visuals, a little under one-third. But, even though the visuals occupy less than one-third space, the space taken up by them in the absence of many advertisements shows the concern of the editorial department to illustrate the editorial content. Such an approach helps the supplement to appeal to the aesthetic sense of the readers.

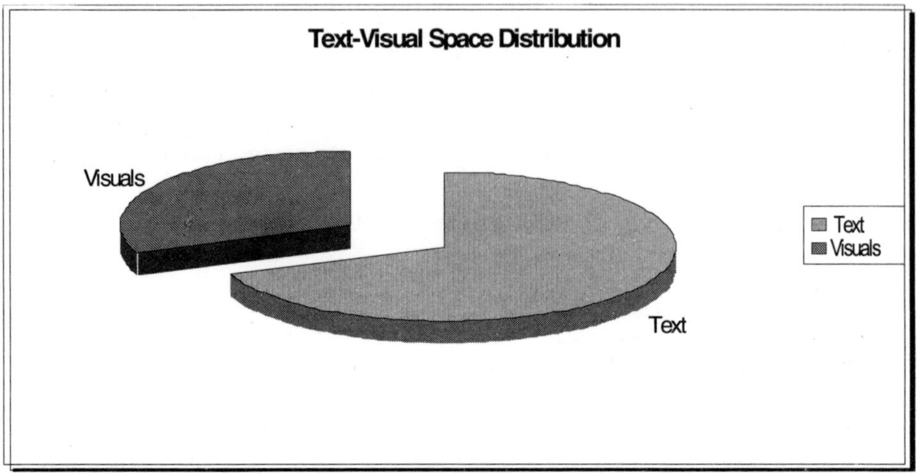

Figure III.20

III.1.c.iii. *Form-Based Edit Space Distribution*

Table III.22

Parameters	**Total**	**Average**	**%age**
Soft News	1885.68	471.42	7.58
Regular Column	2309.36	577.34	9.29
Poetry	1578.68	394.67	6.35
Memoirs	192	48	0.77
Review	336	84	1.35
Fiction	480	120	1.93
Feature	12022.68	3005.67	48.36
Miscellany	6056.6	1514.15	24.37

Of all the forms used in this supplement, features take up the maximum space, occupying 48.36 per cent of the edit space. Miscellaneous items are the next to occupy a sizeable chunk of the edit space. They occupy 24.37 per cent of the edit space. The other forms take up marginal share of the edit space. In descending order of importance, these are regular columns (9.29%), soft news (7.58%), poetry (6.35%), fiction (1.93%), reviews (1.35%), and memoirs (0.77 %). Obviously, the supplement is based on features which act as its fulcrum, followed by the miscellany.

III.1.c.iv. *Subject-Based Feature Space Distribution*

Table III.23

Parameters	Total	Average	%age
Health	440	110	3.66
Celebrity	3149.32	787.33	26.2
Travel	2840	710	23.62
Lifestyle	1566.68	391.67	13.03
Social issues	3242.68	810.67	26.97
Education	784	196	6.52

The table shows that the sample issues of the supplement carry features on the subjects of social issues, celebrities, travel, lifestyle, education and health. The maximum feature space is taken up by social issues (26.97%), followed by celebrities (26.2%), travel (23.62%), lifestyle (13.03%), education (6.52%) and health (3.66%). The distribution of feature space among various subjects shows that the supplement rates these subjects in the descending order of their importance for readers' interest. While social issues indicate an inclination to engage with matters of social importance, the high preference for celebrities, travel and lifestyle shows the growing tendency of the language newspapers to engage with the salacious and the eye-catching. Hallmarks of page-3 journalism, such subjects do not demand a serious research but exhibit the ability to excite interest.

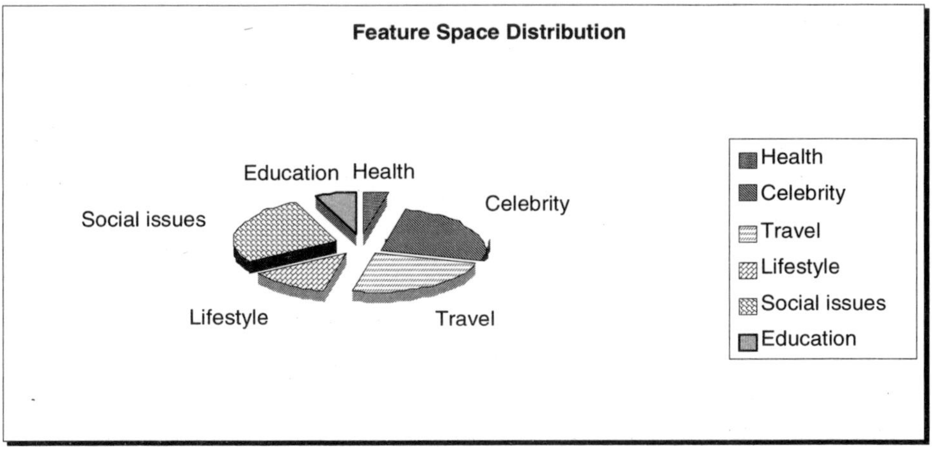

Figure III.21

III.1.c.v. *Review-Based Edit Space Distribution*

Table III.24

Parameters	Total	Average	%age
Book	336	84	100.00
Movie	0	0	0.00
Art	0	0	0.00
Theatre	0	0	0.00

All the reviews in the sample issues of the supplement are of books. There are no reviews of films, art, and theatre. The patronage for theatre and art has more or less vanished in tradition-bound towns and cities of this region of India. So, their absence over here is understandable. Though films do attract people's attention, but the absence of good cinema halls seems to be the reason behind no film reviews.

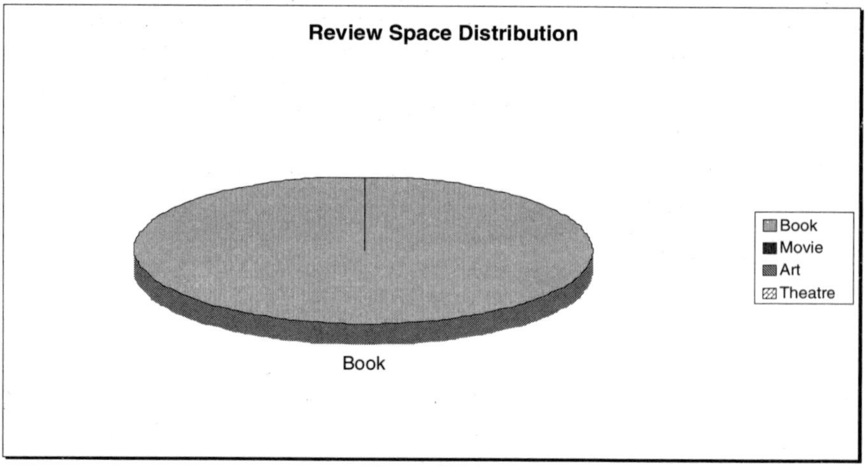

Figure III.22

III.1.c.vi. *Distribution of Visuals*

Table III.25

Parameters	Total	Average	%age
Human Visuals	84	21	67.74
Non-human Visuals	40	10	32.26

Of the 124 visuals in the sample issues of the supplement, 84 display human pictures and 40 non-human pictures. Clearly, the scale is tilted in favour of the human pictures. In percentage terms, it works out to human visuals being 67.74 per cent of the total number of visuals and non-human visuals 32.26 per cent.

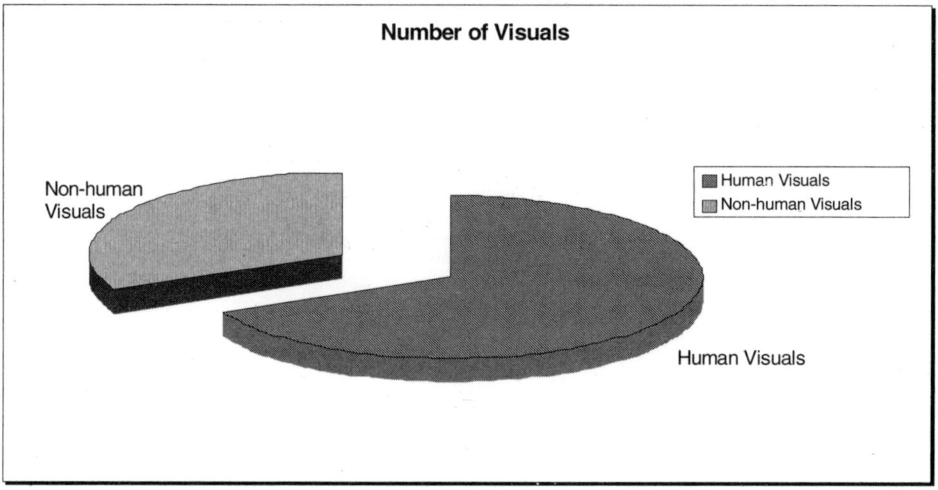

Figure III.23

III.1.c.vii. *Role-Based Human Visuals Distribution*

Table III.26

Parameters	Total	Average	%age
Political	4	1	4.76
Sports	4	1	4.76
P-3	0	0	0
TV & Films	4	1	4.76
Artists	4	1	4.76
Others	68	17	80.96

Human beings have been presented in this supplement in the roles of political, sports, fine arts and celluloid personalities apart from other sundry roles. Most of the pictures in the selected sample, 68 in number, present people in sundry/nondescript roles in the features. The other pictures are evenly distributed over the identified roles of political, sports, TV & films, and fine arts personalities. In percentage terms, pictures of political, sports, TV & films and fine arts personalities are 4.76 per cent of the total numbers of human visuals, while the unidentified role-based human visuals are 80.96 per cent of the total. So, obviously, there is no attempt at presenting any role models. The human pictures are primarily included in the editorial content to give a human touch to the features included in the supplement.

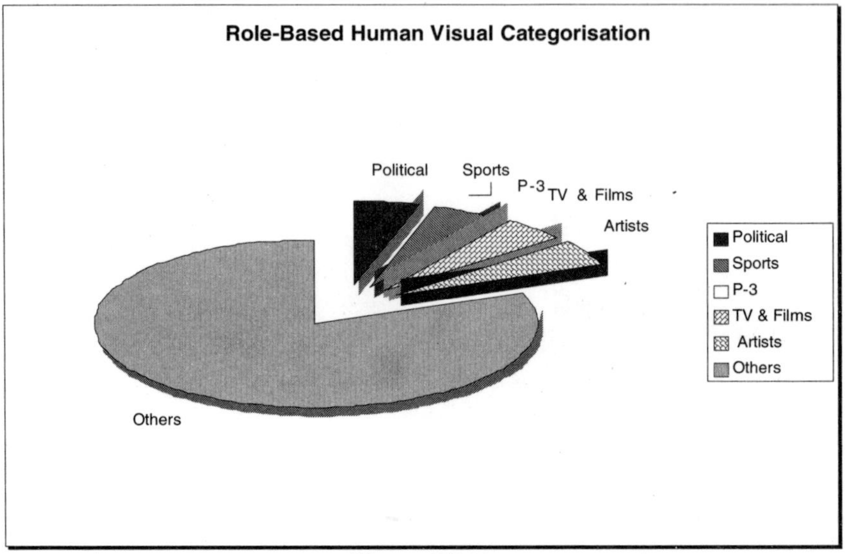

Figure III.24

III.1.c.viii. *Gender-Based Distribution of Human Visuals*

Table III.27

Parameters	Total	Average	%age
Male	42	10.5	50
Mixed	10	4	11.9
Female	32	8	38.1

The gender-based distribution of human visuals as represented in Table III.27 reveals that out of the 84 human visuals in all, 42 were all male and 32 all female. In percentage terms, the all-male pictures are 50 per cent of the total while the all-female visuals are 38.1 per cent. Though the all-female pictures are fewer than the all-male pictures, the sheer size of the all female pictures shows an increasing acceptance of female participation in public life in the hinterland of the state.

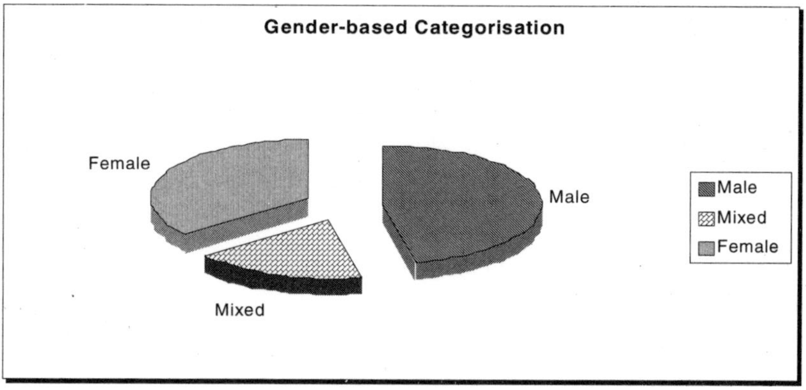

Figure III.25

III.1.c.ix. *Exposure-Based Distribution of Human Visuals*

Table III.28

Parameters	Total	Average	%age
Minimally-exposed	60	15	71.43
Moderately-exposed	24	6	28.57
Maximally-exposed	0	0	0.00

Of the 84 human pictures in the sample, 60 are minimally exposed and 24 moderately exposed. There are no visuals falling in the category of maximally exposed. In percentage terms, the minimally-exposed pictures are 71.43 per cent, while the moderately-exposed ones are 28.57 per cent. From the percentage figures, it is clear that the moderately-exposed pictures are more than one-fourth of the total number of pictures, showing the growing tendency to expose even in the Hindi heartland, where the moral fiber of the society has often been considered to be strong enough to frown upon such exposure.

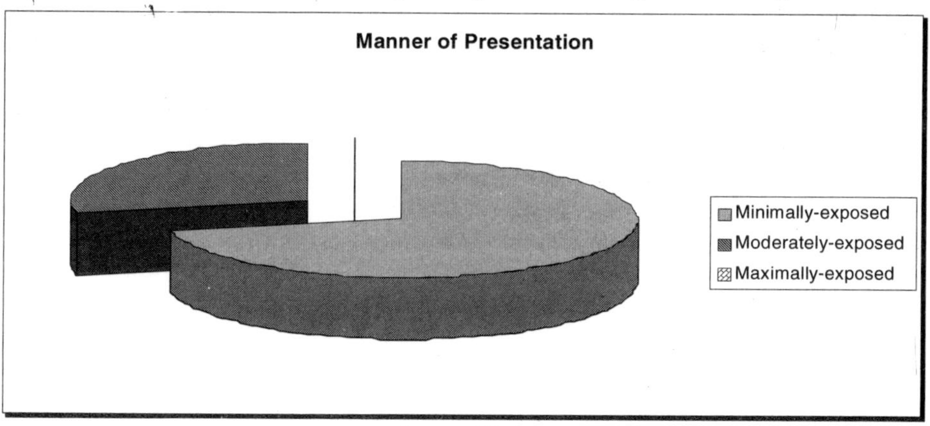

Figure III.26

III.1.c.x. *Manner of Presentation of Visuals*

Table III.29

Parameters	Total	Average	%age
Bordered	104	26	83.87
Borderless	20	5	16.13

Of the 124 visuals in the sample, as many as 104 are bordered, while only 20 are borderless. In percentage terms, 83.87 per cent of the total number of visuals is designed conventionally to have a proper border and only 16.13 per cent unconventionally to let the pictures spill over into the text space and at times dominate it.

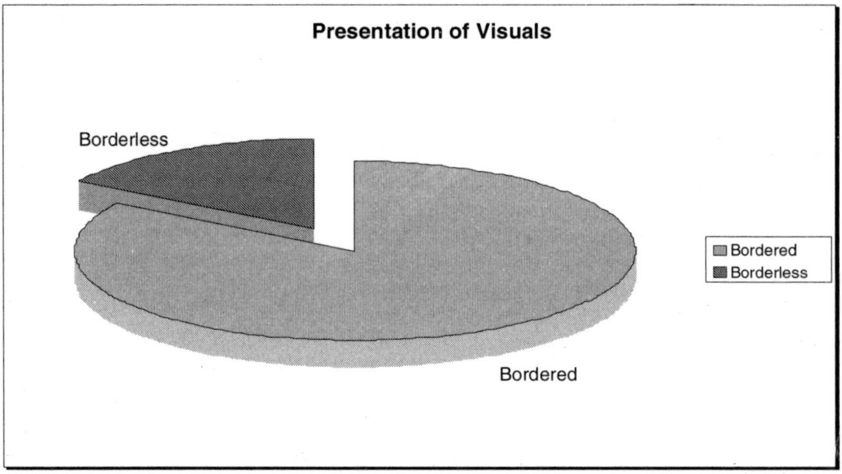

Figure III.27

III.1.d. *Bal Bhaskar*

As the title of this magazine pullout indicates, it is primarily dedicated to the reading pleasure of children. The subjects covered in the sample issue attest to the veracity of this inference. The magazine covers the subjects of children, personality development, interesting historical and scientific facts, sports, mythology, food, art and craft, recreation, vocabulary building, nature, mind games, cooking, poetry and jokes. Carrying on an average 40 pages of newsprint, the magazine is attractive in design and content for children. Bal Bhaskar comes out as a fortnightly magazine. Interestingly, it comes out as a bilingual magazine.

III.1.d.i. *Edit-Ad Space Distribution*

Table III.30

Parameters	Total	Average	%age
Edit Space	34884	17442	100.00
Ad Space	0	0	0.00

As the table depicts, the entire magazine space is devoted to editorial content. The sample issues too have no advertisements. Out of the total magazine space, the edit content occupies 100 per cent of the space.

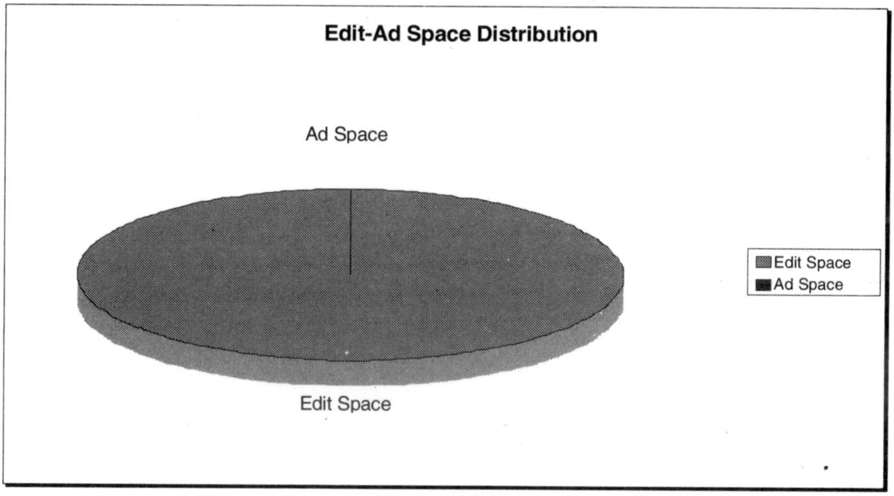

Figure III.28

III.1.d.ii. *Form-Based Edit Space Distribution*

Table III.31

Parameters	Total	Average	%age
Poetry	900	450	2.58
Fiction	1800	900	5.16
Feature	3600	1800	10.32
Miscellany	22284	11142	63.88
Folklore	6300	3150	18.06

The sample shows the use of four main forms apart from other miscellaneous forms. Of the four main forms used in the magazine (poetry, fiction, feature, folklore), folklore occupies the maximum space of 18.06 per cent of the total edit space, followed by features (10.32 %), fiction (5.16%), and poetry (2.58%). The remaining 63.88 per cent of the space has been used for sundry forms that provided variety and diversion to the readers. The high percentage of space accorded to folklore shows the respect for cultural traditions.

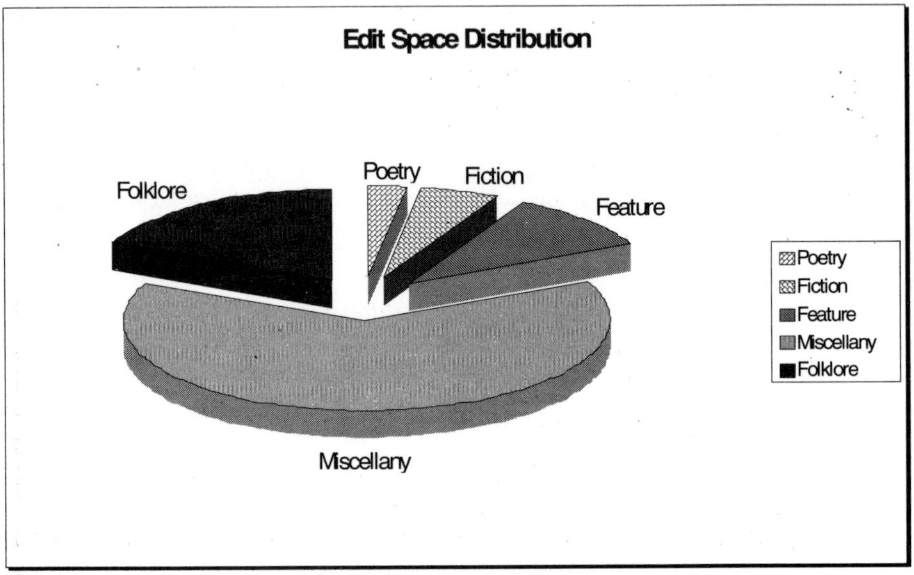

Figure III.29

III.1.d.iii. *Subject-Based Feature Space Distribution*

Table III.32

Parameters	Total	Average	%age
Hobby	900	450	50.00
Environment	900	450	50.00

Only two subjects have been touched upon in the sample issues of the magazine. These are hobbies and environment. Both the subjects have been accorded equal feature space. Obviously, the magazine seeks to inculcate a respect for the environment and the need for incorporating hobbies to do away with the boredom of idle hours.

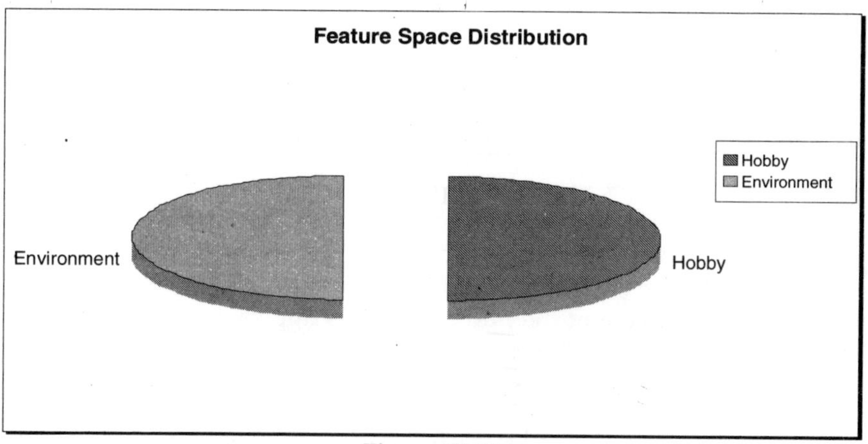

Figure III.30

III.1.d.iv. *Distribution of Human and Non-human Visuals*

Table III.33

Parameters	Total	Average	%age
Human Visuals	178	89	70.08
Non-Human Visuals	76	38	29.92

The human visuals in the sample issues of the magazine account for 70.08 per cent of the total number of visuals, while the non-human ones for 29.92 per cent. The large percentage of human visuals reflects the fascination of children for human pictures.

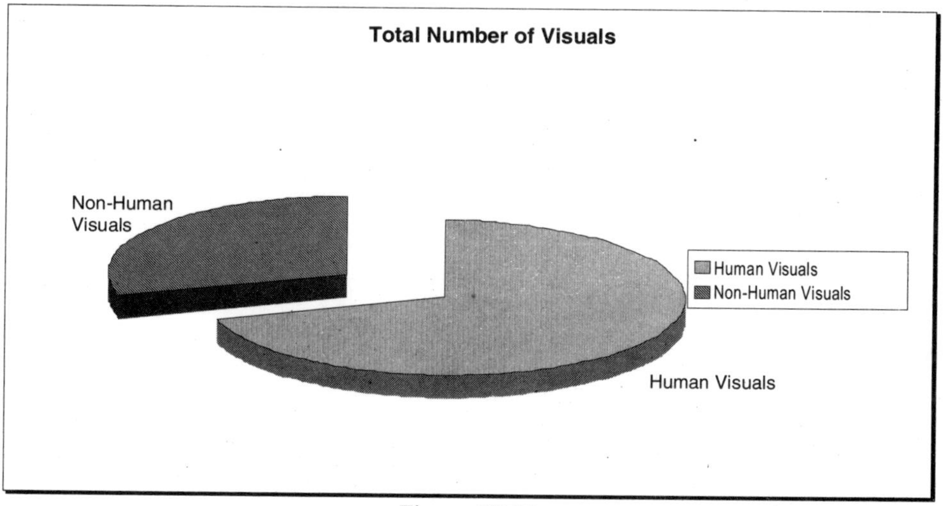

Figure III.31

III.1.d.v. *Role-Based Distribution of Human Visuals*

Table III.34

Parameters	**Total**	**Average**	**%age**
Political	4	2	2.25
Sports	4	2	2.25
Films	2	1	1.12
Others	168	84	94.38

As many as 94.38 per cent of the human persons depicted in the magazine are fictive. Of the remaining, 2.25 per cent each are of political and sports persons, followed by 1.12 per cent of film personalities.

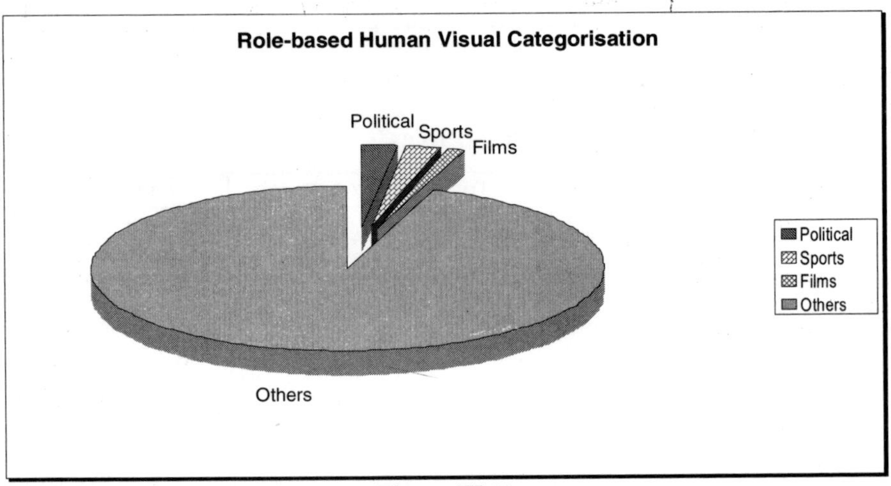

Figure III.32

III.1.d.vi. *Presentation-Based Distribution of Visuals*

Table III.35

Parameters	**Total**	**Average**	**%age**
Bordered	168	84	66.14
Borderless	86	43	33.86

Of the 254 visuals in the magazine, as many as 168 are bordered, whereas 86 are borderless. In percentage terms, 66.14 per cent of the pictures are conventionally encased in borders, while 33.86 per cent, defy all conventions of bordering and spill over the text to splash across the page and thereby acquire a larger than life image.

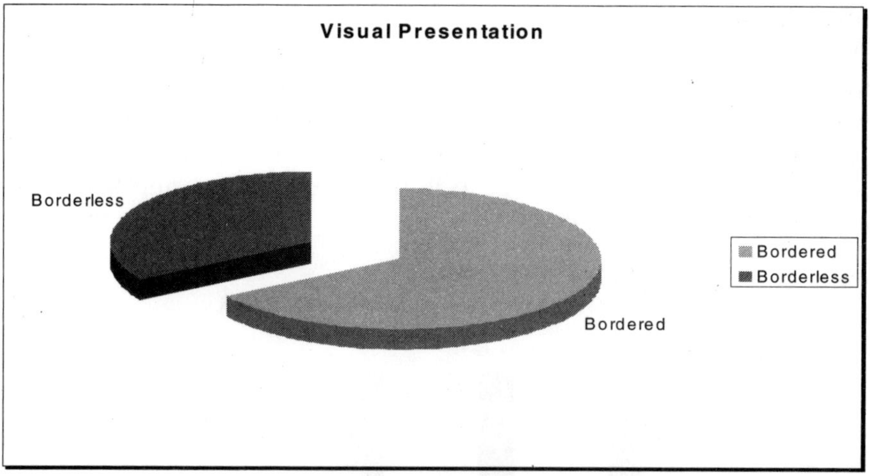

Figure III.33

III.2 Summary

III.2.a. *General Parameters of Dainik Bhaskar Supplements*

Table III.36

Name of Supplement	Periodicity	Paper Quality	Paper Size
Madhurima	Weekly	Newsprint	Tabloid
Navrang	Weekly	Newsprint	Broadsheet
Rasrang	Weekly	Newsprint	Broadsheet
Bal Bhaskar	Fortnightly	Newsprint	Magazine

As the table reveals, Dainik Bhaskar comes out with four supplements namely Madhurima, Navrang, Rasrang and Bal Bhaskar. All the four come out on newsprint. However, with the exception of Madhurima and Bal Bhaskar, the other two supplements of Dainik Bhaskar come out on broadsheet. While Madhurima comes out in tabloid size, Bal Bhaskar comes out in the magazine format.

III.2.b. *Distribution of Ad-Edit Space*

Table III.37: Ad-Edit Space Distribution (in percentage terms)

Name of Supplement	Ad Space	Edit Space
Madhurima	15.54	84.46
Navrang	6.45	93.55
Rasrang	6.23	93.77
Bal Bhaskar	0	0

Of the four supplements brought out by DB, the ad-edit ratio varies from 1:5.43 in Madhurima to 1:infinity in Bal Bhaskar. Between these two yawning extremes, the ratio in Navrang is as high as 1:14.5 and in Rasrang 1:15.05. While in TOI the ad-edit ratio is skewed in favour of advertisements, in DB it is skewed in favour of the editorial content. As the advertising support for DB is much lower compared to that for TOI, the potential for bringing out a large number of supplements is much lower in case of DB as compared to TOI.

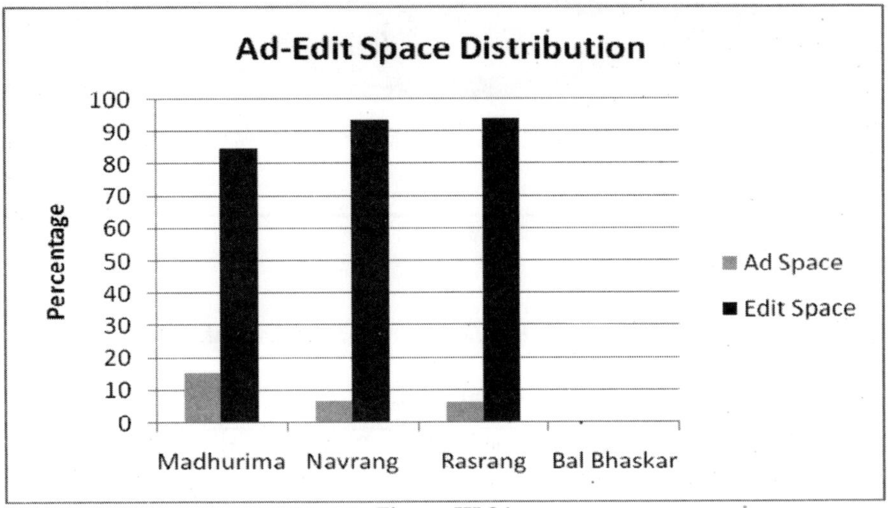

Figure III.34

III.2.c. *Text-Visual Space Distribution*

Table III.38: Text-Visual Space Distribution (in percentage terms)

Name of Supplement	Text Space	Visual Space
Madhurima	64.14	35.86
Navrang	48.71	51.29
Rasrang	68.91	31.09
Bal Bhaskar	65.7	34.3

The text-visual space ratio in DB is skewed in favour of the text in all the supplements but for Navrang where it is 1:1.45. The text-visual ratio is the highest in Rasrang (11:5) followed by Bal Bhaskar (19:10) and Madhurima (9:5). The high priority accorded to visuals in DB supplements is actuated by a concern for making the supplements visually appealing to the readers with a view to spurring the circulation figures. It is interesting to note here that many of the pages in DB carry visually-dominant pictures, with many of them stretching from end to end longitudinally.

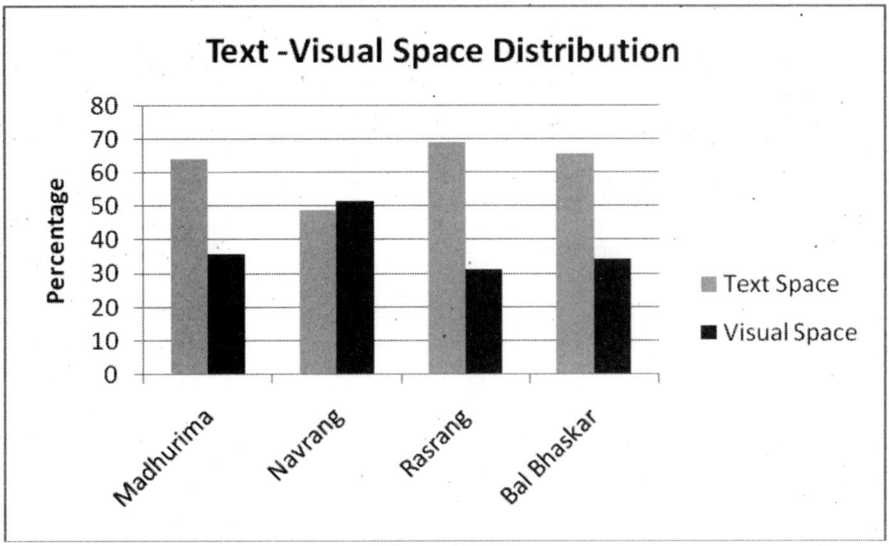

Figure III.35

III.2.d. Edit Space Distribution

Table III.39: Edit Space Distribution (in percentage terms)

Parameters	Madhurima	Navrang	Rasrang	Bal Bhaskar
Interviews	5.99	71.8	0	0
Features	19.39	4.49	48.36	10.32
Memoirs	4.44	1.07	0.77	0
Review	0	5.95	1.35	0
Folklore	0	0	0	18.06
Soft News	0	8.22	7.58	0
Poetry	2.4	0	6.35	2.58
Fiction	41.98	0	1.93	5.16
Miscellany	25.8	5.21	24.37	63.88
Regular Column	0	3.26	9.29	0

Of the various forms of editorial items used in DB supplements, features, interviews and folklore dominate the editorial content. In Madhurima and Rasrang, features take up the maximum editorial space, 19.39 per cent and 48.36 per cent respectively. In Navrang, interviews take up as high a percentage of space as 71.8 per cent whereas in Bal Bhaskar, folklore takes up the maximum space of 18.06 per cent. There is a variation in the kind of editorial content forms used in DB. Only two supplements share a similar pre-occupation while the other two accord space to two divergent forms. This could be because of the fewer number of DB supplements. But one thing that emerges for sure is the reliance on features as the pivotal form of most supplements. This is obvious in view of the function of a feature to appeal to the heart than to the mind and thereby create a feeling of relief in the mind of the reader.

III.2.e. *Feature Space Distribution*

Table III.40: Feature Space Distribution (in percentage terms)

Feature Type	Madhurima	Navrang	Rasrang	Bal Bhaskar
Children	41.6	0	0	0
Women	58.4	0	0	0
Fashion	0	50	0	0
Films	0	50	0	0
Wellbeing	0	0	3.66	0
Celebrity	0	0	26.2	0
Lifestyle	0	0	13.03	0
Travel	0	0	23.62	0
Social Issues	0	0	26.97	0
Education	0	0	6.52	0
Hobby	0	0	0	50
Environment	0	0	0	50

Of the four supplements being brought out by DB, only one supplement, that is Rasrang, has features across the broad spectrum of subjects which include well being (3.66%), celebrity (26.20%), lifestyle (13.03%), travel (23.62%), social issues (26.97%) and education (6.52%). In comparison, the features in Madhurima, Navrang and Bal Bhaskar are concentrated in a few subjects only. While the feature space in Madhurima is shared between features on children (41.6%) and women (58.4%), the feature space in Navrang is shared by features on fashion and films equally. Similarly, in Bal Bhaskar the feature space is shared equally by hobbies and environment. The comparison shows that each of the supplements of DB focuses exclusively on a few segments of readers. It is seen that DB completely skirts past subjects that could be considered taboo in a traditional society.

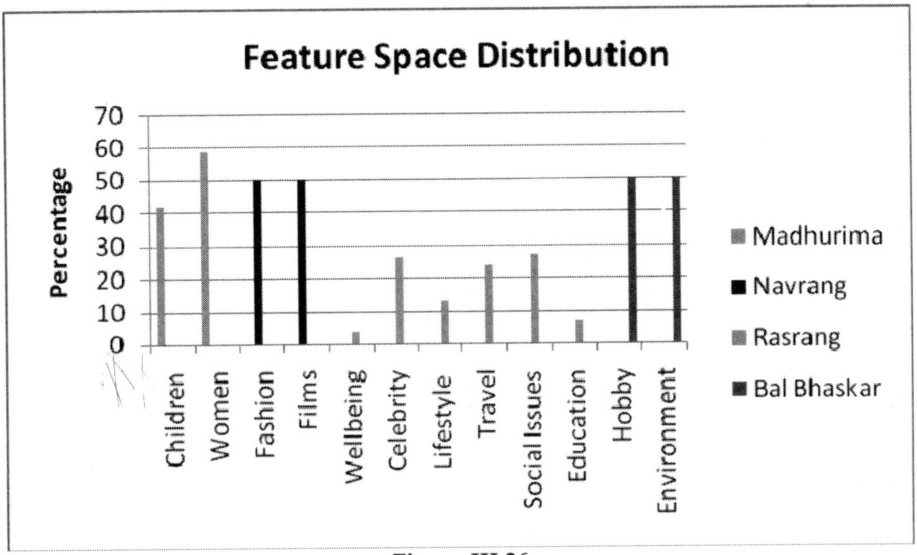

Figure III.36

III.2.f. *Categorisation of Human Visuals*

Table III.41: Human Visual Categorisation on the Basis of Societal Roles (in percentage terms)

Name of Supplement	Page-3	TV & Films	Political	Sports	Non-Celebrities	Artists
Madhurima	7.69	7.69	0	0	76.93	7.69
Navrang	0	100	0	0	0	0
Rasrang	0	4.76	4.76	4.76	80.96	4.76
Bal Bhaskar	0	1.12	2.25	2.25	94.38	0

The visuals in DB supplements happen to be mainly of non-descript characters with a view to adding a visual appeal and human touch to the features published in them. The distribution of human visuals among the various social roles is almost uniform, being 7.69 per cent for page-3, TV & films and artistic personalities in Madhurima; cent per cent for celluloid personalities in Navrang; 4.76 per cent for TV & films, political, sports and artistic personalities in Rasrang and 1.12 per cent for celluloid personalities and 2.25 per cent for political and sports personalities in Bal Bhaskar. There is no focus on celluloid personalities in DB supplements with the exception of Navrang.

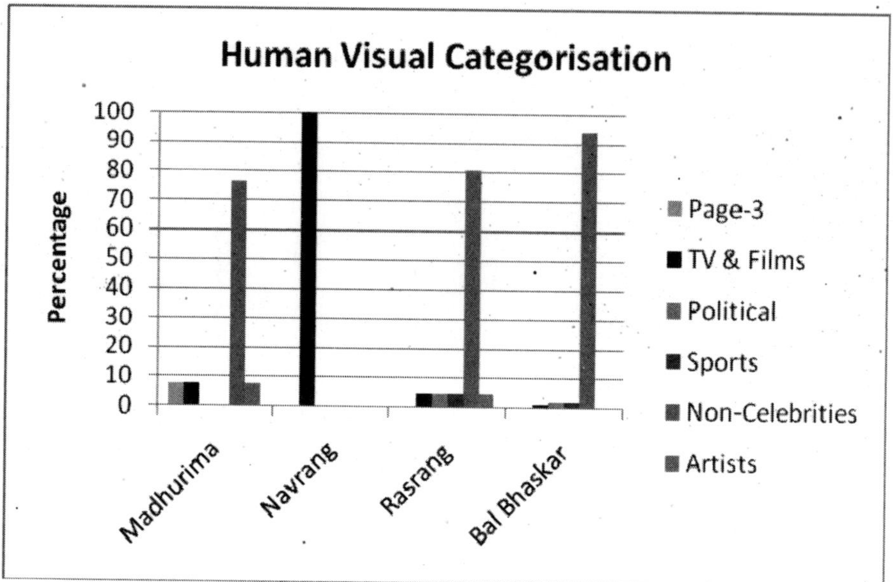

Figure III.37

III.2.g. *Gender-Based Human Visual Categorisation*

Table III.42 Human Visual Categorisation on the Basis of Gender (in percentage terms)

Name of Supplement	Male	Female
Madhurima	7.69	92.31
Navrang	45.36	54.64
Rasrang	56.76	43.24

The gender analysis of human visuals shows that DB supplements are not far behind TOI supplements in including female visuals. While 92.31 per cent of the human visuals are of females in Madhurima, 54.64 per cent of the human visuals are of females in Navrang and 43.24 per cent are female visuals in Rasrang. Obviously, visuals of women are copiously splashed all across the pages of DB supplements. The prominent place occupied by visuals of women in DB supplements shows that not only in the modern society of Gurgaon but even in the traditional societies which constitute the readers of a Hindi language newspaper, visuals of women constitute a strong centripetal force for attracting the attention of readers.

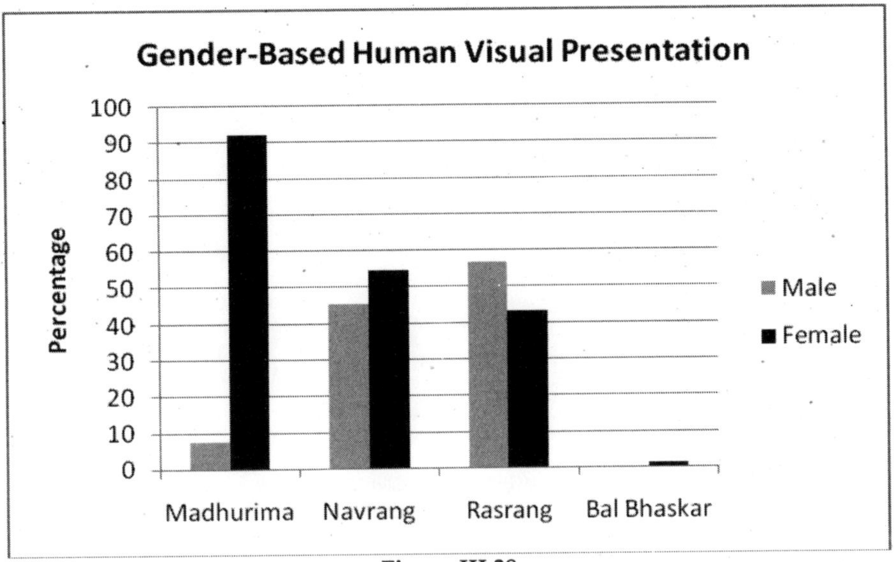

Figure III.38

III.2.h. *Human Visual Presentation*

Table III.43 Manner of Human Visual Presentation (in percentage terms)

Name of Supplement	Minimally Exposed	Moderately Exposed	Maximally Exposed
Madhurima	100	0	0
Navrang	89.29	10.71	0
Rasrang	71.43	28.57	0

Interestingly, even though the visuals of women are plenteously used in DB supplements, their use is buffered for the traditional societies by avoiding maximal exposure.

While in Madhurima all the human visuals are minimally exposed; in Navrang 89.29 per cent are minimally exposed and only 10.71 per cent moderately exposed; and in Rasrang 71.43 per cent are minimally exposed and 28.57 per cent moderately exposed. The exposure level in Rasrang happens to be the maximum among all the DB supplements. This shows that even traditional societies in India have come to accept moderate exposure of human body.

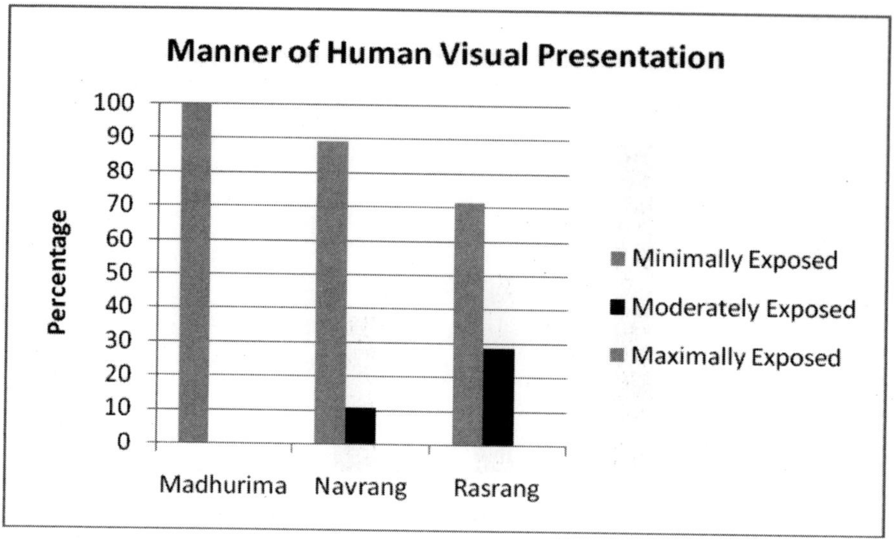

Figure III.39

CHAPTER IV

SURVEY OF SUPPLEMENT READING HABITS

This chapter presents the findings of the survey carried out on the basis of 500 respondents each from Gurgaon and Hisar---two cities of Haryana state of India--- that are at different stages of development. Gurgaon, with its proximity to Delhi, the political centre of India, and of late a happening place in terms of economic development as well, is in popular belief a "modern" city; while Hisar, in the hinterland of Haryana, is in popular perception a traditional society. A survey of supplement readers in these two cities is expected to throw up interesting facts regarding the differences in readers' tastes and preferences which could then be correlated to the content and style of the supplements of Dainik Bhaskar and The Times of India, as read in Hisar and Gurgaon, respectively.

IV.1. Newspaper Preference

Table IV.1: Most Read Newspaper

(%)

Newspaper	Gurgaon	Hisar
The Hindu	2 (0.4%)	8 (1.6%)
The Times of India	330 (66%)	32 (6.4%)
Hindustan Times	86 (17.2%)	16 (3.2%)
The Indian Express	12 (2.4%)	0
The Statesman	6 (1.2%)	0
Economic Times	8 (1.6%)	6 (1.2%)
Dainik Bhaskar	4 (0.8%)	348 (69.6%)
Navbharat Times	18 (3.6%)	0
Punjab Kesri	12 (2.4%)	22 (4.4%)
Dainik Jagran	8 (1.6%)	38 (7.6%)
Amar Ujala	8 (1.6%)	18 (3.6%)
Hindustan	6 (1.2%)	12 (2.4%)

The survey reveals that the maximum number of respondents in Gurgaon prefer to read The Times of India whereas in Hisar the maximum respondents prefer to read Dainik Bhaskar. As Table IV.1 shows 330 respondents (66%) prefer to read The Times of India while 348 respondents (69.6%) prefer to read Dainik Bhaskar in Hisar.

Interestingly, the maximum read paper, The Times of India in Gurgaon and Dainik Bhaskar in Hisar, has a substantial and similar share of total readership in each of their relative areas of circulation. The next most read newspaper in Gurgaon is Hindustan Times with 86 respondents (17.2%) while at Hisar the next most read newspaper is Dainik Jagaran with 7.6 per cent of readership.

The third most read newspaper in Gurgaon is Navbharat Times with 3.6 per cent of readership where as the third most read newspaper in Hisar is The Times of India with 6.4 per cent of readership.

A comparative analysis of the three most read newspapers in each of the two places shows an overwhelming support for English language newspapers in Gurgaon, with a huge gap of readership between the second and the third most read newspaper. In contrast, an overwhelming number of respondents prefer to read Hindi newspapers in Hisar. The third most read newspaper in Hisar, however, happens to be in English with very little interval of readership between the second and the third most read newspapers.

The preferential pattern of languages in two places indicates the level of development/"modernization" in each of these cities. Gurgaon emerges as a modern city while Hisar comes off as a traditional city as is the popular belief. The third place won by an English newspaper, The Times of India, in Hisar indicates the changes taking place in a largely traditional society of Hisar.

The following bar graph (Figure IV.1) visually represents the information given in the table.

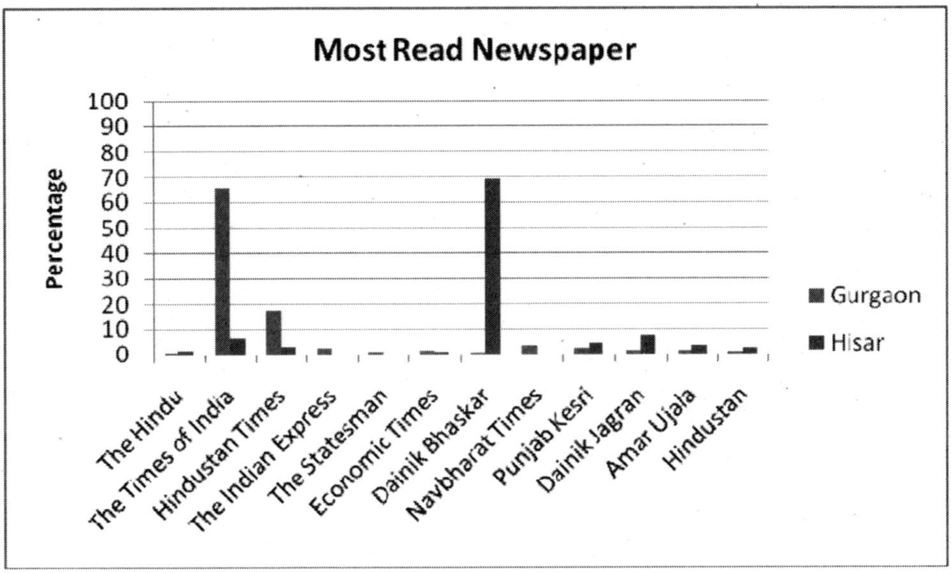

Figure IV.1

IV.2. Time Spent on Reading Newspapers

Table IV.2: Time Spent on Reading Newspapers

Frequency	Gurgaon	Hisar
0-10 min	0	50 (10%)
10-20 min	222 (44.4%)	96 (19.2%)
20-30 min	184 (36.8%)	146 (29.2%)
More than 30 min	94 (18.8%)	208 (41.6%)

The maximum number of respondents in Gurgaon spends 10-20 minutes on reading newspapers while in Hisar maximum number of respondents spends more than 30 minutes on reading newspapers. In Gurgaon, 44.4 per cent of respondents spend 20-30 minutes of their time on reading newspapers while in Hisar, 208 respondents (41.6%) spend more than 30 minutes of time on reading newspapers.

Interestingly, 184 respondents (36.8%) in Gurgaon spend 20-30 minutes on reading newspapers while 146 respondents (29.2%) in Hisar spend 20-30 minutes of time on reading newspapers. When these results are taken together, they highlight that in Gurgaon maximum number of respondents read newspapers between 10-30 minutes while in Hisar maximum number of respondents read newspapers for 20 minutes and above, indicating thereby that newspaper reading is understandably enough a greater leisure time activity in Hisar compared to that in Gurgaon.

As Gurgaon happens to be part of Delhi NCR metropolitan area, the people here are more hard pressed for time than their counterparts in Hisar. As things stand, most of the residents of Delhi NCR happen to be employed in the industrial hubs rather than in government departments, which is the case in Hisar. Considering the long working hours and the long hours of commuting between the work place and residences, the people here are hard pressed for time. As a result, they are unable to spend as much time on reading newspapers as readers in Hisar are.

The bar graph compares the time spent on reading newspapers by the respondents in each of the two cities.

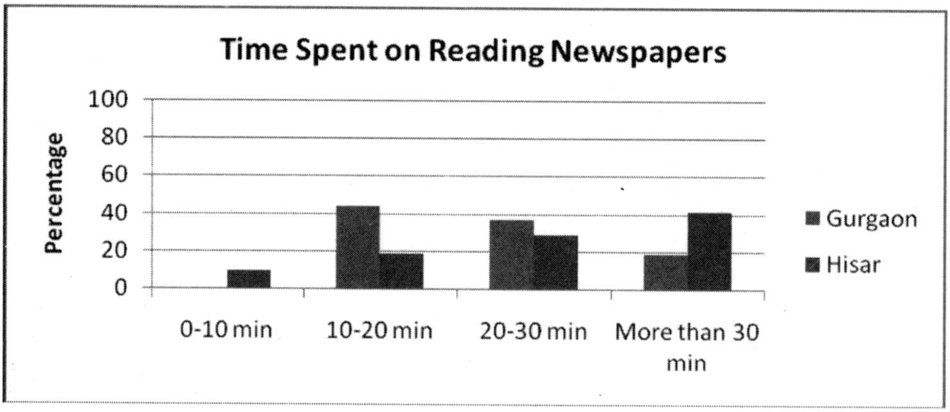

Figure IV.2

IV.3. Reading Frequency of Supplements

Table IV.3: Reading Frequency of Supplements

Response	Gurgaon	Hisar
Regularly	340 (68%)	348 (69.6%)
Sometimes	160 (32%)	152 (30.4%)
Never	0	0

Interestingly enough, both in Gurgaon and Hisar the pattern of reading frequency of supplements happen to be similar. A 3-point scale was used to map the respondents' reading frequency of supplements. As Table IV.3 shows,

340 respondents (68%) in Gurgaon read supplements regularly while 348 respondents (69.6%) in Hisar reflect the same reading pattern.

Similarly, 160 respondents (32%) in Gurgaon and 152 (30.4%) in Hisar read supplements sometimes. There is no such respondent in Gurgaon and Hisar who does not read supplements. As around 70 per cent of the respondents in each of the two cities read supplements, we can safely assume that supplements are popular among the respondents in both the places. Besides, even the remainder does not go without reading supplements though they do so infrequently. This goes to show that supplements have become an integral part of the newspaper reading behaviour of the people in the two cities. The information discussed above has been graphically presented in the form of the bar graph.

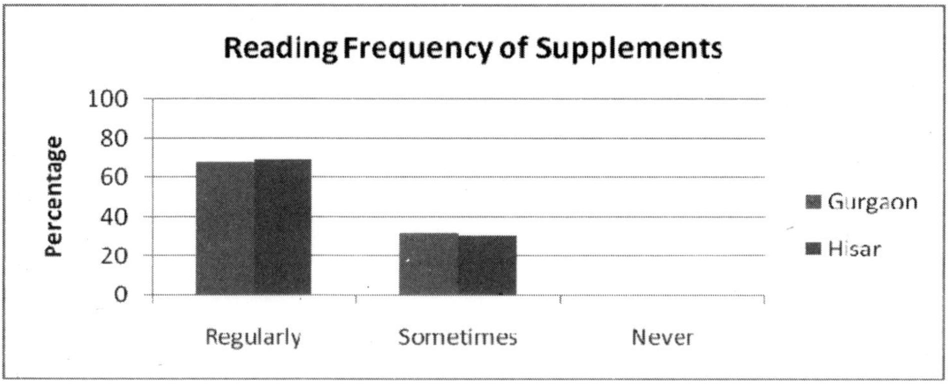

Figure IV.3

IV.4. Main Paper vis-à-vis Supplement Reading Pattern

Table IV.4: Main Paper vs Supplement Reading Pattern

Readers' Preference	Gurgaon	Hisar
Main	342 (68.4%)	388 (77.6%)
Supplement	62 (12.4%)	16 (3.2%)
Sometimes Main Paper, Sometimes Supplement	96 (19.2%)	96 (19.2%)

As Table IV.4 shows, only 62 (12.4%) respondents in Gurgaon read the supplement first compared to 342 (68.4%) respondents in Gurgaon reading the main newspaper first. The picture is not rosier in Hisar where only 16 respondents (3.2%) read supplements first while 388 respondents (77.6%) prefer to read the main newspaper first. An equal number of 96 respondents

(19.2%) in both the cities switch between the main paper and the supplements as their first preferred destination.

The pattern of reading in relation to the main paper and the supplements shows that supplements have not as yet overtaken the main newspaper as the first port of call for the newspaper readers in the two cities. The results are contrary to the popular belief that most newspaper readers prefer to browse through newspaper supplements even before going through the main newspaper. This finding has important implications for advertisers who support supplements under the influence of this popular belief.

Besides, it goes to show that the information dissemination function of the print media still holds precedence over the entertaining and cultural cohesion function of mass media particularly in reference to the print media. As an aside, we may add over here that newspapers evolved to satisfy people's pressing need for information. The information given in Table IV.4 has been lucidly presented in the graph given below.

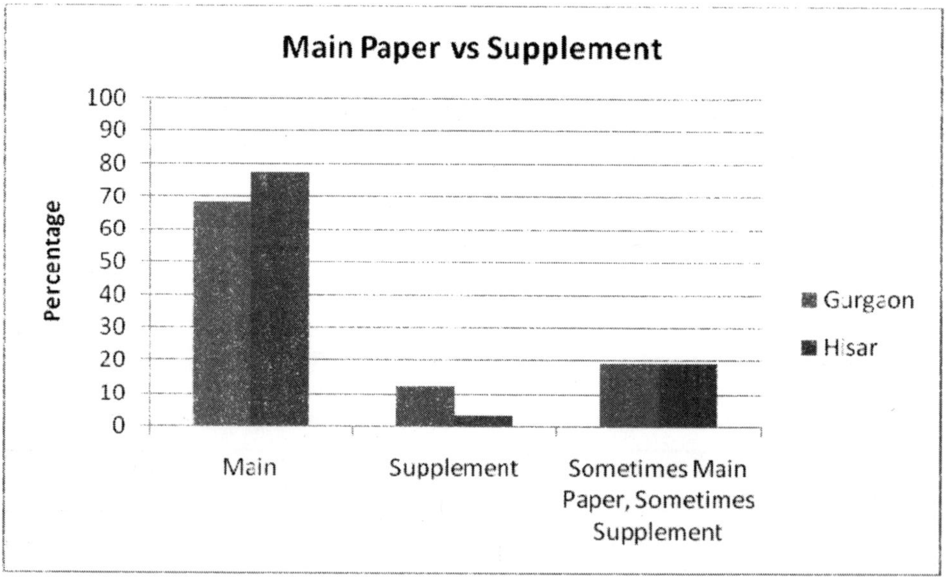

Figure IV.4

IV.5. Time Spent on Reading Supplements

Table IV.5: Time Spent on Reading Supplements

Frequency	Gurgaon	Hisar
0-10 min	214 (42.8%)	222 (44.4%)
10-20 min	160 (32%)	198 (39.6%)
20-30 min	42 (8.4%)	37 (7.2%)
More than 30 min	84 (16.8%)	44 (8.8%)

As Table IV.5 shows 84 respondents (16.8%) in Gurgaon and 44 respondents (8.8%) in Hisar read supplements for more than 30 minutes. The maximum number of respondents i.e. 214 (42.8%) in Gurgaon and 222 (44.4%) in Hisar read supplements for under 10 minutes.

The low percentage of respondents reading newspaper supplements for more than 30 minutes and the high percentage of respondents reading newspaper supplements for under 10 minutes shows that newspaper readers do not spend much time on going through the supplements. This finding complements the one presented in the sub section IV.4. Together the two findings run counter to the belief that newspaper supplements attract and hold the attention of readers which can be sold off to the advertiser at a price higher than that charged for the main paper. The finding is underscored by the recent closure of Life magazine for want of advertising support.

Besides, this finding further endorses the contention that people's information needs continue to dominate over the entertainment need despite changing social, cultural and economic scenario. Furthermore, this finding needs to be understood in the light of the emergence of supplements as print media's answer to the entertaining and captivating function of television which was presumed to have eroded the market share of newspapers because these were primarily information-oriented. That people still continue to give precedence to the main newspaper over the supplements shows that people continue to regard the information function of mass media as a primary function compared to its entertainment function. The data given in Table IV.5 has been graphically represented in the following figure:

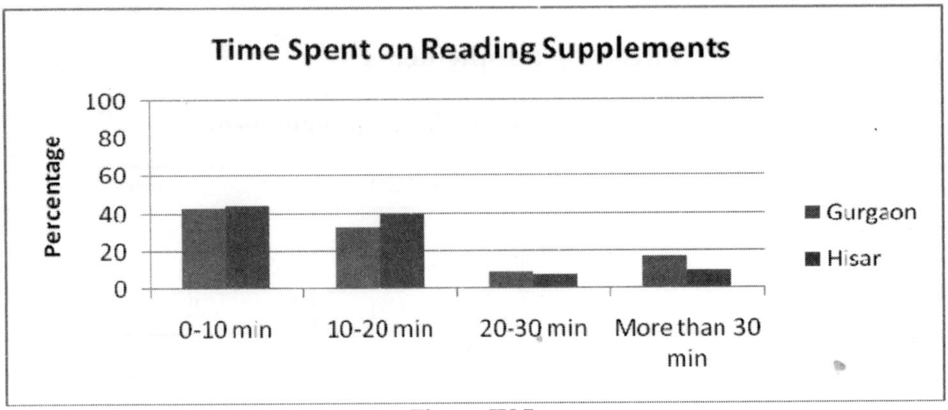

Figure IV.5

IV.6. Number of Supplements Read

Table IV.6: Number of Supplements Read

Supplements Read	Gurgaon	Hisar
All of them	82 (16.4%)	222 (44.4%)
Some	418 (83.6%)	278 (55.6%)
None	0	0

As shown in Table IV.6, only 82 respondents (16.4%) in Gurgaon read all the supplements of the newspapers they subscribe to, whereas 222 respondents (44.4%) in Hisar read all the supplements of the newspapers they subscribe to. A whopping 418 respondents (83.6%) in Gurgaon read only some newspaper supplements of their respective newspapers.

In comparison, 278 respondents (55.6%) in Hisar read only some supplements of their respective newspapers. It is clear that most of the newspaper readers do not read all the supplements. While this number is substantial in Gurgaon, it is no less considerable in Hisar. This finding further reinforces the drift of argument emerging from the findings presented in the previous sub sections. Obviously, newspaper supplements do not attract as much attention as main newspapers do. Also, it follows that readers still look up to newspapers for satisfying their hunger for information than mere entertainment. The following figure graphically presents the information in regard to the number of supplements read.

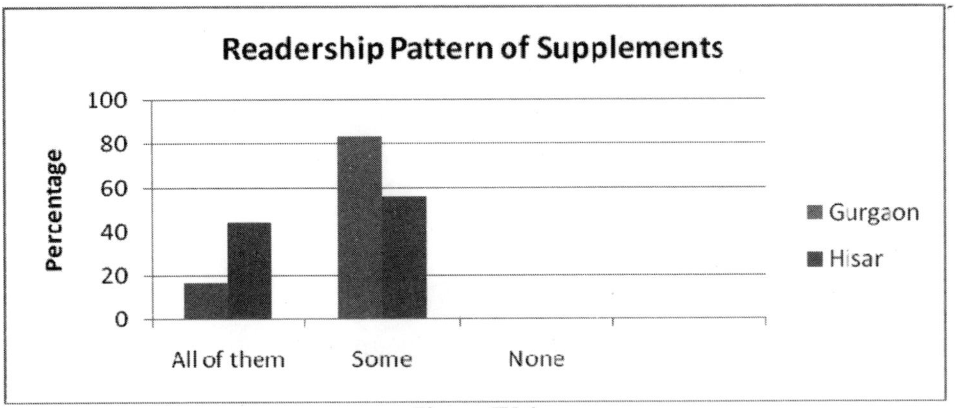

Figure IV.6

IV.7. Frequency of Exposure to Advertisements

Table IV.7: Frequency of Exposure to Advertisements

Readers' Response	Gurgaon	Hisar
Always	418 (83.6%)	142 (28.4%)
Never	0	64 (12.8%)
Sometimes	82 (16.4%)	294 (58.8%)

Table IV.7 shows that 418 respondents (83.6%) in Gurgaon regularly see advertisements given in the supplements. On the other hand, only 142 respondents (28.4%) in Hisar regularly go through advertisements published in various supplements. Furthermore, 294 respondents (58.8%) in Hisar occasionally look up advertisements in supplements. Also, 64 respondents (12.8%) in Hisar do not pay attention to advertisements published in the supplements at all. The low percentage of respondents in Hisar paying attention to advertisements is an outcome of the occupational structure over there.

As people in Hisar happen to be largely employed in the public sector rather than the private sector, advertisements not only happen to occupy less space in the supplements but also attract less attention. In comparison, as Gurgaon is a major industrial/business hub where most of the people are (self) employed in the private sector. Obviously, advertisements not only occupy greater space in the supplements but also attract greater attention. One other factor for greater number of people paying attention to advertisements in Gurgaon is the relatively higher paying capacity of people and their keenness to acquire superior goods. The data given in Table IV.7 has been graphically represented as below:

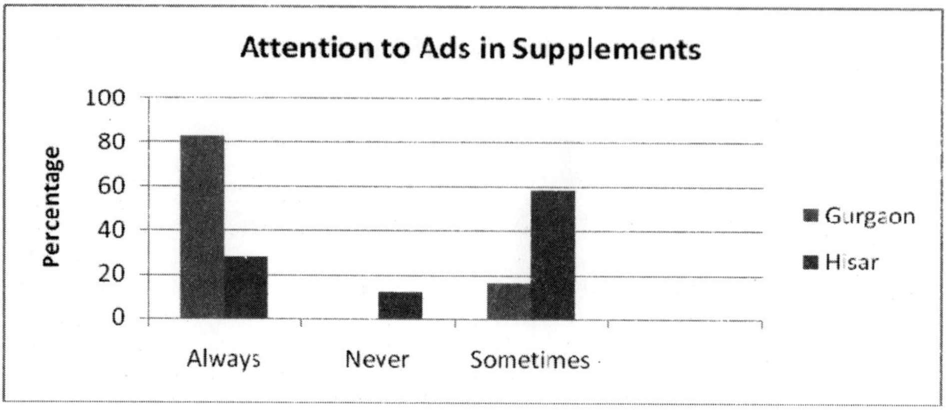

Figure IV.7

IV.8. Favourite Advertisement Category

IV.8.a. *Presentation-Based Classification*

Table IV.8

Advertisement Category	Gurgaon	Hisar
Visually-dominant	370 (74%)	290 (58%)
Text-Heavy	130 (26%)	210 (42%)
Can't Say	0	0

Table IV.8 shows that 370 respondents (74%) in Gurgaon are more interested in visually-dominant advertisements as against 290 respondents (58%) in Hisar. Out of the 500 respondents who were administered the questionnaire at Gurgaon, 130 (26%) pay more attention to advertisements with more text than visuals. In Hisar, 210 respondents (42%) prefer text-heavy ads to visually-dominant ads. The data has been graphically represented below:

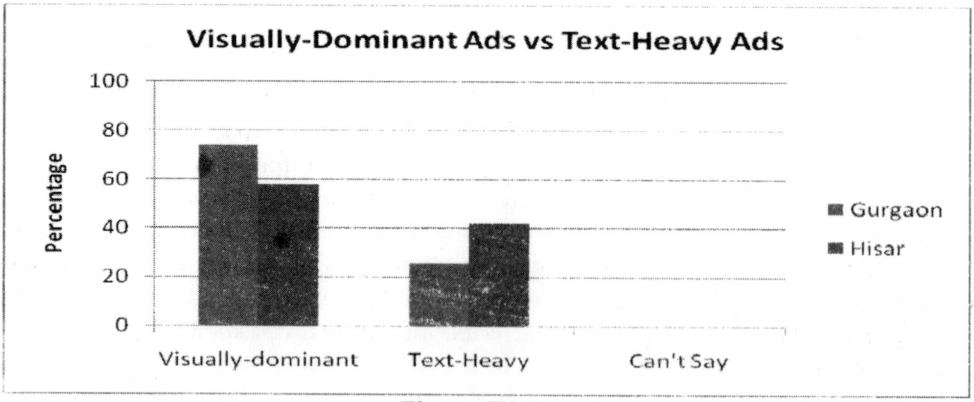

Figure IV.8

IV.8.b. *Content-Based Classification*

Table IV.9: Content-Based Classification

Frequency	Gurgaon	Hisar
Political	136 (27.2%)	226 (45.2%)
Social	100 (20%)	136 (27.2%)
Developmental	82 (16.4%)	72 (14.4%)
Government	68 (13.6%)	40 (8%)
Product/service	54 (10.8%)	26 (5.2%)
Others	60 (12%)	0

That the people of Haryana are deeply involved in politics is reflected in their advertisement preference. In this light, it is not surprising to note that political ad category is the favourite category of 226 respondents (45.2%) in Hisar and 27 per cent of the readers in Gurgaon. In Hisar, 136 respondents (27.2%) prefer going through social advertisements in supplements, thus making it the second most favourite advertisement category of the people of Hisar. Hundred respondents (20%) in Gurgaon feel that social advertisements attract their attention the most.

Exactly the same number of respondents 72 (14.4%) in Gurgaon and Hisar go through developmental advertisements first. Government advertisements make the favourite advertisement category of 68 respondents (13.6%) of Gurgaon as against only 40 respondents (8%) in Hisar. Table IV.9 has been graphically represented in the form of a comparative bar chart as follows:

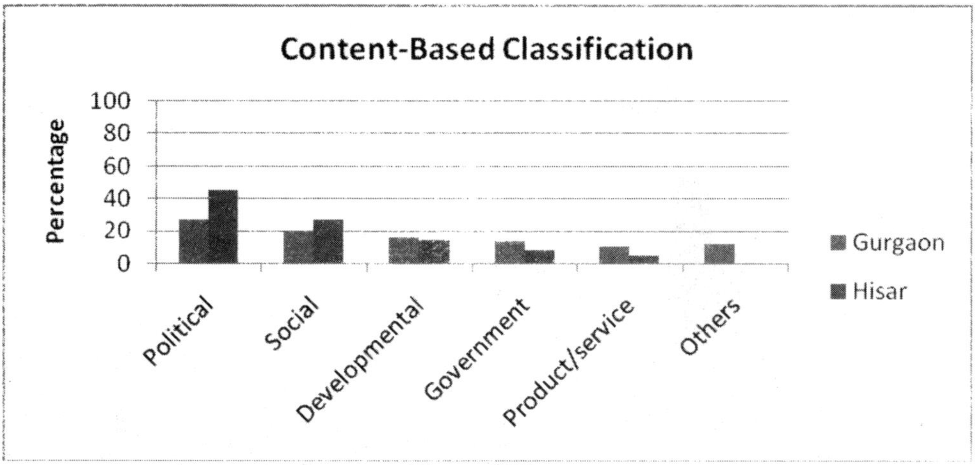

Figure IV.9

IV.9. Reasons for Liking Supplements

Table IV.10: Reasons for Liking Supplements

Categories	Gurgaon	Hisar
Content	250 (50%)	464 (92.8%)
Design	92 (18.4%)	14 (2.8%)
Headline	102 (20.4%)	2 (0.4%)
Visuals	56 (11.2%)	20 (4%)

Table IV.10 depicts that people at Hisar as well as Gurgaon go more by the content of supplements rather than its designing, visuals etc. In Hisar, as many as 464 respondents (92.8%) like reading supplements because of its content as against 250 respondents (50%) in Gurgaon. In Hisar, only 20 respondents (4%) read supplements for visuals whereas as few as 14 respondents (2.8%) attribute their liking of supplements to attractive page make up. Interestingly, only 2 respondents (0.4%) in Hisar like supplements for their attractive and interesting headlines as against 92 respondents (18.4%) in Gurgaon.

In Gurgaon, readers like supplements mostly for its content but at the same time they also pay considerable attention to its designing and headlines. Ninety-two respondents like reading supplements for their designing. Supplements, especially mixed and lifestyle supplements, are splashed with blow ups/pictures. However, even in Gurgaon, just as in Hisar, only a small percentage of respondents go through supplements for visuals. In Gurgaon, only 56 respondents (11.2%) like supplements primarily for the visuals they carry. The data represented in Table IV.10 has been graphically represented as below:

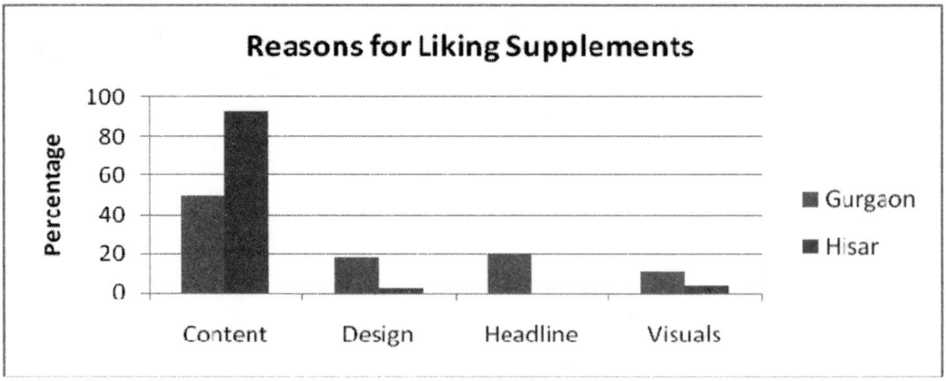

Figure IV.10

IV.10. Readers' Satisfaction with Supplement Content

Table IV.11: Readers' Satisfaction with Supplement Content

Response	Gurgaon	Hisar
Yes	176 (35.2%)	260 (52%)
No	16 (3.2%)	124 (24.8%)
Partially satisfied	250 (50%)	116 (23.2%)
Can't say	58 (11.6%)	0

Table IV.11 shows that the pattern of readers' satisfaction with supplement content in Gurgaon and Hisar is dissimilar in most respects. While a large percentage of readers is satisfied with supplement content in Hisar, a large percentage of readers in Gurgaon is partially satisfied with the supplement content. Of the 500 respondents quizzed to know their satisfaction level with their supplement content, 260 respondents (52%) in Hisar expressed their satisfaction with the content of the supplements they read whereas only 176 respondents (35.2%) in Gurgaon felt so. Clearly, the gap is substantial. This is because 250 respondents (50%) in Gurgaon are partially satisfied with supplements.

Obviously, those liking the supplements comprise the second largest group while those partially liking the supplements comprise the largest group in Gurgaon. In comparison, in Hisar those not satisfied with the content of the supplements comprise the second largest group. 124 respondents (24.8%) in Hisar are not satisfied with the content of the supplements they read. Interestingly, the third largest group of respondents in Hisar is comprised of those partially liking the supplements. 116 respondents (23.2%) in Hisar partially liked the supplements. The difference in percentage between those partially liking and not liking is minimal. In comparison, in Gurgaon the third largest group consists of only 58 respondents (11.6%) who are indecisive. A careful study of the pattern of readers' satisfaction with supplement content shows an overwhelming acceptance of supplements in Hisar compared to that in Gurgaon. The data in Table IV.11 has been graphically represented as below:

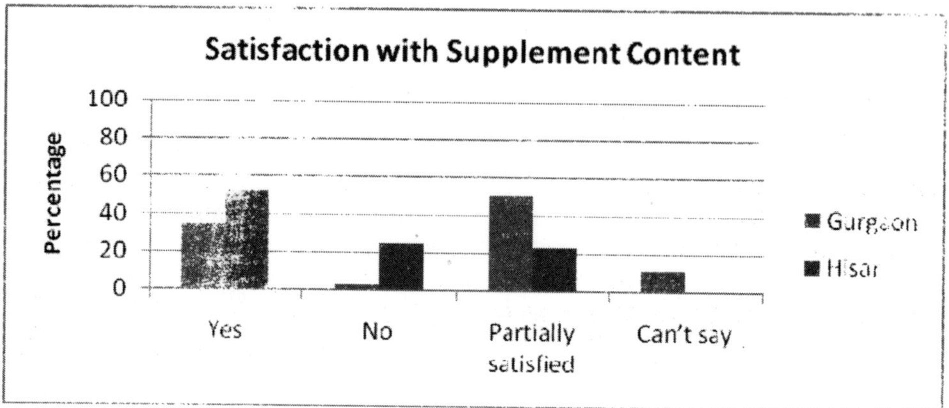

Figure IV.11

IV.11. Harmony Between Supplement Content and Indian Culture: Readers' Perception

Table IV.12: Harmony Between Supplement Content and Indian Culture

Response	Gurgaon	Hisar
Yes	276 (55.2%)	250 (50%)
No	140 (28%)	60 (12%)
Can't say	84 (16.8%)	190 (38%)

Table IV.12 shows a more or less similar pattern of readers' perception regarding the harmony between supplement content and Indian cultural values. Almost an equal number, which incidentally is a substantial one, considers the supplement content to be in conformity with the Indian traditions. As many as 250 respondents in Hisar and 276 respondents in Gurgaon think that the supplements do not transgress Indian cultural values. In percentage terms, as much as 50 per cent of the respondents in the hinterland of Hisar believe that the content published in various supplements that they read was in harmony with the Indian culture. Compared to this, 55.2 per cent of the respondents who were administered the questionnaire in the city of Gurgaon also perceived the content of supplements to be harmonious with the Indian culture.

Interestingly enough, if we were to leave out those who are non-committal then in Gurgaon the total number of respondents who feel that the supplement content is not in harmony with the Indian culture is more than double that in Hisar. As many as 140 respondents (28%) in Gurgaon consider the supplement content in disharmony with Indian culture compared to 60 respondents (12%) in Hisar.

While the percentage of respondents assessing the supplement content favourably from the cultural point of view is more than 55 per cent in Gurgaon, the percentage of respondents viewing it unfavourably is also substantial (28%). Such entrenched positions notwithstanding, we may safely deduce that respondents in Gurgaon by and large assess the supplement content favourably. Furthermore, this assessment is much more favourable in Gurgaon than in Hisar.

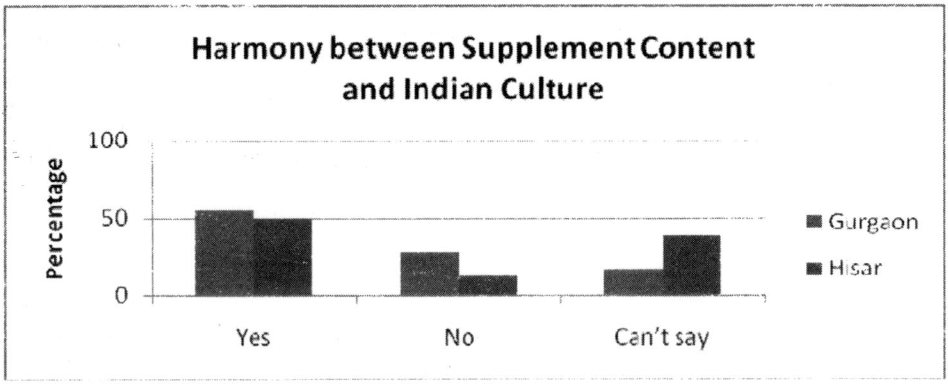

Figure IV.12

IV.12. Readers' Perception of Supplement Content and the Changing Socio-Cultural Values

Table IV.13

Response	Gurgaon	Hisar
Yes	265 (53%)	250 (50%)
No	105 (21%)	174 (34.8%)
Can't Say	130 (26%)	76 (15.2%)

Table IV.13 shows that the pattern of readers' perception regarding supplement content reflecting the changes in the socio-cultural landscape is more or less similar in both the cities. If 250 respondents (50%) in Hisar feel that the supplement content reflects these changes, 210 respondents (42%) in Gurgaon think the same. Those who disagree constitute 34.8 per cent of the respondents in Hisar and 28 per cent in Gurgaon. Surprisingly, 130 respondents (30%) in Gurgaon and 76 respondents (15.2%) in Hisar are non-committal.

The table helps us to understand the results obtained in the previous section where most of the respondents felt comfortable with the content of the supplements. The table also highlights the dynamic character of the socio-cultural milieu in the two places. The following graph represents the data graphically:

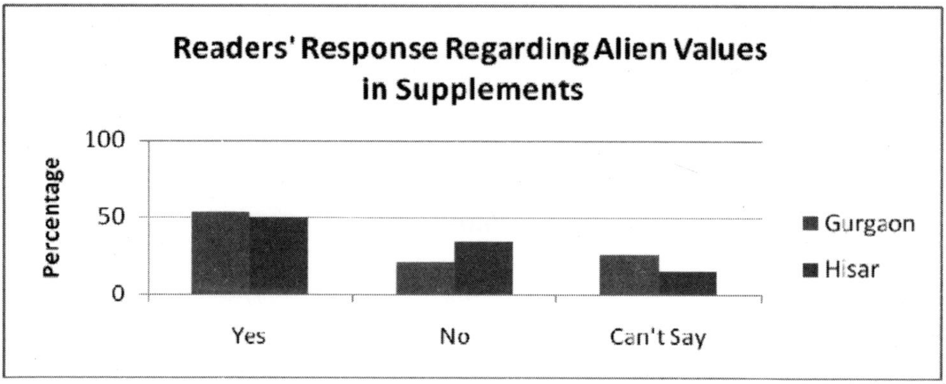

Figure IV.13

IV.13. Portrayal of Women and Gender Relations in Supplements

Table IV.14: Readers' Perception of Portrayal of Women and Gender Relations

Response	Gurgaon	Hisar
Matter of factly	304 (60.8%)	340 (68%)
Provocatively	104 (20.8%)	118 (23.6%)
Entertainingly	92 (18.4%)	42 (8.4%)

Table IV.14 implies that an overwhelming number of respondents in Gurgaon and in Hisar feel that women and gender relations are depicted in supplements in a matter of fact way. Contrary to general perception, very few respondents think that the portrayal of women and gender relations in supplements is provocative. As many as 104 respondents (20.8%) in Gurgaon and 118 respondents (23.6%) in Hisar feel that the portrayal is provocative.

Interestingly, 92 respondents (18.4%) in Gurgaon and 42 respondents (8.4%) in Hisar feel that the portrayal is entertaining. These results confound the generally held perception that supplements portray women and gender relations provocatively. The data of Table IV.14 has been represented in the form of bar graph.

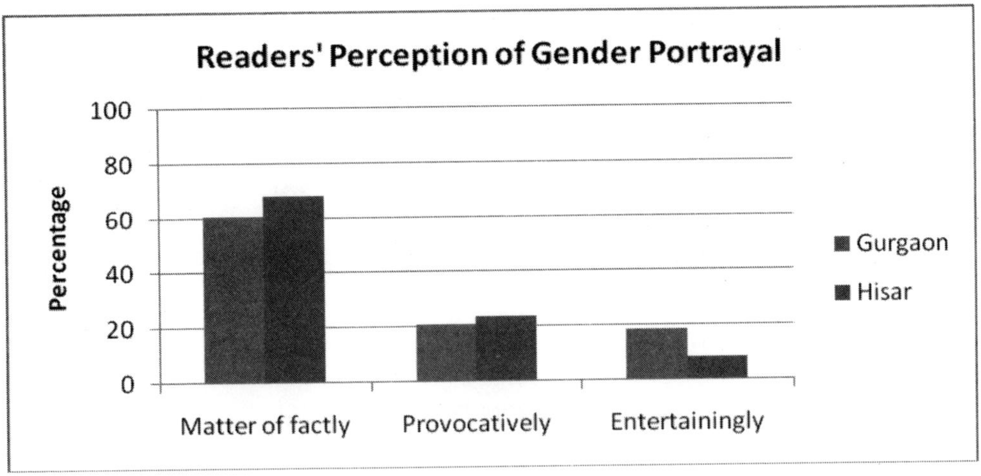

Figure IV.14

IV.14. Readers' Frequency of Satisfaction with Supplements

Table IV.15: Readers' Frequency of Satisfaction with Supplements

Response	Gurgaon	Hisar
Always	76 (15.2%)	180 (36%)
Never	64 (12.8%)	30 (6%)
Can't say	50 (10%)	256 (51.2%)
Sometimes	310 (62%)	34 (6.8%)

Table IV.15 shows that readers on the whole are partially satisfied with the content of the supplements. As many as 310 respondents (62%) in Gurgaon are satisfied with supplements only sometimes. This is in keeping with the results obtained in Table IV.15 where a substantial number of respondents show partial satisfaction with the supplement content. While on the other hand, in Hisar 180 respondents (36%) are always satisfied with supplement content. This again corresponds favourably with the results obtained in table.

While 76 respondents (15.2%) in Gurgaon are always satisfied with supplement content, 64 respondents (12.8%) in Gurgaon are never satisfied with supplement content. In contrast, in Hisar as few as 34 respondents (6.8%) are sometimes satisfied with supplement content and as few as 30 respondents

(6%) are never satisfied with supplement content. The graph given below represents the data in Table IV.15:

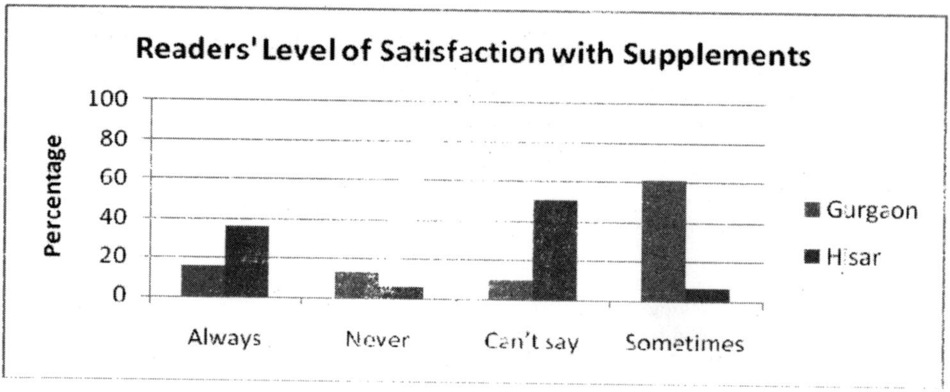

Figure IV.15

IV.15. Level of Credibility of Information for Decision-Making

Table IV.16: Level of Credibility of Information for Decision-Making

Response	Gurgaon	Hisar
Yes	106 (21.2%)	112 (22.4%)
No	240 (48%)	254 (50.8%)
Sometimes	154 (30.8%)	134 (26.8%)

The level of credibility of information for decision making as represented in Table IV.16 shows that the largest number of respondents, 240 (48%) in Gurgaon and 254 respondents (50.8%) in Hisar, do not consider the information given in supplements credible enough to take decisions. In comparison, 112 respondents (22.4%) in Hisar and 106 respondents (21.2%) in Gurgaon are, however, of the opinion that the information given in the supplements is credible enough to take decisions. Similarly, as many as 134 respondents (26.8%) in Hisar and 154 respondents (30.8%) in Gurgaon think that the information is sometimes credible enough to take decisions. The results though split between high and low credibility show that supplements do by and large give information useful enough to take decisions. Table IV.16 has been represented in the following graph:

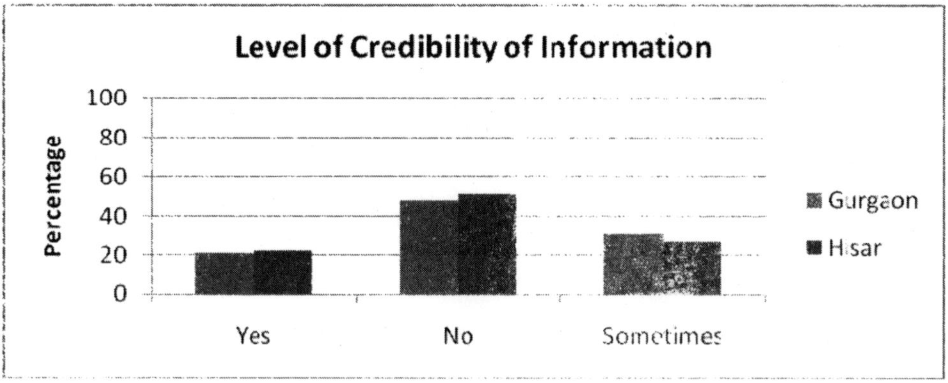
Level of Credibility of Information
Percentage
100
80
60
40
20
0
Yes
No
Sometimes
Gurgaon
Hisar

Figure IV.16

CHAPTER V

CONCLUSION

This chapter sums up the findings drawn from the results and discussion of the research undertaken. This study attempted to analyse and compare the supplements of The Times of India, as circulated in a modern urban centre in the National Capital Region of India and Dainik Bhaskar, as circulated in a traditional urban centre of India, and readers' perception of each of the two, with the objective of mapping the categories of content in the respective supplements of The Times of India and Dainik Bhaskar and comparing and contrasting the two categories of content in the respective supplements. Also, the study attempted to situate the evolution of supplement journalism in the matrix of the sociological and communication theories.

The study also attempted to map readers' perceptions about supplements in Gurgaon and Hisar cities/towns of the Haryana state of India by comparing and contrasting the supplement reading habits of the newspaper readers in both the cities with an objective of exploring the social, cultural and economic underpinnings of the comparative points of departure and similarity in the newspaper reading habits of members of a *gemeinschaft* community like Hisar and *gesellschaft* society like Gurgaon. The study also drew a comparison between the content and the readership pattern of the supplements of the two papers and aimed at relating these differences to the differential development of the two cities. The study explored whether the content of supplements satisfied the supplement readers.

The study reveals that The Times of India (TOI) is the most read newspaper in Gurgaon, while Dainik Bhaskar (DB) is the most read newspaper in Hisar. The survey of respondents in Gurgaon and Hisar shows that a whopping 66 per cent of them read TOI while a similarly significant 69.6 per cent of the newspaper readers in Hisar read DB. The ranked preference of newspapers in Gurgaon and Hisar, therefore, makes each of the two papers representative of the cultural affinities and media habits of the two respective places. Consequently, the supplements of TOI become emblematic of the 'modernised' city of Gurgaon and those of DB emblematic of the tradition-bound town of

Hisar in Haryana. This co-relation between each of the two newspapers and each of the two places in Haryana forms the bedrock of the analysis, both content and survey research.

Dainik Bhaskar comes out with four supplements namely Madhurima, Navrang, Rasrang and Bal Bhaskar. All the four come out on newsprint. However, with the exception of Madhurima and Bal Bhaskar the other two supplements of DB come out on broadsheet. While Madhurima comes out in tabloid size, Bal Bhaskar comes out in the magazine format. In comparison with TOI, only DB has a supplement which comes out in magazine form. Both the papers come out with one supplement each in tabloid form. What's Hot for TOI and Madhurima for DB. However, the most striking comparison between the two papers is the wide gap in the number of supplements brought out by them. While TOI comes out with 7 supplements, DB comes out with only 4. The wide variation between the two is indicative of the marketing strategies suitable for each of the two. While TOI caters to the high-end audience in Gurgaon, DB caters to the middle, the lower middle and the lower end audiences in the Hindi hinterland of Haryana. The difference in the audiences of the two calls for a difference in space marketing exercise. The variety of supplements available in TOI is indicative of the advertisers' desire to reach out to different segments of the consumer-audience. As the segmentation of consumer-audience happens to be more complex in an urban center like Gurgaon compared to that in a relatively less developed town like Hisar, the number of supplements reaching out to these niche audiences of TOI happens to be more. The writing is clear on the wall: supplements have become the vehicles of advertisers attempting to reach out to their prospects. The greater the number of supplements, the greater the ad revenue generated. Supplements therefore fit into a marketing strategy designed to counter the strangle hold of the electronic media on advertising revenues.

The research further reveals non-adherence to any uniform pattern in the number of pages and the size of the supplements and the quality of paper used in the case of TOI supplements while a uniform pattern is discernable in the case of DB supplements. Once again the variations can be attributed to the exigencies of circumstances created by the advertising inflows.

The edit-ad space distribution in the case of TOI supplements is tilted in favour of the advertisement space in comparison with DB supplements where the balance is tilted in favour of the edit space. Of the four supplements brought out by DB, the ad-edit ratio varies from 100:543 in Madhurima to 1:infinity in Bal Bhaskar. Between these two yawning extremes, the ratio in Navrang is as high as 2:29 and in Rasrang 20:301. In comparison with TOI, these ratios are very much on the higher side for the editorial content. While in TOI, the ad-edit ratio was skewed in favour of advertisements, in DB it is skewed in favour of the editorial content. As the advertising support for DB is much lower compared to that for TOI, the potential for bringing out a large number of supplements is much lower in case of DB compared to TOI. This variation can be attributed to the space selling exercise undertaken in each of the two newspapers. While the space selling exercise is more competitive in the case of TOI which has strong rivals like Hindustan Times and other national dailies, Dainik Bhaskar does not have to face that kind of competition in its marketing exercise. Interestingly, the newspaper reading time pattern in Gurgaon and Hisar justifies the preponderance of advertisements in TOI compared to those in DB. As newspaper advertisements demand a much less attention span compared to what the editorial matter demands, the fact that more than 80 per cent of the readers in Gurgaon spend 10-30 minutes of their time on reading newspapers while 41.6 per cent and 48.4 per cent of the readers in Hisar spend more than 30 minutes and 10-30 minutes respectively on reading newspapers, shows that the readers in Gurgaon do pay attention to the advertisements pushed through the variety of supplements, while the readers in Hisar preoccupy themselves more with reading the editorial content. This is corroborated by the fact that 83.6 per cent of the readers in Gurgaon always go through the advertisements, whereas only 28.4 per cent of the readers in Hisar go through advertisements without a miss.

The text-visual space ratio in DB is skewed in favour of the text in all the supplements but for Navrang where it is 1:1.45. The text-visual ratio is the highest in Rasrang (11:5) followed by Bal Bhaskar (19:10) and Madhurima (9:5). However, the text-visual edit space ratio in DB is much lower compared to that in TOI where it is tilted heavily in favour of the text. The high priority accorded to visuals in DB compared to that in TOI is actuated by a concern for making the supplements visually appealing to the readers with a view to spurring the circulation figures. It is interesting to note here that many of the pages in DB carry visually-dominant pictures, with many of them stretching from end to end longitudinally. Interestingly enough, the survey results show the obverse picture. A whopping 92.8 per cent readers in Hisar compared to a mere 50 per cent of readers in Gurgaon prefer to read the content than to view the visuals.

Of the various forms of editorial items used in DB supplements, features, interviews and folklore dominate the editorial content. In Madhurima and Rasrang, features take up the maximum editorial space, 19.39 per cent and 48.36 per cent respectively. In Navrang, interviews take up as high a percentage of space as 71.8 per cent whereas in Bal Bhaskar folklore takes up the maximum space of 18.06 per cent. Compared to TOI, there is a variation in the kind of editorial content forms used in DB. Only two supplements share a similar pre-occupation while the other two accord space to two divergent forms. This could be because of the fewer number of DB supplements. But one thing that emerges for sure is the reliance on features as the pivotal form of most supplements. This is obvious in view of the function of a feature to appeal to the heart than to the mind and thereby create a feeling of relief in the mind of the reader.

Of the four supplements brought out by DB, only one supplement, Rasrang, has features across the broad spectrum of subjects which include well being (3.66%), celebrity (26.20%), lifestyle (13.03%), travel (23.62%), social issues (26.97%) and education (6.52%). In comparison, the features in Madhurima, Navrang and Bal Bhaskar are concentrated in a few subjects only. While the feature space in Madhurima is shared between features on children (41.6%) and women (58.4%), the feature space in Navrang is shared by features on fashion and films equally. Similarly, in Bal Bhaskar the feature space is shared equally by hobbies and environment. The comparison shows that each of the supplements of DB focuses exclusively on a few segments of readers.

In comparison with the supplements of TOI, DB has a very limited variety of subjects. Especially DB completely skirts past subjects that could be considered taboo in a traditional society. While TOI devotes 58.11 per cent of its relationship feature space to the discussion of intimate relations in DT, 100 per cent in What's Hot and 67 per cent in Times Life, none of the DB supplements touches upon intimate relations. The difference in approach is understandable as TOI caters to the uptown *gesellschaft* society and DB caters to the downtown *gemeinschaft* society tucked away in the Hindi speaking hinterland of the state of Haryana.

Interestingly enough, the survey results endorse the findings emerging from the content analysis. The survey reveals that 85.2 per cent of the readers in Gurgaon and 75.2 per cent of the readers in Hisar are satisfied with the content of the supplements. Furthermore, 55.2 per cent of the readers in Gurgaon and 50 per cent of the readers in Hisar consider the content of their supplements to be in conformity with the traditions of the Indian culture. Simultaneously, 53 per cent of the readers in Gurgaon and 50 per cent of the readers in Hisar perceive the supplement content as truly reflective of the changes happening in the Indian cultural landscape. Obviously, readers in Gurgaon have come to accept the bold representation of reality as something inhering with the essence of Indian culture. So, the inclusion of bold and taboo subjects in the TOI supplements becomes reflective of a changing society which is modernizing, rather westernizing itself.

The visuals in DB supplements happen to be mainly of non-descript characters with a view to adding a visual appeal and human touch to the features. The distribution of human visuals among the various social roles is almost uniform in the various supplements of DB, being 7.69 per cent for page-3, TV & films and artistic personalities in Madhurima; cent per cent for celluloid personalities in Navrang; 4.76 per cent for TV & films, political, sports and artistic personalities in Rasrang and 1.12 per cent for celluloid personalities and 2.25 per cent for political and sports personalities in Bal Bhaskar. The comparison between TOI and DB supplements shows that the variety of role models highlighted in TOI supplements is larger compared to that in DB. Again, the role models highlighted in TOI are more specific than in DB where non-descript human visuals happen to abound in each of the supplements. However, while in TOI supplements, the focus is on celluloid personalities, there is no such focus in DB supplements with the exception of Navrang.

The gender analysis of human visuals shows that DB supplements are not far behind TOI supplements in including female visuals. While 92.31 per cent of the human visuals are of females in Madhurima, 54.64 per cent of the human visuals are of females in Navrang and 43.24 per cent in Rasrang. Obviously, visuals of women are copiously splashed all across the pages of DB supplements. The prominent place occupied by visuals of women in DB supplements shows that not only in the modern society of Gurgaon but even in the traditional societies which have largely readers of Hindi language newspapers, visuals of women constitute a strong centripetal force for attracting the attention of readers. The survey results endorse the results obtained from the content analysis. Around 61 per cent of readers in Gurgaon and 68 per cent in Hisar consider that women are portrayed matter of factly in the supplements they read. Though this is a substantial section of the readership yet 20.8 per cent readers in Gurgaon and 23.6 per cent readers in Hisar feel that women are portrayed provocatively in the supplements. So, even though there is a minority opinion against the portrayal of gender relations in both the places, the majority feels unperturbed by the manner of portrayal of women in the supplements.

Interestingly, even though the visuals of women are plenteously used in supplements that accompany Dainik Bhaskar, their use is buffered for the traditional societies by avoiding maximal exposure. While in Madhurima all the human visuals are minimally exposed; in Navrang 89.29 per cent of the human visuals fall in the category of minimally exposed and only 10.71 per cent moderately exposed; and in Rasrang 71.43 per cent are minimally exposed and 28.57 per cent moderately exposed. The exposure level in Rasrang happens to be the maximum among all the Dainik Bhaskar supplements. This shows that even traditional societies in India have come to accept moderate exposure of human body. In stark contrast, The Times of India gives 7.54 per cent of human visuals as maximally exposed in Delhi Times; 6.94 per cent in What's Hot and 12.5 per cent in Times Life. The sharp contrast between the supplements of the two newspapers again shows the high acceptance of maximal exposure in human visuals among readers in a modern society compared to none among readers in a traditional society. This is indicative of the dynamics of change in the cultural values in two different kinds of society in India.

The survey results show that 15.2 per cent and 62 per cent of the readers in Gurgaon are 'always' and 'sometimes' satisfied respectively with the supplements, while 36 per cent and 6.8 per cent of the readers in Hisar are always and sometimes satisfied respectively with the supplements. The comparison shows that by and large the readers in Gurgaon and Hisar are satisfied with the supplements, though the readers in Gurgaon happen to be more satisfied than those in Hisar. However, this could be because 51.2 per cent of the readers in Hisar couldn't decide their response to this query. By implication, both TOI and DB supplements seem to have a satisfying effect on their readers. This indicates that each of the two newspapers have felt the pulse of their readers and hence have structured the content of their supplements in keeping with the taste and preferences of their respective readers.

The survey reveals that a miniscule minority, 21.2 per cent in Gurgaon and 22.4 per cent in Hisar, considers the information given in the supplements credible enough to facilitate decision making. This implies that readers consider the information given in the supplements as something that facilitates their amusement and helps them unwind.

Polyphony of communication helps to break the restrictive and selective control imposed by media on the dissemination of information through its gatekeeping function. The variety of supplements brought out by mainstream newspapers such as TOI and DB helps to add a number of voices in the public domain. Earlier, it was only political news which captured the limelight. But with the launching of multiple supplements, issues pertaining to other aspects of society and its dynamics have started entering the public domain. Unwittingly, it has helped to loosen if not break the stranglehold of the editor on the number of voices entering the public discourse through the pages of a newspaper. Information has become richer in its diversity of content and more broad-based. This, in a way, has helped in bringing mass communication closer, at least by a step, to its apotheosis, communication. Supplement journalism, therefore, comes in as a whiff of fresh air that attempts to resurrect communication in its own small way.

Simultaneously, supplements have also transmuted the character of public discourse which till supplement journalism came to the fore was restricted in its subject matter to the political and 'high' culture. In other words, political events occupied highly visible slots and pages and economic and sports events were pushed to the low visibility slots and pages. Subjects of popular discourse were dismissed as 'lowbrow' and unfit for publication. In fact, a distinction was created between the mainstream media and the tabloid press with the latter stigmatized for highlighting issues of popular taste. The emergence of supplement journalism has led to the tabloidisation of the mainstream media. It is evident from the wide variety of content in supplements of papers of TOI. It is, therefore, but natural that the mainstream media, custodian of high and bourgeoisie culture, should have resisted this tabloidisation in iconic newspapers like TOI. But as the tide turned, the rest of the mainstream media soon followed suit as is evident from the supplements of Dainik Bhaskar.

Most newspapers before the emergence of supplement journalism were preoccupied with the meta-narratives of the national and state politics and national and state economy. The mini-narratives concerned with the travails and successes of the individuals were often forgotten. There was an unnatural imbalance between the meta-narratives and mini-narratives of cultural discourse. Supplements have reversed this trend by focusing on the individual lives of ordinary and extraordinary citizens, thereby focusing on mini-narratives of social discourse.

This revolutionary change in media content is a fall out of the role of advertisements in lining the pockets of the media owners. In the attention economy of the late twentieth century and the early twenty-first century, media has become the purveyor of its readers'/audience's attention to the marketeers and advertisers. The higher the circulation figures, the greater the attention that the media can sell to a potential advertiser. Similarly, the greater the media penetration among different segments of the society, the greater the possibility of advertisements making it to the various segments of its potential customers. This, in effect, calls for niche journalism/narrowcasting which supplements support and nurture. By providing a variety of supplements targeted at different segments of readers, TOI is one of the first papers to initiate this trend and to benefit from it.

The pivotal role played by the advertisements in raising the circulation and advertising revenue figures has led to the emergence of supplement journalism as a manifestation of market driven journalism. As a vehicle of market-driven journalism, print media had to reach out to the least common multiple of the audiences/readers. This meant a deepening, more than broadening, of the audience base by going beyond the highbrow middle class to the subaltern and the marginalized sections of the society. Here, it is pertinent to mention that consequent upon an economic upturn in the post-liberalised phase of the Indian economy, the surplus income levels have risen sharply at different levels of socio-economic hierarchy, in particular 'the bottom of the pyramid'.

In other words, the lower income group, which comprised skilled and unskilled blue collar workforce drawn mainly from the other backward communities and schedule castes and tribes, has started having disposable income which they can spend on consumer goods. To put it in the words of the management Guru, C.K. Prahlad, "The bottom of the pyramid became as attractive a proposition as the middle class was to the marketeers." Quick to realize the gains hidden in such a policy thrust, the English press followed by the vernacular press has been all for adding pull outs/supplements. The marketeers, in particular, have identified the youth as the new segment with the greatest potential of consuming the fast moving consumer goods (FMCG). This has translated into most supplements acquiring a youthful hue in their content and layout. As youth prefers to read about beauty, celebrities, fashion, lifestyle, education, job prospects etc, newspapers have started incorporating these subjects in a big way in their supplements. Incidentally, the average age of an Indian, as on date, is 25-26 years. In other words, newspapers reflect the mood of a youthful nation in their supplements and encash it to their advantage.

From the preceding discussion, it is evident that supplement journalism caters to three major players—the advertiser, the media house and the reader/consumer—through segmentation of information and a consequent fragmentation of mass audience/readers into identifiable homogeneous sub groups within the faceless mass audience. By bringing out a variety of supplements on a variety of subjects ranging from fashion, beauty, lifestyle, tourism on the one hand to career, education and investments on the other hand, supplements reach out to different sub groups within the faceless heterogeneous mass audience. The media sells the attention of these sub groups to the advertiser at a price profitable to it while the advertiser benefits from the media penetration by being able to reach out to the target prospects. The reader benefits from the nexus between the media owner and the advertiser by getting media content that serves his/her specific demands from the media. In view of the atomization of the society and high levels of stress in an industrialized/urbanized society, the readers' demand for amusement, information updating and lifestyle updating calls for a subject matter that the newspapers have been providing in their subject-specific, mixed and geographically-specific supplements. In other words, the functions of this study vindicate the claims of the commercial/*laissez faire* theory, play theory and uses and gratification theory.

However, the application of all these theories is contingent upon a socio-economic transformation of the society. A society that is deeply riven into rigid class stratifications and bogged down with low incomes and subsistence levels at the bottom of the pyramid and low-surplus incomes at the middle class levels can scarcely facilitate the emergence of supplement journalism. The India of post-1990s has been socially and economically resilient nation. Thanks to the social and economic welfare policies pursued by socialistically minded governments at the Centre and in the states. So, when liberalization and globalization opened the floodgates of opportunity, the people at every rung of the social and economic hierarchy stood to gain. It is this overall transformation in the social and economic matrix of the Indian society that has underpinned the success of supplement journalism in India.

The social and economic transformation of the society has also been accompanied with a cultural liberation brought about by globalization through an increasingly unrestricted exchange of, rather import of, cultural products from the developed West. These cultural products, in the form of music videos, films and celebrity pageants, have overwhelmed the traditional Indian cultural mores and planted, to the chagrin of the *swadeshi* zealots, a new culture symbolic of the confluence of the East and the West. The changing cultural landscape and the desire to imbibe the western cultural values with a view to identifying with the West, particularly among the youth, have transformed readers' tastes and preferences and their information and lifestyle needs. This cultural transformation has played an instrumental role in the acceptability as well as the desirability of supplements.

So, in the final analysis, we may safely conclude that the successful emergence of supplement journalism in both the *gesellchaft* and the *gemeinschaft* centres of the Indian society has been actuated by the transformation of the social, cultural and the economic landscape of India and is explained by the application of the commercial, play and uses and gratification theories.

INDEX